Economic Policy in the 21st Century

Economic policy is facing crises on multiple fronts. With the effects of the last financial crisis still with us, it is now faced with the new challenges of post-Covid economic recovery and dealing with the negative effects of over consumption on the climate. This book explores the future of economic policy in relation to what the author sees as the four great policy challenges of the first half of the 21st century: the after effects of the last financial crisis and the catastrophic impact of the Covid pandemic, secular stagnation, growing poverty and inequality, and globalization. The existence of these economic problems has become increasingly relevant since some of the tools available to public action have become useless. As economists begin to suggest new instruments of economic policy, this book will help the reader understand the nature of the economic and political facts that influence both current and future generations.

NICOLA ACOCELLA is Emeritus of Economic Policy at the Sapienza University of Rome.

Economic Policy in the 21st Century

The Four Great Challenges

NICOLA ACOCELLA

Sapienza University of Rome

CAMBRIDGE
UNIVERSITY PRESS

Shaftesbury Road, Cambridge CB2 8EA, United Kingdom

One Liberty Plaza, 20th Floor, New York, NY 10006, USA

477 Williamstown Road, Port Melbourne, VIC 3207, Australia

314–321, 3rd Floor, Plot 3, Splendor Forum, Jasola District Centre, New Delhi – 110025, India

103 Penang Road, #05–06/07, Visioncrest Commercial, Singapore 238467

Cambridge University Press is part of Cambridge University Press & Assessment, a department of the University of Cambridge.

We share the University's mission to contribute to society through the pursuit of education, learning and research at the highest international levels of excellence.

www.cambridge.org
Information on this title: www.cambridge.org/9781009209137

DOI: 10.1017/9781009209106

First published 2022

A catalogue record for this publication is available from the British Library.

Library of Congress Cataloging-in-Publication Data
Names: Acocella, Nicola, 1939– author.
Title: Economic policy in the 21st century: the four great challenges / Nicola Acocella.
Description: Cambridge; New York, NY: Cambridge University Press, 2022. | Includes bibliographical references and index.
Identifiers: LCCN 2022023677 (print) | LCCN 2022023678 (ebook) | ISBN 9781009209137 (hardback) | ISBN 9781009209151 (paperback) | ISBN 9781009209106 (epub)
Subjects: LCSH: Economic policy. | Economic history–21st century. | BISAC: BUSINESS & ECONOMICS / Economics / Macroeconomics
Classification: LCC HD87 .A28134 2022 (print) | LCC HD87 (ebook) | DDC 338.9–dc23/eng/20220614
LC record available at https://lccn.loc.gov/2022023677
LC ebook record available at https://lccn.loc.gov/2022023678

ISBN 978-1-009-20913-7 Hardback
ISBN 978-1-009-20915-1 Paperback

To Anna Maria and our grandchildren, Flavia, Elena, Viola and Matteo, and to their parents, Francesca and Valerio, Roberta and Francesco

Contents

Figures

Tables

Boxes

Abbreviations

ECB	European Central Bank
EIB	European Investment Bank
EMDEs	emerging market and developing economies
EMU	European Economic and Monetary Union
ESFM	European Financial Stabilisation Mechanism
ESM	European Stability Mechanism
EU	European Union
EZ	Eurozone
FDI	foreign direct investment
GATT	General Agreement on Tariffs and Trade
IBRD	International Bank for Reconstruction and Development, World Bank
ILO	International Labour Organization
IMF	International Monetary Fund
LDCs	less-developed countries
LICs	low-income countries
OECD	Organization for Economic Cooperation and Development
S&P	Standard & Poor's
SGP	Stability and Growth Pact
UNCTAD	United Nations Conference on Trade and Development
UNDP	United Nations Development Program
UNIDO	United Nations Industrial Development Organization
WHO	World Health Organization
WTO	World Trade Organization

Introduction

The Proliferation of Problems and the Reduction of Instruments: Economic Policy as a 'Lame Duck'

In this book we aim to look first at the main problems which arose or were aggravated in the recent years, with respect to the economic crises, stagnation, inequalities, and globalisation. These are partly old problems, which have however become deeper in the last decades. We also analyse the relationships between these four problems.

The existence – or aggravation – of so many problems that must be faced by public action is so much more relevant and pernicious because, for a number of circumstances, at least some of the tools available to public action have become useless. This is the case of monetary policy, whose effectiveness has decreased for at least two reasons. On the one hand, it has been substantially blocked by the length and depth of the crises, which have constrained the central banks to maintain the interest rate at its floor, that is, at a zero level, as negative interest rates are not conceivable (or are limited to very specific circumstances). In fact, nobody would lend their money if they had also to pay interest to the borrower. On the other hand, monetary policy has revealed to be ineffective at limiting bank credits in a situation of euphoria, from which a crisis of the financial system can spring. In addition, fiscal policy has largely remained more or less blocked, due to: the roof at the absolute level of debt in the USA; the Stability and Growth Pact, setting a maximum of 3% with respect to the GDP, and the fiscal compact, a rule establishing the reduction of this limit in order to reduce by 1/20 yearly the excess of the debt/GDP ratio with respect to the value of 60%, in the European Union.

In addition, in various countries there are oppositions to implementation of price and incomes policy (i.e., of a policy establishing the rule for changes in prices, wages and other types of incomes) as well as to other economic policy instruments. Finally, at an international level countries do not engage in other than generic coordination of national economic policies.

Actually, the fantasy of economists has led to the suggestion of the possibility of making use of new instruments of economic policy, in the field both of monetary policy (e.g., the unconventional monetary policies implemented by both the Federal Reserve and the European Central Bank and other central banks) and fiscal policy (limits to debt, rather than to the deficit). In addition, new policy instruments such as macro-prudential tools have been devised, in order to limit excessive bank loans in times of market euphoria.

This notwithstanding, facing the multiplication of problems there has been a reduction in the number of unconstrained instruments, which implies the impossibility for the government to reach its economic policy targets. In fact, the classical theory of economic policy states that fulfilment of a given number of (fixed) policy targets is possible only if a number of instruments at least equal to the number of those targets is available. If some instruments are unavailable, the government becomes a 'lame duck', an expression indicating the institution (such as the government or the president) that cannot use its (his) prerogatives for a number of reasons. For instance, the President of the Republic in Italy cannot dissolve Parliament in the last six months of his mandate (the so-called white semester). In the USA, the President-elect has no powers before the inauguration and has limited powers when he has lost the majority of the Congress.

The four economic situations needing policy interventions are linked one to the other. In addition, all of them have a negative influence on the life of most people. This explains part of the title of this book: the four great challenges.

The plan of the book is as follows: in Chapter 1 we deal with the crises. Chapter 2 deals with secular stagnation; Chapter 3 with poverty and inequalities. Chapter 4 is dedicated to globalisation. Chapter 5 pulls together the threads of the previous issues, emphasizing, on the one hand, the relations between the 'terrible four' and, on the other, the economic policy rule stating equality of the number of targets and instruments, from which the observation of insufficiency of the latter in order to reach the former derives.

As said, the first chapter deals with the crises. Almost the entire world – and in particular Europe – has recently suffered from a situation of economic crisis, which in some cases has considerably reduced the average levels of income and employment. This happened first as an effect of the burst of the financial bubble in the United States, which rapidly transmitted to Europe and many other developed countries, lasting in Europe for many years. More recently, since the beginning of 2020 the crisis has rekindled due to the burst of the pandemic. And this crisis threatens to be deeper and wider than the previous one, thus threatening to repeat the negative experience of the Great Crisis begun in 1929.

The crises of these last years have accentuated the risk of a second negative event that had been looming for a long time – especially in Europe, as an effect of the deflationary[1] institutions of the European Union (EU) and the European Monetary Union (EMU)[2] –

---

[1] The term *deflation* means 'reduction' in economic jargon. In particular, in this book it is used with two meanings, which are generally clear from the context. Literally, it has a meaning opposite to that of inflation and indicates a reduction in prices and wages. In this book it is sometimes used also as a synonym for the reduction of economic activity. The two situations – price and wage reduction and reduction of economic activity – are related one to the other.

[2] This is the set of European Union countries that adopt a common currency, i.e., the euro. The European Union is a supranational political and economic organisation, which – after the UK's exit in January 2020 – includes twenty-seven European countries. Its origins date back to the European Coal and Steel Community (ECSC), born in 1952, and then to the European Common Market and Euratom of 1957. It is currently governed by the Lisbon Treaty of 2007. The EU is administered by various bodies, among which at least the European Commission should be mentioned.

without emerging clearly. We refer to secular stagnation, that is, to the tendency of the rate of growth of GDP to decline in the long run. This is the object of Chapter 2, where we show – among other things – that the rate of growth of advanced countries fell by 1 percentage point in the thirty-five years after 1971.

An aspect of the crises and stagnation is the reduction in the average income (and/or its rate of growth) and employment. The negative effects on these variables of the financial crisis begun in 2007 declined with its termination, but resumed in the last couple of years, due to the pandemic. Another effect of the crises and stagnation is the worsening of distribution and the rise of the poverty rate, especially in some European Union countries. Inequality also rose in other countries, especially in the USA and the UK. In Chapter 3 we highlight the effects of the crises on both the rise of poverty and inequalities and the reduction of the efficiency of economic systems. Inequalities have increased, with few exceptions not only in each country, but also at the world level, between the different countries, due to globalisation (with which we deal in Chapter 4), which can be defined as a rise in the movements of people, goods and capital. Some aspects of globalisation have merits, since they correspond to a more intense relationship between peoples, but others imply also some possible disadvantages, such as the rise of the degree of monopoly, due to the formation of international oligopolies or monopolies, as a consequence of some types of capital movements. International movements of people are potentially more beneficial for various reasons, as the historical experience shows. However, their concentration in the space and time can cause no minor problems of economic, social and political nature. Finally, the rise in the international exchange of goods has in some cases displaced old trades and professions, negatively affecting

---

Another body is the European Parliament, which, however, performs reduced functions compared to those of national parliaments. Instead, the EMU is mainly governed by the European Central Bank (ECB).

the distribution of income. All these effects can largely be charged to the absence of institutions capable of governing globalisation, as this role is in the real world attributed almost completely to the pure operation of markets. As mentioned, we deal with these issues in Chapter 4.

The threads of the analysis carried out in these four chapters are reconnected in Chapter 5, which shows more clearly the reciprocal relations between the economic phenomena we have been dealing in those chapters.

The issues the book deals with involve use of concepts of economic analysis and policy (in some cases also of true political concepts) as well as of statistics. The book is recommended for the reader interested in economic problems even if he/she does not have a specifically economic culture, since understanding of many terms is facilitated first by their careful explanation in a very succinct way offered immediately after their use or in footnotes, when the explanation can be given in a few lines, and in addition by a large final glossary. (The terms contained in the glossary are underlined at first mention in the text.) Some boxes contain very detailed explanations of some concepts for readers familiar with an economic culture. Then, the book develops at three levels: a level that allows understanding concepts for all readers with some culture (even if not a specific economic one), through short explanations of the meaning of some terms; another one, involving understanding through consultation of the glossary; and, finally, through use of boxes for readers having some knowledge of economics.

The actuality of the problems enquired implies some difficulties in dealing with them, due to the rapidity of the resulting changes. Think, for example, of the effects of the crisis due to the pandemic, which change almost incredibly from one month to another, faster than the publication of this book.

Some parts of this book reproduce some previous contributions of mine (sometimes reworked also for the necessary updates), especially those contained in Acocella (2020a, b, c).

I am grateful to my friends Guido Candela, Grazia Ietto Gillies and Vincenzo Macchia, who have overhauled my previous versions of the book with great care, allowing me to have a better outcome. Thanks also to Augusto Frascatani for having prepared the figures with his usual skill.

I The Great Recession and the Pandemic

Negative economic consequences on <u>GDP</u> and employment have derived in the last fifteen years or so from two types of recessions, one tied to the financial crisis and the other, more recently, to the pandemic. We will deal with both in the following sections of this chapter, starting from their determinants and then going to their effects and some possible solutions.

I.I RECESSIONS THROUGH TIME

I.I.I Previous Financial Crises of a Speculative Nature until the 2000s

A premise is indispensable referring to the nature of the Great Recession – and in effect to other previous crises. In this chapter we first deal with a crisis of an essentially financial origin or nature, not being the result of a purely cyclical fluctuation of the real economy, that is, of the economy directly tied to production of goods. The latter are in fact intrinsic to the capitalist development, which does not proceed in a linear manner, but, precisely, through cyclical fluctuations. In fact, it is normal that firms producing for the market can be mistaken in their production plans, producing more than can be absorbed by the market (thus leading to supply exceeding demand), which leads to a fall in prices, production and employment. By contrast, firms can produce less than demanded by the market, thus leading to price rises. If this happens for important sectors of the economy or, in any case, for more firms at the same time – due to euphoria or pessimism – a crisis, respectively, of over- or underproduction can arise. The nature of the crisis due to the pandemic is more complex and, from some points of view, similar to a typical capitalist crisis, even if originating from an exogenous shock.

As to financial crises, their history is very long and can be traced back to the 'Tulip Mania', which hit the Netherlands when this country began growing tulips, after having imported them from Turkey. Practically, contracts were devised for these flowers that can be considered the forerunners of the current *futures*.[1] Bulbs were bought together with flowers for the value guaranteed by the flowers that would originate from them. The peak of speculation took place at the turn of 1636–1637. Within two to three months the price of bulbs rose by fifteen times and more, until an auction of bulbs went deserted, originating a wave of panic, which resized the value of bulbs, leading it more or less to the initial one.

After this crisis, forerunner of financial crises, other crises took place in the subsequent centuries. Notable are those of 1792 and 1825, linked to bank positions and speculative activities, but the first crisis of a truly big dimension was that begun in Vienna in 1873, called the Great Depression, whose roots were sales of shares as a consequence of a wave of panic.[2]

At the end of October 1929, instead, the Great Crisis erupted in the USA. This financial crisis was grafted on to a good trend that the economy had shown throughout the 1920s, due also to the numerous innovations introduced in those years or in previous decades. The crisis derived from the development of financial instruments and the role played by the stock market. Expectations of a further real growth, possibly at higher rates, were largely diffused and stimulated a

---

[1] These are forward contracts that are drafted with standard rules so that they can be traded easily on the stock exchange. With them you undertake to make a deferred purchase at a predetermined price.

[2] It may be important to realise with Minsky that purely financial crises 'do not rely upon exogenous shocks to generate business cycles of varying severity' (Minsky, 1992: 9). Minsky's financial instability hypothesis holds that capitalist economies exhibit inflations and debt deflations having the potential to spin out of control: '[T]he economic system's reactions to a movement of the economy amplify the movement–inflation feeds upon inflation and debt-deflation feeds upon debt-deflation' (Minsky, 1992: 2).

stock market speculation, starting from 1922. In the next seven years, the average index of stock values had grown by about six times and stock ownership, direct or indirect (through *investment trusts*, forerunners of today's mutual funds[3]) had largely diffused, based on the expectation of strong earnings in the value of stocks due to the economic growth.

At the end of October 1929 with Wall Street's Black Thursday (October 24), euphoria was followed by panic and a series of falls in equity values of the order of magnitude of 40% in a month's time, with uncontrolled sales of shares. Obviously, the nature of the circuit that had made the boom possible could not limit the effects of panic to the stock market. The banks themselves, which were at the origin of the financial chain, were involved in the wave of panic. The fear of insolvency in relation to credits granted involved depositors, causing them to fear the insolvency of the banks themselves and triggering a bank run. As a consequence of this, in 1930 the large Bank of the United States bankrupted, followed by other banks (almost 10,000 from 1930 to 1933) of all sizes, with a loss for depositors of about 20%. From the financial sector the crisis moved to the real one, influencing first the prices of primary products and then the level of industrial production. Both collapsed. The prices of raw materials dropped to a variable extent from 40% to 60%.

The solution that was initially taken was support, through customs protection, of the non-agricultural raw materials and industry. However, foreign countries replied to these measures with similar measures, resulting in a general reduction of demand and, then, of production, income and employment in advanced countries. Unemployment rose to levels never seen before, touching values equal to 25% in the USA. The price collapse also determined a rise in the values of debt in real terms (i.e., in terms of ability to purchase

---

[3] These are a pool of money collected from many investors and used to invest in various types of securities (stocks, bonds and/or other assets).

goods),[4] thus creating further difficulties for firms, which are usually operators for whom debts incurred in order to make investments exceed credits.

The first financial crisis of the period after World War II has to do with the continuous US balance-of-payments[5] deficits, which undermined other countries' confidence in the convertibility of the dollar into gold. Therefore, on 15 August 1971, US President Nixon was compelled to declare inconvertibility of the dollar into gold, ending the system in place since 1945, with the convertibility rate of US$35 per ounce. This decision determined a long period of instability in the currency markets, with the devaluation of the dollar with respect to other currencies in the following years, the rise in the margins of fluctuations of exchange rates and the passage to a system of flexible exchange rates.

Despite the significant tensions that emerged during the period under review and the absence of a well-thought-out and substantial reform, the system of international payments has been able to operate without further traumatic ruptures since that of August 1971, except that for the crisis of the European Monetary System (EMS)[6] in the early nineties, which hit some European countries, and those of some

---

[4] More generally, the expression 'real terms' refers to a value derived from a nominal value (i.e., expressed in the current value of the money) that has been adjusted to take into account the effects of inflation. If, e.g., one's wage has increased from 100 to 110, i.e., by 10%, and prices have risen by 5% in the same period of time, i.e., have increased from 100 to 105, one can say that the value of the new wage in real terms is $110/105 = 1.0476$, i.e., while nominal wages have risen by 10% at current prices, they have risen by only 4.76% in terms of purchasing power. If, instead, prices have increased by 15%, the new wage in real terms is $110/115 = 0.9565$ (at constant prices the wage has reduced by almost 4.35%).

[5] The balance of payments records the economic transactions between residents and non-residents of a country. It is made up of two parts. The first, also known as current account, basically includes exports and imports of goods, including services. The second part is called the capital account. The algebraic sum of the balance of the two accounts gives the change in official reserves, which is shown in balance in the capital account.

[6] The EMS, which entered into force in 1979, was a monetary agreement between the member countries of the then–European Economic Community which ceased to exist on 31 December 1998 with the creation of the EMU. The system tended to maintain a fixed exchange rate parity (within the limits of ± 2.25% or ± 6% for Italy

South East Asian countries, Russia and some emerging countries, including Argentina, since 1997.[7]

I.I.2   *The Great Recession*

The determinants and the evolution of the financial crisis in the USA are well known.[8] In Europe, it appeared initially in forms similar to the American ones, but they soon took on a very different guise. This was due first to the different type of financial system, lacking control, supervision and rescue instruments common to the whole EMU, also called Eurozone (EZ) or Euroarea (EA), even if also in the USA deregulation had dismantled the centralized control on the financial system. An additional role was played by the specific financial imbalances that appeared in the EMU as a consequence of the formation of a monetary area. As mentioned, the accumulation of private debt in some countries (in particular the PIIGS countries, i.e., Portugal, Ireland, Italy, Greece and Spain, which constitute the so-called peripheral countries of the EMU) was inherent in the modalities of the common institutions, which caused macroeconomic imbalances.

The pre-existing imbalances became more intense when Germany decided to deal with the difficulties of a mature economy and the unification with the Eastern *Lander* by adopting a growth model driven by exports, supported by a real devaluation and a careful remodelling of its productive role and specialisation, especially with respect to Eastern European countries. There was freedom in capital movements and deregulation of the financial sector, as in the USA, but within a framework of asymmetrical structures of the different

and a few other countries). The currency turmoil of 1992 led to the exit of Great Britain and Italy and the revision of the agreement.

[7] Argentina has experienced a crisis also since 2018.

[8] The main components were: high levels of speculative bubbles for stocks and real estate, stemming in part from US housing policy; a mix of high lending and borrowing; extensive bankruptcies of financial institutions that do not accept time deposits; malfunctions in the system of corporate governance, i.e., for regulation of companies, particularly with respect to oversight of directors' activities; systematic violations of accountability and ethics in the financial sector; deregulation of the financial sector; and unpreparedness of policymakers and regulators for the crisis.

European countries, market rigidity and imbalances in the current account and public finance.

Finally, the EMU lacked the support of common active policies, in particular fiscal policies. After about 2005, the 'peripheral' countries began to run current account deficits also[9] with countries outside the EMU (China, Central and Eastern European countries) as well, due to trade liberalisation and the appreciation of the euro. These deficits were also filled by capital account surpluses with the 'core' EMU countries.

In the USA, instability had begun in 2007 and soon turned into a deep crisis in terms of the main macroeconomic indicators. It also immediately affected Europe, where it led to a long and deep recession, the Great Recession, as the reduction in levels of economic activity that began in 2008–2009 is known. In 2009, GDP fell by 3.1% in the USA and 4.4% in the EZ. Initially, the shock that hit Europe was symmetrical, involving practically all EMU countries, not just the peripheral ones. However, it became asymmetrical after the announcement in 2009 of false government statements about the state of Greek public finances and the solution given to Greek debt the following year.[10]

The solution – with the transfer of the exposures of the Greek banks to the EU and the IMF[11] – freed, on the one hand, the French, German and Italian banks from bad debts towards Greece (respectively for 60, 30 and 10 billion euros) and, on the other hand, the respective governments that would have had to cope with the crisis resulting from the insolvency of their banks. Greece was required to implement repeated budget restrictions and wage cuts for civil servants, together with liberalisation, privatisation and other structural

---

[9] They had continuously run current account deficits vis-à-vis core countries after 1999.

[10] The newly elected government announced that the deficit/GDP ratio for 2009 was approximately 15%, as opposed to the 6% announced by the previous government.

[11] This is the International Monetary Fund, an organisation founded in 1944 in Bretton Woods that aims to facilitate cooperation in the currency field. We will deal with it extensively in Section 4.3.1.

adjustments. This country received credits amounting to 110 billion euros over three years from the European Financial Stabilisation Mechanism (EFSM).[12]

When the financial crisis triggered by the Anglo-Saxon countries caused panic in the European financial system and affected the peripheral countries, capital returned to their countries of origin. The banks found themselves in difficulty and the states had to intervene with loans, which burdened the public debt and in turn threatened a sovereign debt crisis. More recently, this debt has been absorbed in part by the banks, causing problems for them as well and then again for the public debt.

Therefore, in addition to the private debt problem – and to a large extent as an effect of the public measures implemented to deal with it – a public debt problem arose in peripheral countries. The sovereign debts of these countries were hit by speculation and a 'flight to quality' by financial institutions. The spreads[13] between the interest rates paid on them and those on German *Bunds* – which had fallen to almost zero after entry into EMU – grew to unsustainable levels.

Markets misjudged the risks. Until 2007, they were dominated by overly optimistic forecasts that underestimated risks, as can be seen in Figure 1. Instead, after the first signs of the crisis they suddenly assumed pessimistic attitudes. There was thus a pendulum swing from a 'flight to risk' to a 'flight to safety' (De Grauwe and Moesen, 2009). In particular, Figure 1 shows that, especially in the first months of the Greek crisis, the spread on Greek ten-year government bonds over German rates (indicated by the line with the greatest increase, above that of Portugal) rose to incredible levels, raising their

---

[12] This Mechanism acquired funds from the financial markets guaranteed by the EU budget. As of 2012 it was replaced by the ESM, which will be discussed below.

[13] Spread is the yield differential between two securities (shares, bonds, government bonds) of the same type and duration. Normally, the yield of Italian bonds and of those of other governments in the EMU are compared with that of the *Bunds* issued by the German state (*Bundesanleihe*), considered fully solvent, and thus the spread indicates the higher yield of Italian bonds attributable to the risk of insolvency of that state.

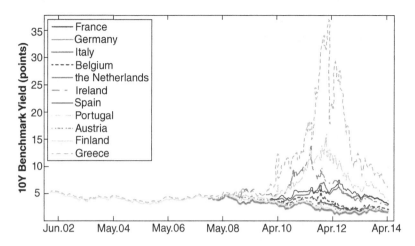

FIGURE I Government bond yields, March 2002–May 2014, EMU
(*Source*: Sensoy et al., 2015)

interest rate to around 35% in April 2012, reducing immediately thereafter, also as a result of the Outright Monetary Transactions (OMT).[14] The solution given to the crisis hit the Greek economy, causing it to fall into a depressive spiral, as had been predicted by a few analysts many years before.

The governments of the other countries also reduced public spending and raised taxes in an attempt to increase market confidence and to comply with European regulations. Thus, in a short time practically the entire EMU economy plunged back into recession. In light of this, the rules dictated by the EU appear to be self-destructive, also because they do not take into account the values of the multipliers. The core countries also suffered from this policy. In fact, their exports to other EMU countries declined. Meanwhile, the US economy had largely recovered.

[14] OMTs were the operations carried out by the ECB to purchase short-term government bonds issued by countries in serious and overt difficulty, following Draghi's famous speech in 2012 in which the ECB president declared that he would do 'whatever it takes' to save the euro.

Table 1. *Comparison of growth, unemployment and inflation, 2007–2016, EMU, USA*

	2007-16		2010-16	
Variable/Data	EMU	USA	EMU	USA
Annual growth (%)	0.4	1.3	0.9	2.2
Unemployment r. (differences in p. p.) *	2.0	0.2	−0.5	−4.9
Inflation rate (%)**	1.4	1.6	1.2	1.6

Source: OECD 2020a
* Change in the unemployment rate refers to EU 16, rather than EZ
** The inflation rate is measured through the CPI, i.e., the Consumer Price Index.

As can be seen from Table 1, in the six (nine) years after 2010 (2007), the EMU GDP grew at a rate of 0.9 (0.4)%, compared to 2.2 (1.3)% growth in the USA. Its unemployment rate in 2016 was -4.7 (+1.6) percentage point (p.p.) higher than in 2010 (2007), while the EMU unemployment rate grew by 0.5 (2.0) p.p. over the same period. The US inflation rate (1.6%) was higher than in the EMU (1.4 and 1.2%) for the entire period and particularly in the second, but this is largely due to the deflation that hit the EZ until 2014.[15]

The different performance in terms of unemployment and inflation, however, demonstrates a higher inflationary bias of the USA that in part stems from the relative interdependence between the Fed (i.e., Federal Reserve) and the US government.

The following section deals with one of the determinants of the financial crisis, the deregulation of the financial sector. Section 1.3 studies the dynamics of the crisis in its two components, the one of private debt and that of public debt.

---

[15] In the tables and figures presented in this chapter, the time references are often not to the most recent years for which data are available, but to the years even a little earlier. In fact, these data are more significant, in that they highlight the more violent impact of the crisis, which instead in more recent years is somewhat muffled.

I.2 THE CRISIS: EMU'S FINANCIAL AND FISCAL FRAGILITY

I.2.I Financial Deregulation

As with the USA, a central role for the EZ was played by the substantial deregulation of the financial sector and the disorganisation of the residual supervisory system. The financial sector had been significantly influenced by the Single Market, which played a decisive role on international trade in services in the European Community first and then in the EU, even more so than for other goods. In addition to currency controls, the barriers were (and to a lesser extent still are) mainly represented by the various regulatory systems adopted by member countries. In the field of financial services, these systems, justified by the need to safeguard systemic stability, certainly imposed different restrictions and rules from country to country, thereby segmenting individual national markets. However, they were not replaced by an appropriate regulation at the EU level.

The Community and the EU sought to reduce the existing barriers between the various financial markets, with a series of interventions, principally: (1) complete liberalisation of capital movements, as envisaged by the Delors Report of 1989; (2) harmonisation of some crucial parts of financial legislation, including the adoption of the universal bank model and minimum requirements and ratios between equity and assets (i.e., leverage[16] and, in the long run, solvency ratio); (3) automatic mutual recognition by other countries of the financial institutions (banks or investment companies) authorized to operate in an EU member country (single banking license); (4) home country supervision of all activities of a bank, including those of its foreign subsidiaries, with little EU regulation or supervision. Only after 2014 were partial regulation and supervisory powers introduced for the largest banks by the ECB, with a relatively small bailout fund

---

[16] Leverage or financial leverage is the ability to mobilise credit offered by the availability of a certain equity capital, which increases the availability of external financial means for investment purposes.

(the ESM, i.e., the so-called Bailout Fund); (5) introduction of a system (called TARGET) that allows banking systems in the centre to finance peripheral countries for their balance of payments deficits, making it possible to avoid the onset of a crisis when capital inflows no longer offset current account deficits, as happened in 2009–2010.

1.2.2 The Functioning of TARGET and the Resulting Problems

In order to understand this last point and also to provide a picture of the imbalances that have emerged between the various EU member countries, it is appropriate to briefly indicate the trends of their balances of payments. In practice, as we have said, until the outbreak of the crisis there were current account surpluses in the core countries and deficits in the peripheral countries. These surpluses resulted from the lower price dynamics in the countries of the first group, caused by a cut in wages. On the other hand, peripheral countries had the advantage of borrowing abroad precisely because – at the same nominal interest rate (given the free movement of capital) – they experienced higher inflation and therefore paid a lower real interest rate. This contributed to the creation of speculative bubbles, particularly for real estate, which reinforced the inflationary trend.

With the crisis that started in 2007–2008, investors from core countries feared the insolvency of peripheral countries and withdrew their loans to banks or states in these countries. The overall deficit that was created – in addition to the current account balance, as was the case before – also on the capital movements side was financed through the TARGET system. Banks in peripheral countries that were faced with a liquidity crisis due to liquidation and repayment of claims by other banks or creditors in core countries could turn to their central bank on behalf of the European Central Bank for credit, which actually happened from 2009 to 2010. The opposite was the case for banks in the core countries, whose liquidity was absorbed by their central bank. In this way the banking systems of the centre through the ECB financed the peripheral countries for their balance-

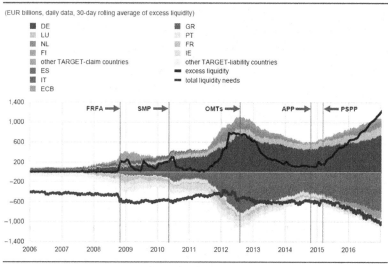

Source: ECB.
Notes: Excess liquidity reflects the sum of banks' account balances at their NCB and banks' recourse to the deposit facility, less the liquidity needs of the banking system. Liquidity needs are expressed as a negative number and reflect the sum of (net) autonomous factors and reserve requirements. FRFA stands for the fixed rate full allotment policy effective from 15 October 2008, SMP stands for the Securities Markets Programme launched in May 2010, OMTs stands for the Outright Monetary Transactions announced in August 2012, APP stands for the asset purchase programme that was initiated in October 2014 and PSPP stands for the public sector purchase programme that started in March 2015.

FIGURE 2 TARGET balances, total liquidity needs and excess liquidity (*Source*: Eisenschmidt et al., 2017)

of-payments deficits, making it possible to avoid the onset of a crisis when capital inflows no longer compensated for current account deficits, as was the case starting in 2009–2010 (see Figure 2).

1.3   THE DYNAMICS OF THE CRISIS IN THE EMU

The EZ crisis is usually characterized by the dynamics of public debt in certain countries, particularly the peripheral ones. This characterisation should be corrected or completed for several reasons.

First of all, the imbalances considered in Sub-section 1.1.2 originated to some extent before the creation of the EZ, although they later increased in some countries, due both to errors of approach in the EZ institutional framework and the inaction of national and European policymakers. In addition, some imbalances were inevitably symmetrical: deficits in some countries corresponded to surpluses in others, even within the EZ. However, the burden of adjustment fell largely on the deficit countries. Third, imbalances in private debt were more important than those in public debt (especially at the time of the US financial crisis) and, to a large extent, the pre-existence of the former gave rise to the latter (a 'transformation' problem, as we shall see). In turn, the public debt crisis generated a new private debt crisis, as in a 'diabolical loop'. Fourth, the fundamental determinants of the crisis of European private debt were often different from those that had triggered the financial crisis in the USA, stemming from countries' balance of payments imbalances in a situation of incomplete economic union. Finally, the American financial crisis only served as a trigger for the specific European crisis. To understand the reasons for this, it is necessary to analyse the causes, dynamics and effects of the crisis, in terms not only of the complex links between private and public debt, but also of the characteristics of the growth process in the EMU.

Let us analyse the formation of the debt crisis in Europe, also as an effect of the characters assumed by growth in different countries. We show that the public debt crisis was essentially a consequence of the private debt crisis and then of how the policies decided by the Union concurred to translate the debt crisis into a depression (Acocella, 2015). Under Section 1.3.1 below we show the relevance of the direction of capital flows before and after 2007. Under 1.3.2 we examine the progression of public deficit and debt.

1.3.1 The Trend in the Direction of Capital Movements before 2007 and Its Reversal

One source of the debt problem in Europe is strictly related to the US financial crisis. As mentioned above, the European crisis was triggered by the American one, but it germinated and developed in very different forms. Many European financial institutions – especially Irish and British – had invested in American Certificates of Deposit (CDs) for a total of around one-third of Asset Backed Securities (ABS) and were therefore exposed to the same risks as American banks. Indeed, they suffered even greater total losses (50%) from the end of 2007 to the end of 2008.

Another source of the debt problem in the EMU has to do with its institutions. With the monetary union, exchange rates became (irrevocably) fixed and the markets, perhaps too optimistically, ceased to perceive country risks, resulting in the near cancellation of spreads, despite the permanent divergence of inflation rates. The result was to produce low (or even negative) real interest rates in the periphery. The free movement of capital and the common monetary policy triggered a process of financial transfers from the centre to the periphery. Loans granted to the periphery rose to very high values, even higher than GDP, and were used for speculative operations in the real estate and stock markets and to underwrite public debt securities, overheating the sectors concerned, with speculative bubbles and a modest stimulation to income growth. On the other hand, it was convenient for core countries to lend to peripheral countries, because the real interest rate, calculated by deflating the common nominal interest rate by the lower price index of those countries, was higher.

Expectations of high real income growth deriving from bubbles and increased consumption convinced people of the sustainability of debt and made weak and uncertain the signals about imbalances, not only for citizens, but also for banks and policymakers. The analytical work of leading economists helped to induce people not to care about current account imbalances.

A lack of financial regulation in the EMU allowed the bubbles to grow. Their burst, threatening the entire European financial system, as we shall see in a moment, required the intervention of governments to rescue financial intermediaries and, thus, a rise in public deficits. And the absence, once again, of EMU policies forced individual countries to solve the problems on their own, despite the deflationary effects on the entire area that would have resulted from restrictive national policies. Some PIIGS countries actually implemented fiscal policies of this kind, while others preferred to maintain their previous position, resorting to questionable measures to increase labour market flexibility. Greece did not change any of its policies, with the consequences we know. However, inflation differentials with Germany for all PIIGS countries did not diminish, due to the previous wage reduction implemented by this country in 2003–2004. Appropriate wage policies set at the level of the EMU would have prevented the virulent onset of the crisis and, above all, its subsequent evolution.

From the end of 2007 capital stopped flowing into the PIIGS countries and from 2009 returned to the countries of origin, with a reduction in the leverage of banks and companies and the need for public intervention.

I.3.2 The Public Debt

Thus, in order to avoid bank failures, public debt replaced private foreign debt. Before 2007, it had been reduced throughout the EZ, with the exception of France, Germany, Greece, Portugal and the UK. And, as mentioned above, there were no signs of significant tensions in its development. The major difference between the core and the periphery lies in the fact that the former had shaped the economy in such a way as to make it more resistant to the crisis. For this reason, in particular, the public accounts were not overburdened by the need to counteract the shock. The sovereign debt situation after the crisis was heavier for the peripheral countries in particular, but also to some extent for the others (Tables 2 and 3).

The major causes of the sovereign debt crisis are to be found in the sequence of the following factors: (1) a marked increase in the sensitivity of financial markets to *fundamentals*[17] and contagion

---

[17] This term refers to the main characteristics of an economic system, which determine its performance at least in the medium term, beyond the effects of temporary shocks. From the macroeconomic point of view, they refer to the level of production factors that determine potential output and to the variables that influence consumption and economic growth, such as employment and unemployment rates, household disposable income, company profits and demographic factors.

Table 2. *Government budget balance/GDP (%), various years from 1999 to 2020, various EU countries*

GEO/TIME	1999	2007	2013	2016	2019	2020
UE 28 (27 since 2020)	−1.4	−0.5	−2.9	−1.4	−0.5	6.9
EZ 19	−1.5	−0.6	−3.0	−1.5	−0.6	7.2
Germany	−1.7	0.3	0.0	1.2	1.5	4.2
Ireland	3.5	0.3	−6.2	−0.7	0.5	5.0
Greece	−5.8	−6.7	−13.2	0.5	1.5	9.7
Spain	−1.2	1.9	−7.0	−4.3	−2.9	11.0
France	−1.6	−2.6	−4.1	−3.6	−3.0	9.2
Italy	−1.8	−1.3	−2.9	−2.4	−1.6	9.5
Portugal	−3.0	−2.9	−5.1	−1.9	−0.1	5.7
UK	0.6	−2.6	−5.5	−3.3	−2.3	n. a.

Source: Eurostat

Table 3. *Government debt/GDP (%), various years from 1999 to 2020, various EU countries*

GEO/TIME	1999	2007	2013	2016	2019	2020
UE 28 (27 since 2020)	n.d.	57.5	86.3	83.8	79.2	90.7
EZ 19	70.7	65.0	92.6	90.1	84.0	98.0
Germany	60.0	63.7	78.7	69.3	59.6	70.0
Ireland	46.6	23.9	119.9	74.1	57.4	59.5
Greece	98.9	103.1	178.4	180.8	180.5	205.6
Spain	60.9	35.6	95.8	99.2	95.5	120.0
France	60.5	64.5	93.4	98.0	98.1	115.7
Italy	109.7	99.8	132.5	134.8	134.7	155.8
Portugal	51.0	68.4	131.4	131.5	117.2	133.6
UK	39.9	41.9	84.2	86.8	85.4	n. a.

Source: Eurostat

Note: Data for 1999 and 2007 are not strictly comparable with others

followed by a 'wake-up call' among peripheral countries, absent before the crisis, when markets did not fully reflect fundamentals, for example, in terms of interest rates, which were not particularly high due to high country risk; (2) as a consequence of this, a return of capital to their home countries; (3) a significant increase in public deficits and debt in peripheral countries due to the need to bail out troubled banks; (4) a 'herd' effect[18] (which occurs when lenders follow the behaviour of operators considered more informed) that transmits the increase in sovereign debt risk between markets in PIIGS countries; (5) the transmission of contagion between different fiscal positions in peripheral countries; and (6) the diversification of contagion effects across countries, as some of these were hit more than others.

Over time, the ratios of public deficit or debt to GDP depended on the reactions of governments to the private debt crisis, in particular due to the operation of two factors: the public bailout of banks in difficulty and the deflationary policies adopted by all EMU countries since 2010. The former (albeit in various forms and size) was almost generalised, with public commitments for capital increases and guarantees on debts varying from country to country from 20% to 300% and more. The latter derived in part from deleveraging (i.e., a reduction in the leverage) of banks and companies – which reduced investment – and, in addition, from the reduction of the public deficit, tending to lower its ratio to GDP, which, however, also negatively affected the denominator. The absence of a common European fiscal policy and the EMU obligations to implement a 'healthy' fiscal policy

---

[18] This effect is linked to Keynes's 'beauty contest', according to which in choosing the most beautiful face in a competition in which those who had chosen the one they liked the most could have won a prize, instead of expressing their own personal judgement on the beauty of the competitors, people followed the strategy of trying to evaluate the most beautiful face according to the perception of beauty of the majority of the participants in the competition, thus following a second-order reasoning. But it is obviously possible to follow this path further, even arriving at reasoning of a higher order.

by each government, especially in peripheral countries, implied the 'fallacy of composition' and the 'savings paradox' accentuating the deflationary impulse.

The crisis had at least two negative consequences for credit. One consisted in its rationing. The other was the significant increase in the cost of credit in all peripheral countries – according to Neri (2013) on average by an order of magnitude from 60 to 130 basis points,[19] depending on the type of loans, at the end of 2011 – compared to the period in which spreads had remained constant (April 2010). The negative effects of the sovereign debt crisis also manifested themselves in the countries of the centre, with a reduction in economic activity and an increase in unemployment, due to trade links and the effects of this on market confidence.

Some economists believe that these negative effects could have been avoided with a stricter SGP (Stability and Growth Pact)[20] and a credible no-bail-out clause. In reality, on the one hand, Greece would still (or even more so) have contravened the rule; on the other hand, in Ireland the bailout of the banks would have been more difficult, with a further deflationary effect and difficulties for other countries. Indeed, the burden of the bailout was compounded by the poor design of the first EZ bailout fund, the European Financial Stability Facility (EFSF), which, by charging high interest rates, gave the markets a signal of significant risk of failure. Moreover, a stricter SGP would have exacerbated the deflationary effects.

As a tentative conclusion, we can say that institutions played a central role in the impact of the financial crisis in EMU. We will return to this consideration later. Instead, we must note that their

---

[19] The term – used in the financial field – means percentage points, for example with reference to changes in the interest rate; 1 basis point corresponds to a change of 0.01 percentage point and 50 basis points indicate a change of 0.50 percentage points, in case of a change in the interest rate from 2% to 2.50%.

[20] The Stability and Growth Pact is the rule valid in the EMU according to which the ratio between public deficit and GDP cannot exceed the level of 3%.

role was absolutely limited in many respects for the pandemic. Nonetheless, the economic measures adopted to overcome its deflationary effects go in the right direction and, indeed, introduce interesting novelties at the institutional level. We will deal with these in the following sections.

I.4   THE ECONOMIC IMPACT OF THE PANDEMIC SO FAR

At the end of 2019, forecasts for 2020 were positive, indicating a recovery in the global economy. Instead, in the first months of 2020 the negative effects of the pandemic hit the global economy, reflecting on: production, the aggregate demand[21] and supply[22] of all economies, international trade,[23] stock market prices[24] and inflation expectations as well as well as an initial significant increase in the spread in the yield of government bonds in EMU peripheral countries compared to German ones. Inflation has not risen too much so far in the periphery, thanks to the collapse of oil prices and many commodity prices, but it could rise, if the negative effects on supply prevail over those of demand. There would then be 'stagflation', that is, stagnation of production together with an increase in inflation.

In short, the effects of the pandemic were both real and financial (Mann, 2020). The real effects on industrial production may have taken a V-shaped or U-shaped form. In the first case, the fall in activity would be promptly followed by a recovery. In the second, the end of the fall would be followed by a period of stagnation before recovery. And this second case seems to have been the most common one, because of the occurrence of many V-shaped

---

[21] This is the demand for goods and services that occurs over a certain period of time in an economic system as a whole.

[22] Aggregate supply is the quantity of goods and services that are offered over a certain period of time in an economic system as a whole.

[23] The reduction in international trade due to the pandemic looks similar to that of the Great recession but will likely be less profound than initially feared.

[24] Indeed, stock market changes have had little relation to the underlying conditions of the various economies (Capelle-Blanchard and Desroziers, 2020).

changes in the various activities and locations, changes that, added together, gave rise to the other trend, namely, the emergence of a period of stagnation. The evolution of activity in services, on the other hand, was expected to have an L-shaped profile. Demand for energy and raw materials was expected to fluctuate. Forecasts of related price changes -at the end of 2019 and in January 2020 (e.g., a short-term increase of 10% in energy prices) were followed by a fall of, for example, 15% in these prices in February, with negative repercussions for income and business trends in producing countries. Obviously, in mirror terms, there were positive effects of the fall in these prices for the consuming countries.

As to the effects of the closures imposed by many countries, there is evidence that allows us to compare the case of Europe with those of the countries of South East Asia, in particular South Korea and Taiwan, in addition to China. In China there are sophisticated electronic systems on which the possibility of everyone to move about in the country depends, since each person is assigned a daily status. In the first twenty days of October 2020 there were no deaths, while in September there had been only sixteen deaths and the total number of infections was just under 86,000. Since then there have been only limited cases of infections until August 2021. As in China, in South Korea the closures of the first wave were limited to the region in which the outbreak initially developed, and the second wave was much less virulent than the first in terms of number of infections and duration, virtually exhausting itself in August 2020 with a peak in the number of infected involving less than half as many people as in the first. The Korean strategy, called 'test-trace-contain', involves an investigative team that has the task of reconstructing the movements of the infected. It is helped in this by surveillance cameras placed almost everywhere, outdoors and inside many buildings. Technology involving facial recognition is used to identify the infected, even with the cover of masks. The success was such that one per thousand cases of infection caused only a 2–3% drop in employment. In the last week of July 2021, there were a total of a little more than 197,000 infections in South Korea out of a population of just over 51 million. In Taiwan, a country of approximately 24 million inhabitants, there were from ten to twenty weekly infections in July 2021. Another virtuous country, in Oceania, is New Zealand, which has significantly reduced infections with a series of timely total closures. Lastly, the very drastic bans introduced by the South African Republic, which had made it possible to considerably limit contagions, should be noted, but they did not have a long life and in the 2021 summer the number of new cases peaked.

On the other hand, in European countries, and in the United States, more extensive but belated restrictions were adopted.[25] The total number of infected until the last week of July 2021 was: 34.6 million in the USA; 4.4 million in Spain; just under 6 million in France; 5.8 million in the UK and 4.4 million in Italy.

In 2020, there has been an estimated shortfall of 144 million jobs due to the pandemic (International Labour Organization, 2021). Figure 3 gives the time required to return to pre-pandemic levels of employment rates. While East Asian and some European countries will do so in the current year, some, such as the UK and the United States, should wait until the end of 2023, and others (the extreme cases are those of Iceland and Israel, not indicated in the figure) will do so only in 2025.

The effects of falling employment range between 5% and 6% in the United Kingdom and the United States, the difference between the two percentages possibly indicating the specific effects of limitations, which have affected economic relations over a wider area.[26] The reduction in employment is attributable essentially to

---

[25] Han and Mei Jin Tan (2020) point to the various control systems put in place in many countries.

[26] The important point is that the effect of limitations for the entire country is greater than the sum of the effects of limitations adopted in individual provinces. For example, limitations imposed on only one province (take the case of prohibition of movement of goods and people with the rest of the country) reduce the supply only of goods produced in that province, e.g., iron, that would normally be processed in other provinces, thus reducing only the use of iron elsewhere. They do not prevent

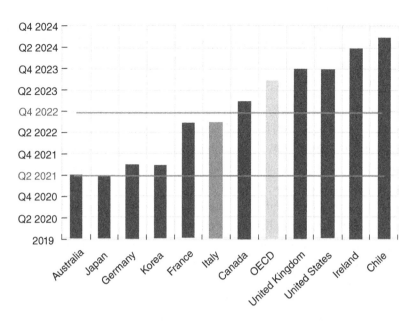

FIGURE 3 Time needed to return to pre-pandemic employment rates, various countries
(*Source*: OECD, 2021)

small businesses. In addition, certain sectors (hotels, restaurants, food, education, real estate and transportation) and less educated, younger and lower-paid workers with temporary contracts have been particularly affected. The removal of restrictions may imply only a limited recovery in employment, unless there is a marked decline in infections (Aum et al., 2020). The evidence available in relation to the United States shows that small businesses have suffered the most from the pandemic, for three reasons: first, their structural weakness, which had led 60% of them to lay off at least one worker before government provisions were introduced; second, owners' expectations, already negative to begin with, deteriorated over time, with

the continuation of economic activity in that province and elsewhere in other areas. On the contrary, restrictions of the same kind imposed throughout the country also reduce economic (and people) exchanges among other areas, thus restricting economic activity to that of survival and self-sufficiency in each of the sub-areas.

37% of respondents initially having negative expectations for the next two years, a percentage that later grew to 46%; and finally, smaller businesses are not at all aware of existing government provisions (Humphries et al., 2020).

In Italy and other advanced countries industrial production and the GDP are estimated to have fallen in the initial months, only to rise again at least until August 2020, but there has been a drop in the second half of 2020. Particularly affected were workers with fixed-term contracts, to the extent that can be inferred from Table 4 (due to the non-renewal or extension of employment contracts and the inability to benefit from extraordinary income support measures) in micro and small businesses that cannot resort to smart working or teleworking.[27]

A recovery in income and employment should take place in 2021, but – as partly seen – this will not always be able to offset the decline of 2020.

The effects on the population of the pandemic and the reduction in income and employment are different, depending on age and economic and social condition. With regard to age, it is true that the elderly are those most directly affected by the virus, but the younger generations have suffered more frequently – at least in many countries like Italy – sharp reductions in employment, due to the non-renewal of temporary contracts, more frequent among those who have recently entered the labour market. In addition, distance learning, which has replaced face-to-face lessons in schools and universities, has certainly reduced training, particularly for young people without computers or access to the Internet.

As for the differentiation of effects according to income distribution, the share of the population that does not have liquid assets to cope with negative income shocks grows considerably over time after the shocks, as shown in Figure 4.

---

[27] Smart working means remote work from a variable location through the digital network. It differs from teleworking, which is performed remotely from a fixed location.

Table 4. *Employees of active and suspended companies according to the nature of the occupation and the sector of economic activity, Italy*

Employment feature and sector	Employed in active firms	% of active people	Employed in suspended firms	% of active people	Total employed	%
Permanent employment industry	1,611,208	40.5	2,362,297	59.5	3,973,505	100
Permanent employment services	4,619,801	70.1	1,966,031	29.9	6,585,832	100
Permanent employment total	6,231,009	59.0	4,328,327	41.0	10,559,336	100
Temporary employment industry	155,400	49.1	161,305	50.9	316,704	100
Temporary employment services	898,260	68.2	419,079	31.8	1,317,338	100
Temporary employment total	1,053,659	64.5	580,383	35.5	1,634,042	100
Total industry	1,766,608	41.2	2,523,601	58.8	4,290,209	100
Total services	5,518,061	69.8	2,385,109	30.2	7,903,170	100
Total	7,284,669	59.7	4,908,710	40.3	12,193,379	100

Source: Centra et al., 2020

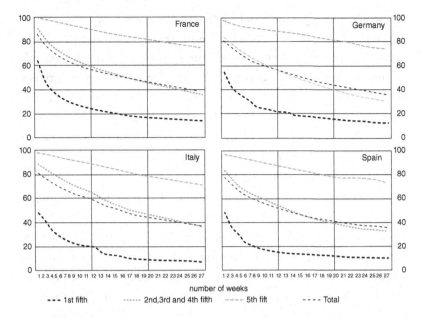

FIGURE 4 Share of population without liquid assets to cope with negative
income shocks by income distribution (%), various countries
(*Source*: Banca d'Italia, 2020)

In all the countries considered, twenty-seven weeks after the
shock, less than 20% of the first income quintile (i.e., the fifth part of
income earners with the lowest incomes, whose position is indicated
by the curve below) had sufficient assets. And the poor in Italy were
even more disadvantaged, also compared with those in Spain, given
that – as shown by the curve at the bottom – less than 7% of them have
such assets. The social and political consequences are easy to imagine.

Furceri and colleagues (2021), after having analysed the impacts
of previous pandemics, suggest the possibility that the distributional
consequences of COVID-19 will be larger than these (see more below,
Section 3.3).

In the Eurozone in October 2020, the European Commission's
estimates had improved somewhat compared to its previous ones.
But the worsening of the pandemic since the second half of the year
has reversed the direction of the changes again. The International

Monetary Fund (International Monetary Fund, 2021) has estimated a fall in GDP in 2020 of 6.5% for the Eurozone (a fall even higher with respect to the Fund's previous estimate, practically the largest fall among all areas). The reduction for the United States is smaller (3.5%). The reduction for Italy (8.9%) is the highest in the Eurozone, after Spain (10.8%). All areas should register a recovery in 2021, but in some cases at rates that will not be able to bring GDP back to the level of 2019, as for Italy and all advanced economies, with the exception of the USA.

As can be seen, not even the sum of the growth percentages in 2021 and 2022 can equal the fall for 2020. In addition to the fall in foreign demand and international tourist flows, the decrease in domestic demand would contribute to the trend in 2020. Similar forecasts were those formulated by the OECD.[28] As shown by Figure 5, the forecasts of the OECD were much worse than those of the International Monetary Fund, which may depend on the fact that, on the one hand, the former were made about three months after the latter and that, on the other, the pandemic has meanwhile extended to countries that were previously exempt from it or were scarcely affected. Instead, the World Trade Organization presents two scenarios for the world GDP trend (the best with a reduction of 2.5%, the worst with a fall of 8.8%) (World Trade Organization, 2021).

Similar data on the impact of the epidemic in the euro area on the basis of three scenarios, related to the intensity and duration of the infection, are produced by the ECB. In the most severe and intermediate scenarios, the decline in the EU GDP can arrive at 12% over the whole year, an increase of this variable, with a return to the values of 2019 that will take place in the years after 2022, while in the other scenarios the return could be anticipated to 2022 (ECB, 2021a).

---

[28] This is an intergovernmental economic organisation with thirty-seven member countries, mainly advanced ones.

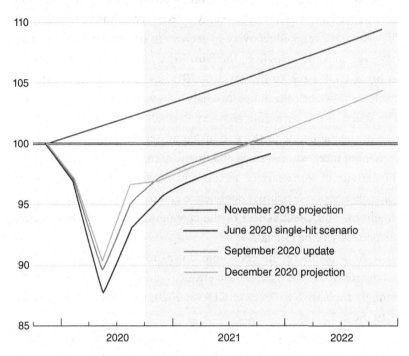

FIGURE 5 World GDP growth projection, 2021–2022
(OECD, 2020b)

If Europe and other areas that have been hit hard do not act in a timely, massive and coordinated manner, in 2020–2021 the decline could be more than double that of 2008–2009. Compared to the financial crisis, this is different: Back then it was an avoidable failure of finance and global demand in some countries, up to the Greek disaster. In that case, the support of demand was (or would have been) sufficient to revive the economy. Today the pandemic shock, in addition to hitting demand, also reduces global supply, as will be seen later.

The speed of recovery will depend on both the duration of the pandemic and the effectiveness of the economic policies that will be implemented. All the data available on the evolution of the GDP of most advanced economies incorporate a strongly negative evolution in the first half of 2021, followed by a recovery in the second half of the year and a marked recovery in activity in the whole 2021, unable, however, in some cases (e.g., the Euro Area, Japan and Latin America) to bring GDP back to the level of 2019, as shown in particular in Table 5; however, the range of analysts' evaluations is very broad. The speed of the economic recovery depends not only on the evolution of the pandemic in the various countries, but also on the development of international trade and financial markets, on the effects on the activity of some service sectors and, as mentioned above, on the consequences on consumer confidence and income. In particular, the timeliness and effectiveness of the economic policy measures being introduced will be crucial.

As a result of the economic downturn and the strong fiscal policy reaction, the general government budget deficit in the EZ strongly increased, to 7.3% of GDP in 2020, whereas it was 0.6% in 2019 (ECB, 2021a).

In various European countries, the use of the redundancy fund has mitigated the impact of the health emergency on the number of employees. The governments have already launched significant expansionary measures to support the health system, families and businesses affected by the crisis, strengthening the social safety nets system, suspending tax payments, declaring a moratorium on bank loans and granting public guarantees on loans for businesses.

Extraordinary monetary measures have been implemented also by European institutions: The ECB has introduced a broad package of measures with more expansionary refinancing operations to reduce the cost of bank funding and support corporate liquidity and a new purchase program of securities for the pandemic emergency. As for the other measures, ESM plans, and the like, have been announced, as will be discussed more extensively in Section 1.7. The European Commission has activated the general safeguard clause provided for in the SGP, which allows temporary

Table 5. *Recorded and projected changes in* GDP *by countries and regions, 2019–2023*

(Percentage change from previous year)

	2018	2019	2020e	2021f	2022f	2023f
World	**3.2**	**2.5**	**−3.5**	**5.6**	**4.3**	**3.1**
Advanced economies	**2.3**	**1.6**	**−4.7**	**5.4**	**4.0**	**2.2**
United States	3.0	2.2	−3.5	6.8	4.2	2.3
Euro area	1.9	1.3	−6.6	4.2	4.4	2.4
Japan	0.6	0.0	−4.7	2.9	2.6	1.0
Emerging market and developing economies	**4.6**	**3.8**	**−1.7**	**6.0**	**4.7**	**4.4**
East Asia and Pacific	6.5	5.8	1.2	7.7	5.3	5.2
China	6.8	6.0	2.3	8.5	5.4	5.3
Indonesia	5.2	5.0	−2.1	4.4	5.0	5.1
Thailand	4.2	2.3	−6.1	2.2	5.1	4.3
Europe and Central Asia	3.5	2.7	−2.1	3.9	3.9	3.5
Russian Federation	2.5	2.0	−3.0	3.2	3.2	2.3
Turkey	3.0	0.9	1.8	5.0	4.5	4.5
Poland	5.4	4.7	−2.7	3.8	4.5	3.9
Latin America and the Caribbean	1.8	0.9	−6.5	5.2	2.9	2.5
Brazil	1.8	1.4	−4.1	4.5	2.5	2.3
Mexico	2.2	−0.2	−8.3	5.0	3.0	2.0
Argentina	−2.6	−2.1	−9.9	6.4	1.7	1.9
Middle East and North Africa	0.6	0.6	−3.9	2.4	3.5	3.2
Saudi Arabia	2.4	0.3	−4.1	2.4	3.3	3.2
Iran, Islamic Rep.[3]	−6.0	−6.8	1.7	2.1	2.2	2.3
Egypt, Arab Rep.[2]	5.3	5.6	3.6	2.3	4.5	5.5
South Asia	6.4	4.4	−5.4	6.8	6.8	5.2
India[3]	6.5	4.0	−7.3	8.3	7.5	6.5
Pakistan[2]	5.5	2.1	−0.5	1.3	2.0	3.4
Bangladesh[2]	7.9	8.2	2.4	3.6	5.1	6.2
Sub-Saharan Africa	2.7	2.5	−2.4	2.8	3.3	3.8
Nigeria	1.9	2.2	−1.8	1.8	2.1	2.4
South Africa	0.8	0.2	−7.0	3.5	2.1	1.5
Angola	−2.0	−0.6	−5.2	0.5	3.3	3.5

Source: World Bank, 2021c
[2] and [3]: GDP growth rates are on a fiscal year basis

deviations from the medium-term budgetary objective or from the path towards the latter. The European institutions have also prepared a substantial expansion of the tools available to cope with the effects of the pandemic.

1.5 FORECASTS ON THE DURATION AND INTENSITY OF THE IMPACT

The pandemic spread from China, where it started at the end of December 2019. After an initially faster start in Italy, until the end of February 2020, the outbreak had spread to some South East Asian countries, Japan and South Korea, while remaining limited to an area of the latter. In Europe, after Italy the virus spread to the rest of Europe (France, Germany, United Kingdom and Spain) and to the Middle East. One or two weeks later than in Italy, the contagion had also begun to spread to the United States, Canada, Russia, Turkey and Latin American countries, especially Brazil. The number of infections and victims was rather low in Germany and some Scandinavian countries. Sub-Saharan Africa was also relatively little affected by the infections, but the economic effects will also be significant for these countries. The geographic distribution of cases recorded up to July 2021 is shown in Figure 6.

It should be considered that to the direct victims of the virus must be added the probable victims deriving both from the delay of medical and hospital visits and treatment (think of oncological diseases) due to the closure of the presidia and the difficulty of movement of the population on the territory. These aspects of the problem have been the subject of studies for Italy by Nomisma researchers (see Piccioni and Perrelli, 2020, Perrelli Branca and Piccioni, 2020), who have evaluated the incidence of lethal cases on visits made in the past, but on the consequences no data are currently available, which, unfortunately, will emerge in the coming months and years from a comparison of mortality with the past.

Figure 7 presents the curves of daily cases of infected, positive, healed and deaths and Figure 8 indicates the vaccines doses

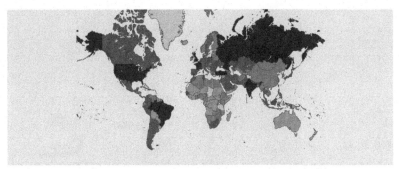

Globally, as of 6:30pm CEST, 30 July 2021, there have been 196.553.009 confirmed cases of COVID-19, including 4.200.412 deaths, reported to WHO. As of 29 July 2021, a total of 3.839.816.037 vaccine doses have been administered.

FIGURE 6 Number of Covid-19 cases detected from the start of the pandemic to 30 July 2021, worldwide
(*Source*: WHO, 2021)
Note: The extent of the infections is indicated by the intensity of the color: lower for the countries indicated in light blue and gradually increasing towards dark blue.

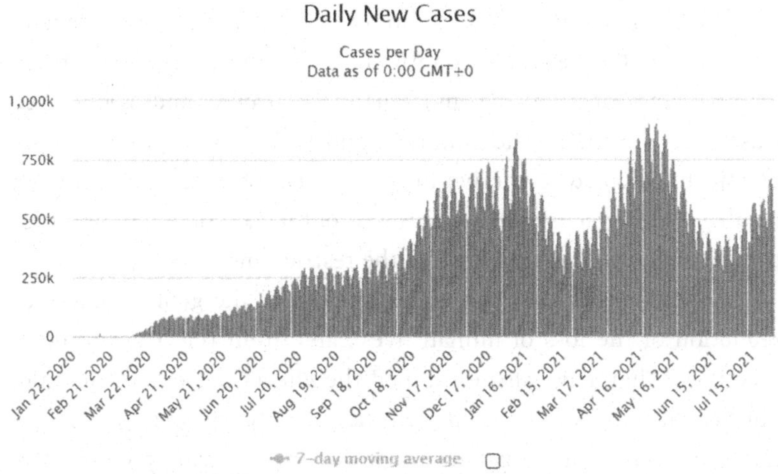

Daily New Cases

Cases per Day
Data as of 0:00 GMT+0

FIGURE 7 Total daily cases, 22 January 2020–15 July 2021, World
(*Source*: www.worldometers.info/coronavirus/)

administered in the period December 2020–July 2021 in some countries. One can see how important vaccination has been for countries such as China, Japan and Brazil, which show data much higher than the world average, and Germany, India, the UK and the USA.

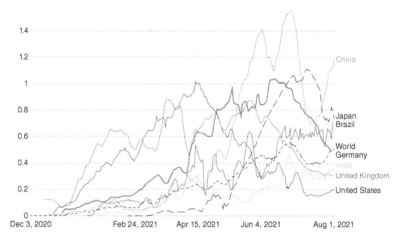

FIGURE 8 Daily Covid-19 vaccine doses administered for 100 people, December 2020–August 2021, various countries
(*Source*: Roser and Ortiz-Ospina, 2019)

The intensity and duration of the consequences[29] depend crucially on the restrictions introduced by the authorities of the various countries on the movement of people and goods (see Caselli et al., 2020). The countries and regions that promptly and drastically adopted restrictive measures have obtained so far a good result – barring subsequent returns of outbreaks, due, among other things, to an untimely removal of the restrictions.

According to Deb and colleagues (2020) the greatest effect of reduction of the loss of human lives came from the ban on public meetings. They have also examined the effects not only economic, but also in terms of pollution, and therefore the possibility of facilitating the spread of the pandemic, of the limitations imposed by the authorities. Another result of their analysis is the inverse relationship between the restriction measures and the emission of nitrogen dioxide, a known pathogen.

---

[29] On the importance of infections deriving by contacts in bars and restaurants, see research carried out by many people (Fisher et al., 2020). On the non-economic consequences, in terms of effects on people's health and well-being, see Giuntella et al. (2021).

Becchetti et al. (2020) present various data and analyses that show the crucial influence of fine particles on the extent of infections. Not surprisingly, in Italy this was higher in the provinces of the areas with higher pollution and less ventilation, such as those of the Po Valley. Similar results are those obtained by Wu et al. (2020) with reference to the United States. This work finds that the increase of a fine dust (the one called PM2.5) in the measure of 1 µg/m3 (that is, of a microgram – or a millionth of a gram – of dust per 1 cubic meter of air) is associated with an 8% increase in the rate of increase in deaths from COVID-19. The reason that can explain the influence of pollution on the extent of infections is relatively simple. In fact, pollution puts the first lines of defence of the respiratory tract at risk, facilitating inflammation and chronic diseases (Conticini et al., 2020).

Apart from the limitations imposed that have been mentioned so far, it should be emphasized that their effectiveness in reducing the spread of the epidemic depends crucially on the behaviour of the population. There are investigations from which it emerges that a high number of initial infections can lead the population to greater caution and the use of fruitful measures to limit the spread of the epidemic (Battiston and Gamba, 2020). From the analyses conducted by various researchers, it also appears that the extent of the infections can be put in an inverse relationship with the social capital of the regions or countries that have introduced the limitations (Bartscher et al., 2020). Similar results are obtained by Durante et al. (2020), who document how after the start of the epidemic and before the restrictions on the movement of people were introduced by the authorities, mobility was reduced much more in Italian areas with a greater social capital (see Figure 9). In fact, in the pre-pandemic period the gap between provinces with the highest civic capital and the others equalled 0.18 movements per day; in the second period it was only 0.076.

Putnam's (1993) analysis actually distinguishes two types of social capital: 'bridging' social capital as differentiated from 'bonding'

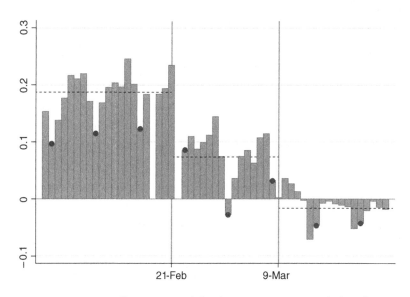

FIGURE 9 Differences in mobility between provinces, including those with the highest 25% social capital and others, 2020, Italy
(*Source*: Durante et al., 2020)
Notes: 1. On the horizontal axis are indicated the dates. On the vertical one, the differences in mobility.
2. Dots indicate Sundays.

social capital. The former refers to trust in relationships between social groups. The second, on the other hand, concerns trust in family relationships. The results of the analysis of Alfano and Ercolano (2020), referring to the different Italian regions, show an opposite effect on the infections of the two types of social capital. In particular, the Southern regions tend to have a higher value of the second type of social capital, while Tuscany, Liguria, Piedmont, Valle d'Aosta and Friuli-Venezia Giulia have a greater value of the first type. And the second type of social capital seems to have the greatest effects in terms of curbing contagion.[30]

---

[30] Obviously, this is a partial analysis, whose results should be considered together with those of other causal factors, such as pollution.

The forecasts on the duration of the pandemic are absolutely uncertain, also because it will be necessary to wait for the results of the easing of restrictions that took place in many locations as well as in light of people's behaviour. The fact is that after August 2020 the contagion curve has soared to levels well above those of the first wave of infections, and in Autumn 2021 the fourth wave was expected. According to some American epidemiologists and immunologists, the duration could be several years, and further outbreaks of infections could occur in the coming winters. To avoid them or reduce their extent, it will be necessary to extend social distances until 2022, and even later outbreaks could resume (Kissler et al., 2020). Obviously, all this is in the event that effective antiviral drugs are not introduced.

Figure 4, already presented, showed the impact of the epidemic in the euro area on the basis of three scenarios essentially related to the intensity and duration of the infection. In the most severe and intermediate scenarios, the decline in GDP can even reach 12% in the whole of 2020, with the return to the values of 2019 in the years after 2022.

The problem is that – even apart from antiviral drugs – the scenarios are not a completely exogenous datum, that is, only due to chance and to the danger itself of the virus. They also depend on the health and social distancing policies, and so forth, adopted by the authorities of a country and on people's behaviour. The results are crucially based on people's trust in the country's political authorities that underlies their behaviour. According to some, the greater success achieved by some Northern European countries in containing infections depends on the greater trust placed in the authorities of those countries (Rothstein, 2020). This can create a vicious (or virtuous) circle: The intensity of the epidemic depends on people's trust in political authorities, but trust in turn depends on the intensity of the epidemic.

Referring to partly different concepts, the economic malaise deriving from the pandemic and the difficulties that originate from it (from the point of view of the ability of individual countries and various international institutions to cope with it) feed the populist attitudes of individuals and political parties, giving rise to authoritarian tendencies and/or the isolation of individual countries. According to Kroll (2020), the extension of these attitudes is linked to the inability of various countries to pursue the goals of sustainable development, ranging from the reduction of poverty, inequality and pollution to the maintenance of peace.

1.6   THE DUAL NATURE OF THE SHOCK, FROM SUPPLY AND DEMAND, AND THE POLICIES NEEDED

The immediate effect of the epidemic on production is to reduce the availability of one of the factors of production – labour – causing a supply shock. Obviously, the ensuing fall in demand for goods due to reduction of employment and income has a further effect of reducing the supply, because the owners of the affected activities decide to close the production sites. And to these negative effects one should add those for the closure of the activities decided by the owners following the lack of bank loans. The effect of the measures imposed by public authorities introducing bans and limitations is similar in nature. The subsequent effect is no longer a supply shock, but again a demand shock. In fact, above all, current incomes are lacking for people affected by the epidemic and, in realistic conditions, there is no possibility of discounting the availability of sufficient income in the future. This implies a more or less generalized fall in demand, which manifests itself in particular when some activities are reopened. This is followed by shocks of supply, first, of demand, then, and again shocks of the first and second type.[31]

Overall, we can identify some lasting negative effects of the epidemic. The resulting unemployment implies depreciation of human capital, due to inactivity and disaffection with work that follows, the possible loss of specific human capital for companies, the separation of existing work capacities from the specific production

---

[31] Brinca et al. (2020) have measured the different impact of the two types of shock, concluding that the shocks of supply, through the reduction of labour input, were more important, but the demand shocks were significant in sectors not affected by the closures and restrictions, such as some manufacturing sectors.

methods they are used to, school closures and the lasting impoverishment of education that results (Portes, 2020), with obvious negative effects on <u>productivity</u> (on this see further Rehman et al., 2020). A particular negative effect on <u>productivity</u> that acted in Italy was the delay in digitalisation (see Cinquegrana et al., 2020). Obviously, the recovery will depend on the measures the government takes to counter supply and demand shocks and to boost production and employment.[32] Another important factor is related to the distribution of losses deriving from shocks. As Gobbi et al. (2020: 1) note, in fact, 'the pace of the recovery of economic activities…will depend in a fundamental way on how the measures undertaken by governments and other authorities will determine the allocation of losses among the different economic actors (companies, banks, households, governments and central banks) as well as the temporal distribution of such losses'.

BOX 1   **The effects of supply and demand shocks in terms of aggregate supply and demand curves**

For the reader who has knowledge of economics, the following representation, which indicates the effects of the pandemic in terms of aggregate demand and aggregate supply, may be helpful. The amount of work used in the economy is represented on the abscissa axis of Figure B1. Labour <u>productivity</u> is indicated on the ordinate. The aggregate demand curve is indicated by the AD. That of the aggregate supply by the horizontal line, which initially is positioned at level g. As part (a) of the Figure shows, when there is a negative supply shock, the aggregate supply curve shifts to position g', recording a reduction in employment, from l⁻ to l'. Obviously, if there were a (negative) demand shock at the same time,

---

[32] The effects of these shocks are illustrated in refined terms in Box 1. The need to adapt economic policies in China to the variability and uncertainty of the development of the pandemic is underlined in Fang (2021). The arguments developed in Fang's book can be referred also to other countries. Baldwin (2021) insists on the role of science and prevention, on the one hand, and of citizen's actions, on the other.

BOX 1   **(cont.)**

the AD curve would shift to the left, with a further reduction in employment. Only a sufficient increase in aggregate demand, indicated by the shift of the aggregate demand curve to the right, in the AD' position, could bring employment back to the initial level.

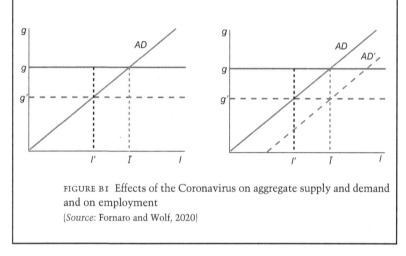

FIGURE B1 Effects of the Coronavirus on aggregate supply and demand and on employment
(*Source*: Fornaro and Wolf, 2020)

In correspondence with the two types of shocks, we indicate the policies necessary for a country like Italy. We distinguish the case of supply policies, which we deal with first, from that of demand policies.

Supply policies must be adopted both immediately and in the longer term. The former must tend, on the one hand, to contain infections – which implies restrictions on supply, for the prohibition to carry out certain activities or in any case for the constraints imposed on production methods – and, on the other, to increase production, particularly of the goods necessary to treat and combat the epidemic (such as masks, disinfectants and the construction or adaptation of fixed structures, in particular those necessary for treatment) or its effects, with the provision of basic necessities for affected families. These measures may require the direct intervention of public entities or the use of incentives to private agents.

The supply policies to be implemented in the longer-term concern, first of all, the rejection of *market fundamentalism*, considering that the market has shown considerable rigidity, not so much in the movement of prices, but in the re-orientation of resources from the sectors where prices are falling towards those where prices rise. Public action will tend to be directed primarily towards the correction of the production structure. For a country like Italy the fields of intervention are numerous, as are the distortions of the economic and administrative structure of this country. In addition, the public sector must be significantly reformed, increasing its efficiency and reducing the high ratio of public debt to GDP both by combating tax evasion and avoidance[33] and by stimulating GDP growth.

The private sector also needs to increase its efficiency (essentially, the low productivity dynamics, due in large part to low investment in R&D) and to increase the small size of companies. There is also a need to increase the role of the green economy, regulation of the environment, of traffic and many other activities.

A field of particular attention is that of the reform of the legal system of the economy, in particular of company, bankruptcy, procedural and competition law. This reform should tend to induce companies to seek profit with competition through prices and even more through the innovations incorporated in new investments and the consequent increase in productivity. A particular aspect of the reform should concern the relations of the public administration with companies, in particular for the procurement or management of infrastructures (Ciocca, 2020).

As for the public budget, both short- and medium-term measures would be needed. Among the former, public transfers to

---

[33] Tax evasion can be defined as the set of methods by which a citizen or a company tends to reduce or eliminate the tax levy by the state, violating existing rules, with the consequence of making a public budget deficit more likely.

Tax avoidance (or elusion) is the circumvention of the laws in force, which – while not constituting an offense (as in the case of tax evasion) – leads to the same result.

companies must be included to compensate them for the losses in turnover and cover current expenses, in order to avoid excessive indebtedness to banks. In the medium term, public financing instruments could be created to restructure the debts of medium and large companies. The financing of these instruments could largely take place through the issuance of long-term debt. Tax incentives could also be introduced to recapitalize businesses (Gobbi et al., 2020).

In June 2020 the Colao Commission in Italy suggested:

- first of all, the strengthening of the economic and productive structure, with innovation, reduction of the fragmentation and undercapitalisation of companies;
- the improvement of infrastructures and the environment;
- the protection and enhancement of tourism, art and culture;
- increasing the transparency and productivity of the public administration;
- the enhancement of education and research;
- finally, the care of people and social cohesion, also with protection from inequalities.

Some of these policies, especially those referring to infrastructures, should be implemented also in other EU countries. As for demand policies, the order of magnitude of the intervention depends on the fall in GDP.

This impulse can be ensured both by monetary policy, with the reduction – down to negative levels – of interest rates (Rogoff, 2020b), and, above all, by fiscal policy. The advantages of coordinated fiscal and monetary policy action are underlined by Pietrunti (2020), who points out the consequences of this coordination in a contained increase in inflation and in a cut in the dynamics of the ratio between public debt and GDP.

With specific reference to this ratio, public investment is required to mitigate or avoid the fall in GDP, also to overcome the drastic cuts made during the Great Recession to meet the EU rules of the SGP, due to the greater flexibility of this expenditure item (see Figure 10).

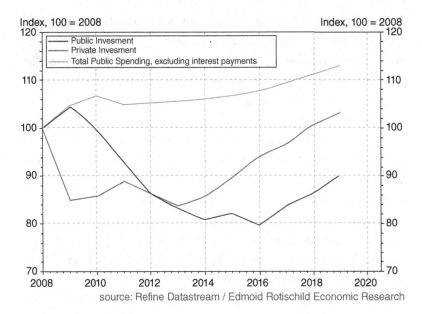

source: Refine Datastream / Edmoid Rotischild Economic Research

FIGURE 10 Public and private investments, total public expenditure, 2008–2020, EU

(*Source*: Badré and Lemoine, 2020)

Note: Public investment is indicated by the lowest line since 2013. In 2019 it decreased by 10% compared to the 2008 level. Private investment (intermediate line from 2013) collapsed in the darkest years of the Great Recession, resumed its initial value in 2018 and grew by a few points in 2019. The line that is always all the way up is that of total public expenditure, excluding interest accrued on public debt, which would cause it to rise even more as the public debt increases.

In particular, public investments with a high underline{multiplier} should be favoured and should grow by at least 1–2 p.p., possibly using the desirable golden rule of public finance. From the point of view of the geographic destination it can be useful to continue to refer to the specific case of Italy. In this country the growth in investment spending should take place above all in the South or, at least, the '34% clause' established by the Gentiloni government in 2016 should be respected, tending to ensure a corresponding flow of public investments, that is, a flow equal to the incidence of the Southern population compared to the national one. The clause was suspended in

2020 on a proposal from the Department for Economic Planning and Coordination, the body of the prime minister that oversees the decisions of the Interministerial Committee for Economic Planning. The justification for the suspension is apparently well founded, if one thinks of some of the effects of the first wave of the pandemic, that is, the need to address the immediate health needs, objectively higher in the North, due to the greater incidence in that constituency of infections in that phase. But if the horizon was broadened to consider the negative effects on demand and production also in the South of Italy, it would have become necessary to maintain compliance with that clause even in the first wave.

From this point of view, it will be important to implement, with the small adjustments required by the pandemic, the Plan for the South presented in February 2020 by the then–Minister Giuseppe Provenzano (Minister for the South and Territorial Cohesion, 2020). Over a ten-year perspective, the Plan tends to pursue five priorities (commitment to young people, emphasis on innovation, social inclusion, ecological compatibility, international openness). Here, however, it should be noted that, particularly for the South, innovation must consist not so much or not only in the use of a new technology or a new device. It must be the product of a territory, with its vocations, its dynamics and its organisational skills, and therefore it is difficult to import it. In short, 'it must rather flourish within a local ecosystem, which exploits existing resources', even if – following Schumpeter – it must overcome the previous order (Costa, 2020).

As for the other items of public spending, there should be: an increase in the role of the welfare state, which requires policies to mitigate inequality and economic insecurity, subsidies to families and businesses in need; the extension of the redundancy fund and also the increase in health expenditure (in particular, with the increase both in the short and in the long term of *public* health expenses,[34] which have

---

[34] In some countries (take Finland, the UK and the USA, only to make a few examples) the total health expenditures/GDP ratio is already high (OECD, https://data.oecd

been cut down in many EU countries), education and research, land and environmental security and other tangible and intangible infra-structures.[35] In the longer term, current public spending should be made more efficient, with the elimination of numerous wastes.

In supporting the need for higher public spending, the solutions for its coverage must also be indicated, through both internal and European sources.

In the first case, it is possible to resort to a greater deficit and therefore to a higher level of public debt. This solution can give rise to debt sustainability problems. This depends on, among other things, its initial level and on the extent of the current deficit, which is linked to the duration of the epidemic. Debt sustainability need not be a worry under certain conditions. There may be a need for monetisation, restructuring or fiscal consolidation,[36] but the persistence of current low interest rates can be very useful to avoid these solutions and ensure both limited budget surpluses and debt reductions. Ultimately, the impact of the pandemic on public debt may be smaller than that of the financial crisis (Barnes and Casey, 2020). A different solution can leverage on the reduction of tax evasion and avoidance (or elusion), which normally takes time and also has international implications, linked to the existence of tax havens and the adoption

---

.org/healthres/health-spending.htm), but the problem is that some of these expenditures are high simply because health functions are delegated to private structures, which are more expensive.

[35] In Germany, more than 1 trillion euros have been foreseen to support the economy, with 130 billion euros to support family income and investments; VAT rates have also been reduced and sums allocated to guarantee loans. Families will receive a contribution of 300 euros.

[36] Monetisation of the public debt is the transformation of public debt into money, which occurs when the central bank buys the public debt of a country in definitive terms, and not temporarily (as it happens for quantitative easing operations: see unconventional monetary policy). The term *restructuring* takes on multiple meanings in economics. When referred to public debt, it normally indicates an agreement between the state and creditors or a unilateral decision of the former to reduce the interest rate or to extend the maturity of a debt tranche or to cancel it. Consolidation takes place by means of a set of policies aimed at reducing public expenses and increasing revenues.

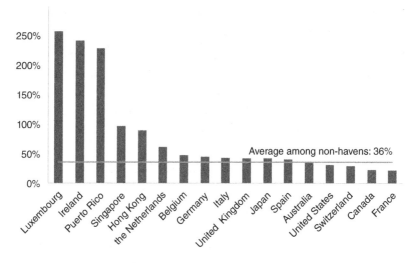

FIGURE 11 Profit-to-wage ratio across various tax-haven and non-haven countries, 2015
(*Source*: Tørsløv, Wier and Zucman, 2020)

of 'tax rulings',[37] by Luxembourg, Ireland, the Netherlands, Belgium, Malta, Cyprus and other countries, with lower revenues for Italy of approximately 5.6 billion euros in 2015.

Figure 11 shows that in 2015 the profit-to-wage ratio did not vary too much across the main non-haven countries, being equal to an average 36%. By contrast, this ratio was as high as around 250% in Luxembourg and Ireland. To be more specific about the profits (and the taxes) lost to one country, Italy,[38] according to the same source (i.e., Tørsløv et al., 2020), the reader can look at Table 6, offering a picture of the sources of lower revenues deriving from the various tax havens.

The same source, namely Tørsløv et al. (2020), indicates the reduction in tax revenues for large districts due to the existence of tax havens that allow the diversion of profits (see Figure 12). The

[37] These consist of specific agreements for the reduction of taxes with individual foreign companies to induce them to locate in the country.
[38] Similar indications can be obtained for specific other countries, by consulting the indicated source.

Table 6. *Taxes on profits and revenues lost by Italy (million $)*
due to the presence of tax havens, 2015

	Lost profits	Lost taxes
All havens	26,476	6,354
EU havens	23,195	5,567
Belgium	2,129	511
Cyprus	14	3
Ireland	6,181	1,484
Luxembourg	11,170	2,681
Malta	191	46
the Netherlands	3,509	842
Extra-EU havens	3,281	787
Switzerland	2,250	540
Others*	1,031	247

Source: Tørsløv et al., 2020
* Bermuda, Caraibi, Puerto Rico, Hong Kong, Singapore and others.

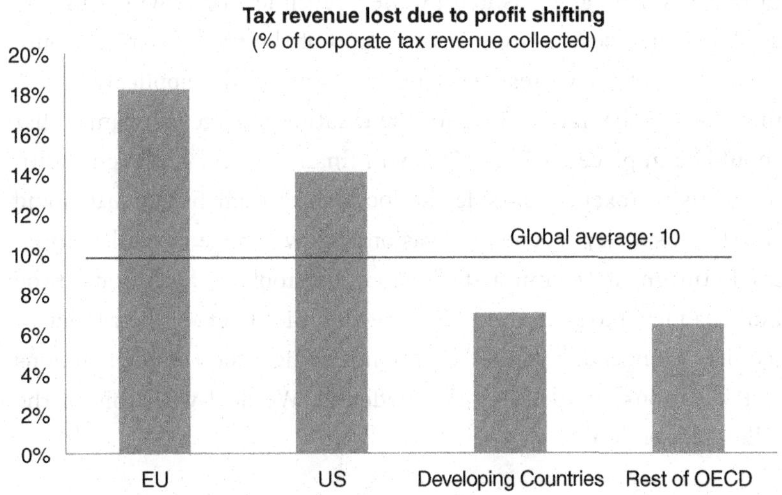

Tax revenue lost due to profit shifting
(% of corporate tax revenue collected)

Global average: 10

FIGURE 12 Tax revenues lost due to profit shifting, 2015, EU, USA,
developing countries, other OECD
(*Source*: Tørsløv et al., 2020)

reduction amounts to 18% of total taxes for the EU and about 14% for the United States, being much higher than the world average (10%), and even more than that of developing countries, and of OECD countries other than the EU and the United States. According to the same source, globally almost 40% of multinational profits are shifted to tax havens. The total amount of worldwide tax revenues lost yearly is likely to amount to 360 billion euros (or some $427 billion yearly) (Tax Justice Network, 2020).

Another form of tax distortion derives from the rule according to which the countries where multinationals (or transnational corporations) have their headquarters have the right to tax the profits gained in those countries. This rule allows the profits of multinationals in the digital field (Facebook, Apple, Amazon, Netflix and Google) to shift these to the countries in which their headquarters are located, that is, the United States, or in some other countries with lower tax rates.[39] A new regulation is being studied at the OECD level that should allow each country in which the companies indicated carry out their activity to tax them in proportion to the activity they carry out in that country, as measured by their revenues. Meanwhile, in July 2021 the finance ministers of the group of the twenty largest countries, the G20, have reached an agreement on the application of a minimum global rate of 15% for the taxation of large companies that should be in place by 2023. This will finally subject Big Tech multinationals to taxation outside the location of their headquarters and should drastically reduce tax evasion and avoidance by multinationals. Returning to the initial discussion, the problem of solutions at the European level to stem the negative economic effects of the pandemic requires a longer discussion, with an initial digression on the reactions of the various countries to the epidemic. We deal with this in the following section.

---

[39] Although located in the USA, these companies are allowed to carry out their activities remotely in other countries.

I.7   SOLUTIONS AT A EUROPEAN LEVEL

The coronavirus has imposed a crossroads on Europe. The various countries of the Union have acted in no particular order both in the adoption of measures to combat the pandemic and in those for its partial overcoming and also in fiscal interventions. In contrasting policies, each country has for a long time adopted its own policies for the containment of infections, staggered in the timing of the regulation and not connected with those of the others (for example, unilaterally suspending the freedom of movement of people, introducing bans on the export of some products such as material and machinery useful for medical treatment). This was partly due to the different timing of the infections and partly to the well-established habit of 'self-service' in Europe.[40]

In March 2020, the European Commission effectively suspended freedom of movements in the Schengen area, recommending for people to avoid non-essential foreign travel and closing the EU's external borders to non-EU citizens. From 3 June 2020 all these restrictions were removed and from the fifteenth of the same month the restrictions on travel to and from the EU countries, the Schengen area and the United Kingdom fell. However, some rules must still be obeyed in moving from one such country to another.

The caution with which the Commission has moved is partly explained by the fact that the size of the flows of people between the various European countries is so high as to prevent, or at least advise against, limitations, because the number of commuters residing in the countries of the Schengen area was almost 1% in 2018, and even more than 5% in Slovakia and 2.7% in Luxembourg. Residents in one of the countries in the area made about 320 million trips with an overnight stay in another EU country, more than 39 million (12%) of them for business purposes (Meninno and Wolff, 2020). Perhaps the position taken by the various countries in the initial phase of the epidemic is

---

[40] The negative effects of the export ban introduced by various countries are indicated in Grassia et al. (2020).

also partly justified by the difficulty of understanding its extent and consequences at that stage. And similar attitudes partly explain the different timing and modalities of the restrictions introduced in the various countries. However, it is difficult not to blame the indiscriminate inward and outward movements abroad (as well as the reduction of precautions in contacts) for the significant increase of infections in European countries since August 2020.

The economic effects for Europe are difficult to predict, also because they are linked to the trends of the epidemic. For this reason, it is necessary to proceed by scenarios.[41] Tancioni (2020) considers a first scenario (S1) in which it is assumed that the shock concerns only one country (in the specific case, Italy) and a second scenario (S2) in which the shock hits with the same intensity the whole Eurozone, with ECB measures not re-tailored to the new situation. Scenario 3 envisages that the ECB provides the system with all the liquidity necessary for the system's solvency, in the actual conditions that have arisen, avoiding deflationary spirals. The fourth scenario assumes sufficient public consumption and national public transfers to households and businesses, with the issuance of national debt. The latter scenario assumes that the ECB absorbs the debt generated by national policies. In general, it can be said that these scenarios contain almost all the ingredients that may be present or absent in the actual responses to the pandemic, but on which its economic consequences essentially depend. The effects on GDP, the unemployment rate and the change in the debt/GDP ratio derived from the analysis of these scenarios are shown in Table 7. Perhaps further elements that could be added are those relating to the situation and evolution of the economy outside the EU.

Also Bénassy-Quéré and Weder di Mauro (2020b) proceed by scenarios. In the most optimistic one, there would be only a few new infections, easily faced at the epidemiological level and without heavy negative consequences from an economic point of view for the

---

[41] On these see also Battistini and Stoevsky (2020).

Table 7. *Effects of pandemic on GDP: Changes in the unemployment rate (UR) and in the debt/GDP ratio in the various scenarios*

Scenario	GDP Ch.%			Unem. rate Ch. %			Debt/GDP changes %		
	T1	T2	T4	T1	T2	T4	T1	T2	T4
S1	−7.9	−11.4	−9.5	4.5	3.8	6.3	12.7	18.7	17.3
S2	−11.2	−17.6	−13.4	6.8	8.0	9.2	18.0	27.5	24.7
S3	−6,6	−10.7	−5.4	3.8	3.6	4.1	7.0	10.7	4.3
S4	−8.6	−13.1	−9.4	5.0	5.0	6.3	16.4	24.6	21.4
S5	−5.4	−8.3	−3.6	3.0	2.0	3.8	6.1	8.7	3.3

Source: Tancioni, 2020

Note. These are deterministic simulations (time profile and size of shocks are fully expected) obtained by the model Be.Ta. T(.) defines the simulation horizon, in quarters.

private and public sectors. The intermediate scenario envisages further outbreaks and contagions at the regional level, which require additional contrasting measures, with uncertain effects on economic balances. The worst scenario arises from the inability to sufficiently deal with contagions and coordinate actions among the various countries, with a very high probability of a financial, social and political crisis, even with the possibility that the unity of the Eurozone and perhaps also of the EU are threatened, unless an appropriate strong reaction in these fora is taken.

As for the contrasting economic measures, the orders of magnitude of the fiscal policies decided in each country range from about 1% of the GDP of the Mediterranean countries to 2% of France and Denmark and up to 8% of Germany. The resources to be invested in public health are partly linked to the state of the public accounts of the various countries. They do depend less on the extent of the infections. However, the deficits needed to cope with the pandemic and the resulting accumulation of debt will require further measures to reduce spending and/or increase revenues to repay the accumulated debt (Cochrane, 2020).

With regard to common interventions, monetary and credit policies were first adopted, implementing a new unconventional monetary policy program, in particular with the purchase of public debt securities of the euro area countries (Pandemic Emergency Purchase Program, PEPP, a program worth €750 billion). At the beginning of June 2020 the ECB announced an increase of €600 billion of the PEPP, bringing the total of the program to €1,350 billion, and then a further addition to €1,850 billion and the extension of the same to March 2022, therefore beyond the initially planned date of December 2020. The reference interest is zero and that on bank deposits with the ECB is −0.50%, again in order to not induce them to deposit their liquid assets with the same central bank and stimulate banks' lending. The operation was not bound to a breakdown of the acquisitions of the securities for the various countries proportional to their share of capital in the ECB, in order to counter the action of speculation on the differentials of the yields of different countries' securities, that is, on the spreads. The banking systems of the various countries have also been refinanced, which has allowed, on the one hand, the maintenance of public securities held by the banks and, on the other, the financing of the private sector, also facilitated by the granting of state guarantees on bank loans to businesses.

The policies adopted by the ECB do not seem, and should not be, influenced by the ruling with which on 5 May 2020 the German Constitutional Court – in contrast to a previous decision of the Court of Justice of the European Union – criticized the expansionary policies of 2015, calling on the Bundesbank not to join such interventions. The ruling created considerable embarrassment, but it does not appear to have influenced the strategy adopted by the ECB, as can be seen from the reactions of its main bodies. The expansionary monetary action will most likely continue for the future, if inflation continues to be low. According to some forecasts it should be until 2029 at a level below 1%, well below the limit set by the ECB for the medium term (Claeys, 2020), even if some more recent forecasts indicate higher values.

With regard to macroprudential policy, temperaments could be introduced to the new accounting standards in relation to expected losses and in the calculation of troubled loans for the assessment of the soundness and capital requirements of banks. Similarly, some capital requirements for banks could be eased (Bénassy-Quéré and Weder di Mauro, 2020b). Angeloni (2020) offers a different argument. In a period in which credit systems are undergoing the impact of the epidemic in various ways – with the need for greater loans to customers and, at the same time, the growth of 'non-performing loans' (NPLs) – the need of capital can be on the order of 200 billion euros in Europe. There is therefore the need to avoid poor management of micro- and macro-prudential policy instruments and a shrewd strengthening of existing institutions, for example, with the possibility of increasing the role of these institutions for liquidation procedures of banks in difficulty.

Apart from the interventions of the monetary authorities and macroprudential policy, new credit measures have been adopted at the Community level. As for the ESM, the details of the financing were only clarified in early May 2020. On the occasion of the epidemic, it was specified that conditionality relates only to the object of expenditure (medical and health care), and not to the adoption of other measures to reorganize the existing public debt, which would otherwise have slowed the use of the Mechanism by heavily indebted countries such as Italy. The loans have a term of ten years and a rate of 0.1% is applied to them. If we consider that the interest rate on Italian ten-year BTPs was 1.83% at the beginning of May 2020, recourse to the ESM became convenient for Italy, as it ensured a lower financing cost of 1.73% per year. On a loan of up to 36 billion, the savings would have been greater than 600 million euros per year (Accademia Nazionale dei Lincei, 2020). Since then the interest rate has lowered in this country by about 1 p.p., but the ESM loans are still convenient. However, it should also be noted that access to the Mechanism by a country could imply a reduction in its credibility and therefore an increase in the cost of other loans.

The EU Commission can authorize state support for: (1) direct subsidies and tax breaks aimed at meeting urgent liquidity needs up to €800,000 per company; (2) guarantees on bank loans; (3) public loans at subsidized rates; (4) aid to banks to finance businesses; (5) short-term export credit insurance; (6) support for research and development against Coronavirus; (7) deferral or suspension of taxes; (8) income support for employees.

In addition, the European Investment Bank (EIB) has created guarantee funds for bank loans to companies with an endowment capable of supporting loans for a total of 240 billion euros. The funds should be financed by EU member countries according to their participation in the Bank's capital. Various funds were then set up such as SURE (Support to mitigate Unemployment Risks in an Emergency) and other funds for a total of 540 billion euros. SURE is a new instrument that should guarantee temporary support to reduce the risk of unemployment in emergency situations and could raise up to 100 billion on the market through a system of guarantees by member countries to finance member countries in difficulty (European Commission, 2020c). In addition, the EIB will set up a pan-European guarantee fund to support European workers and businesses affected by the pandemic crisis, and finally the agreement to channel support through the ESM has been confirmed. In July 2020, the so-called Recovery Fund was also defined. It was renamed Next Generation EU (European Commission, 2020b). With this newly created fund, the European Commission intends to raise up to 750 billion on the market[42], giving long-term funds as collateral. This is made available by a (temporary) increase in the European budget 2021–2027 up to 2% of GDP (therefore doubling the current amount of the budget) for a value of 1,100 billion over the seven years, deriving from new direct contributions (for 390 billion) and greater guarantees from member countries.[43] The funds will be repaid against future budgets, not before 2028 and not after 2058.[44] Coverage will be offered by new EU own resources, such as new corrective border levies for products that involve excessive carbon emissions[45] and a new tax on those

---

[42] In its essential lines, the Fund follows many of the proposals already suggested by Garicano (2020). The general features of the Fund and the repercussions for Italy are outlined in Romano (2020). Various criticisms have been raised, in particular by Clancy (2020), who points out the relative scarcity of the size of the Fund compared to the initial advances of the president of the European Commission, Ursula Von der Leyen. According to the president's initial statements, the total recovery effort would have amounted to 2.4 trillion euros, which is obviously an exaggerated value, perhaps deriving from the sum of inconsistent figures. An in-depth analysis of the issue is in Clancy (2020).

[43] Gros (2020) had made proposals similar to the content of the Fund under consideration, suggesting to activate Coronabonds or, better, transfers from the EU budget, for example, simply by exempting the weaker countries from their contributions to this budget for the next seven years, from 2021 to 2027.

[44] Giavazzi and Tabellini (2020) had already suggested the issuance of very long-term (50- or 100-year) or irredeemable securities (i.e., securities having no maturity and with a fixed coupon or consolidated public debt securities), which would not substantially burden the existing public debt countries and could be bought by the ECB.

[45] In July 2021, a proposal has also been presented for the establishment of a tax on the use of polluting fuels (carbon tax), which will be called the 'border adjustment

multinationals that, as said, can exploit existence of tax havens. On the objectives of the Fund, there have been people who understand them as aimed at short-term purposes, that is, as a tool to support the economy. But various considerations lead instead to favouring those of a structural nature (see in particular in Pisani-Ferry, 2020). Moreover, we can add that the long-term, generational objectives transpire from the denomination of the Fund.

The use of these funds was also allocated by the European Commission to countries with greater difficulties (see Figure 13) – Italy and Spain were in the lead – to carry out investments and reforms necessary for recovery. The reason why the Mediterranean countries, also supported by France, have advocated this tool is that, unlike the others, these are resources that are partly very long-term loans, therefore to be repaid much later in time and at rates lower than those of national bonds, and partly non-repayable. The main recipient will be Italy, which will receive €208.8 billion (of which €81.4 is through non-repayable subsidies and €127.4 in loans). Spain will receive a total of €140 billion (€72.7 of which is non-repayable), France €39 billion, Greece €31.5, Portugal €26.1 and Germany €23.6.

The estimated effects on GDP are shown in Figure 14. They are more favourable in the peripheral countries, Greece and Portugal first, and a little less so for Italy.

The so-called frugal countries (i.e., Austria, Denmark, Finland, the Netherlands, Sweden) have objected to the ratification of the Treaty for some months, but in December 2020 an agreement was reached that led to the approval of the Recovery Fund regulation by the European Parliament. After publication in the Official Journal of the EU, the regulation is operational and the final spending and reform plans have been sent by the end of April to the Commission, which has taken two months to evaluate them. Consequently, the first loans

mechanism'. This would provide a sort of 'climate tariff' for a series of products imported into the Union from countries that do not apply as stringent standards as the European ones against climate change.

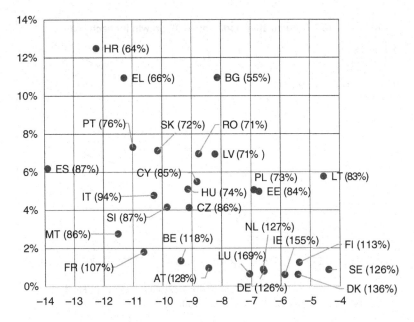

FIGURE 13 Economic shock caused by the Coronavirus and provisions from the Recovery Fund

(*Source*: Darvas, 2021)

Notes: 1. The horizontal axis measures the extent of the shock caused by the epidemic (in terms of the percentage of the change in GDP forecast by the European Commission in Autumn 2020 with respect to Autumn 2019). Thus, for example, for Italy, the 2020 forecasts indicated a reduction of GDP of about 10%. The vertical axis measures the Fund's provisions in percentage terms of the countries' net national income. For Italy they should be around 6%.

2. The numbers in parentheses after the country abbreviation indicate its per capita gross national income compared to the EU average for 2021, according to the forecasts of the EU Commission.

have arrived during summer 2021. For instance, Italy has received in August 2021 13% of its share of the aid. However, it should be noted that, for some countries, the payments from the budget for the next seven years cannot be materially disbursed in 2021 or 2022, if not in minimal part. According to Darvas (2020), which takes up statements from the European Commission, the disbursement of three-quarters of the funds will have to wait until 2023. According to Giovannini et al. (2020), the disbursements for the loan component will be higher

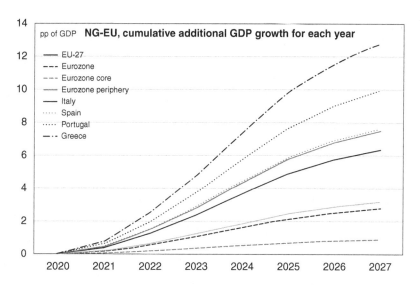

FIGURE 14 Cumulative effects of the Next Generation EU Fund
(*Source*: Codogno and Van den Noord, 2020)

in 2022, while the peak of non-repayable grants should occur in 2024. Therefore, the various governments have been forced to intervene, anticipating the funds of the Next Generation EU for 34.7 billion, beginning January 2021.

Among other measures, the Next Generation EU provides funds equal to 31 billion euros for the recapitalisation of companies, which should mobilize private resources to support economically viable companies in the sectors, regions and countries most affected by the pandemic. Through the leverage effect, €300 billion should be raised. In reality, this intervention, while focused on a well-founded need, that of the recapitalisation of companies, appears insufficient in the face of their growing debt.[46]

Access to funds is not conditional on compliance with the Stability and Growth Pact (which, however, is suspended for now, as

---

[46] Boot et al. (2020) proposed a European Pandemic Equity Fund, particularly in favour of small- and medium-sized enterprises.

we will see shortly) nor obviously on the adoption of 'structural reforms'. The disbursement of funds is subject to the presentation by individual countries of national spending plans that will be evaluated by the Commission and approved by the Council with a qualified majority, that is, with the vote of at least fifteen countries representing no fewer than 65% of the population. The approval will be accompanied by 'country-specific recommendations' (CSR). These will in fact constitute the reference for the evaluation of national spending plans, with particular attention to reforms that improve the potential for growth, employment and economic and social resilience. From interviews released by the competent authorities, the various countries could be required to guarantee policy guidelines such as to ensure the recovery of the economy in a reasonable period of time, the sustainability of the public debt, an improvement in coordination between the different layers of government, the strengthening of health and education and distance learning through digital tools, the improvement of the efficiency of the judicial system and the public administration, the support of the vulnerable groups most affected by the crisis and of small- and medium-sized enterprises and innovative ones, the reduction of unemployment and increased investment in the green economy and digitalisation.

The times within which the use of funds must be made are important, as there is a risk, as noted by Perotti (2020), of a hasty, rash and patronising identification of the projects to be carried out with their use.

The EU's ability to ensure growth by stimulating productivity and innovation will have important effects on the attractiveness of the area for investment and on strengthening the rating of the weaker areas, which could positively affect supply of safe assets by the Eurozone, thus increasing the role of the euro as an international currency (Claeys and Wolff, 2020).

Measures that are halfway between monetary and fiscal ones are represented, among other things, by the 'money dropped from the helicopter' (helicopter money), consisting of the opening of an irredeemable credit by the ECB to governments or by direct purchase at the issuance of public debt securities and their immediate cancellation or the conversion of such securities into irredeemable securities. Many objections would probably arise against such an intervention, starting from the one according to which it would be precluded by the independence of the ECB and by the existing rule that prohibits direct financing by governments or by the fact that it would generate inflation. The first of these objections can be overcome, because the exceptional nature of the situation requires an adaptation of the existing rules, as happened for the purchase of public securities on the secondary market. In addition, the ECB could decide on its own to implement such a policy. The second objection has no basis, given the existing lack of aggregate demand and the need to activate public spending to increase income and employment (Galì, 2020).[47]

As for expansionary fiscal policies in the strict sense, first of all the Stability and Growth Pact was suspended for 2021 and also for 2022, which allows individual member countries to adopt significant expansionary fiscal policies financed in deficit. The ban on state aid to companies has also been suspended since mid-March 2020 to December 2021.[48]

It would also be desirable to transform part of the national debt into European debt (Eurobonds or similar), to reduce the ratio of public debt to GDP, which is particularly high – or destined to become so – in some countries such as Greece and Italy. The advantages of issuing this form of mutualized debt are many. Among them, the lack of dependence on market *ratings* (i.e., assessments) of the reliability of sovereign debts and their variations, the reduction of spreads for the most indebted countries, which would thus reduce their exposure to the

---

[47] There are numerous positions taken by authoritative scholars in favour of this solution. We limit ourselves to mentioning Buiter et al. (2015) and most recently De Grauwe and Diessner (2020).

[48] The apparent generosity of the concession – in the past particularly opposed by Germany – was linked by the media to the fact that German companies have already benefitted from half of the aid measures approved by the European Commission.

financial market and the possibility of banks using <u>Eurobonds</u> to diversify their portfolios, often burdened with lending to domestic securities.

Further initiatives could concern: (1) the creation of a single European institution that should be entrusted with the competences of national institutions, such as the ministries of health, in the event of an epidemic involving more than one country; (2) enhanced cooperation, to carry out a European investment project financed by securities and destined to specific investment fields (for example, bio-medical research, transport infrastructures, information technologies, giving equal access to the market through a level playing field). In the longer term, it is finally necessary to devise a European industrial policy that not only identifies priority sectors in which to invest, but that also favours aggregations between European companies, for example in the energy, telecommunications and bio-genetics sectors, strengthening European research platforms useful for innovative medium-sized enterprises and start-ups, on the model of CERN (European Center for Nuclear Research, Conseil européen pour la recherche nucléaire), ESA (European Space Agency) and EMBO (European Molecular Biology Organisation). Then, various trans-European infrastructures could be enhanced (Accademia Nazionale dei Lincei, 2020).

1.8 PROBLEMS AND SOLUTIONS WORLDWIDE

If at a national and a European level the problems posed by the pandemic are relevant, they are dramatic on a world level. To get an idea of the impact of the pandemic on the economy, comparing it with that of the Great Recession that began in 2007–2008, a weakness index was constructed for the United States, given by the average of the recession probabilities of the various states. Another indicator – which, however, stopped in May 2020 – had been built with the same methodology for the various countries. As can be seen from Figure 15, the weakness index, which in March 2020 was still relatively low compared to 2008–2009, jumped to very high levels in just a few months. The economic recovery in the summer and the limited closures of activities imposed in some countries in the autumn meant

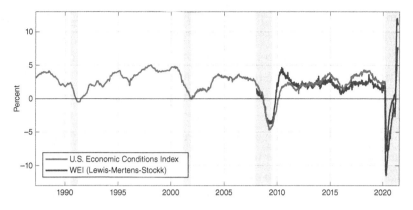

FIGURE 15 Index of the weakness of the US economy, April 1987–May 2021, per cent changes
(*Source*: Baumeister et al., 2021)
Note. The Weekly Economic Index (WEI) starts in 2008.

that the peak of weakness calculated in May 2020 did not rise further until November 2020, but in the following months the recovery was very neat.

At the world level, there are essentially problems of: increasing poverty; imbalances in the supply and demand of goods, with the negative economic, social and political implications that derive from it;[49] and effects of de-globalisation. Therefore, various questions arise on the guidelines to be imprinted in the various fora on international economic policies and related provisions.

As for the immediate responses to the health emergency by international organisations, more than 100 member countries of the International Monetary Fund have requested access to its funding and funds have already been allocated for about half of the requests. In May 2020 the World Bank and the International Monetary Fund urged G20 countries to establish a Debt Service Suspension Initiative of its

---

[49] Consider that profound upheavals such as those created by the pandemic destabilise not only the economy, but also society, giving rise to protests, unrest and overthrow of political regimes.

member countries. This has been done first until the end of 2020 and then again also for the whole of 2021 (World Bank, 2021a).

For interventions on a broader scale, the reduction in employment should be noted, which has cut the incomes of many families and increased poverty. The pandemic has mainly affected some categories of workers: first of all women (who occupy 70% of positions in the health and care sectors and are therefore on the front line of the epidemic); workers in the informal sectors or with casual and temporary jobs; young people, whose employment prospects are more sensitive to fluctuations in demand; the elderly, who are also affected from the point of view of vulnerability to infections; the refugees and immigrants, particularly if employed in certain sectors; micro-entrepreneurs and self-employed workers (ILO, 2020, Palomino et al., 2020). The International Labour Organisation (ILO) itself suggests four pillars of intervention:

1 Stimulation of the economy and employment through traditional macroeconomic policy tools.
2 Support for businesses, employment and income, through the extension of social protection and various measures aimed at avoiding redundancies.
3 Protection of workers in the workplace, for example, with the strengthening of safety measures, the use of teleworking or smart-working.
4 Use of social dialogue to design possible solutions.

A major problem to be addressed concerns the financing of businesses in the period of the depression. Didier et al. (2020) warn that, to avoid meltdowns and bankruptcies, it is important to preserve relationships between businesses and workers, as well as suppliers, customers and creditors. To this end, the credit necessary to overcome the crisis must absolutely be guaranteed. It can be added that the credit system has an important role in this and the guarantee of its proper functioning must be offered, first of all, by the monetary authorities.

As we have seen in Table 5 already presented, a fall in world GDP has taken place in 2020. Aside from this general fall in demand, the Coronavirus has implied a change in the composition of demand, with an increase in demand for food and a fall in demand for durable goods (e.g., cars). While in normal times this sudden change in the composition of demand could be dealt with in particular by a change in relative prices, during the pandemic the readjustment risks are much more difficult. Problems with the availability of food were noted not only due to the increase in demand for these goods, but also due to the embargo introduced by the countries that produce the raw materials (Russia and Kazakhstan for wheat and India and Vietnam for rice) and at the same time for the accumulation of reserves by others (such as Egypt and the Philippines). This has led to an increase in the prices of these raw materials (for example, by 40% for wheat), which has hit hard 110 countries – of which 50 are developing countries that make up three-fifths of the world population (Reinhart and Subbaraman, 2020). In particular, developing countries, already struggling with growth problems, suffer further from the pandemic, especially due to the fall in demand for their goods – as some of them based growth on these goods – and, moreover, because of the reduction of remittances from their own emigrant citizens and of capital inflows.

Obviously, the impact of the increase in the prices of essential goods affects the various income earners differently, worsening the distribution of income and wealth, to the detriment of the less well off. The availability of food and the worsening of this distribution could cause social unrest and, in any case, will affect the political structures of many countries.

Absolute poverty will be increased, as will be seen better in Chapter 3. Perhaps the only positive effect of the pandemic has been the improvement of the environment, in terms of lower energy consumption and reduced carbon dioxide emissions.

International trade, with an upward trend that had already declined since 2008, will also suffer further from the pandemic. As Figure 16 shows, in this case two scenarios also have been identified, with reductions in the volume of trade of goods ranging from 13% to 32% in 2020.

With respect to the previous year, Chinese exports have increased by 4% in 2020. All other top ten economies suffered a

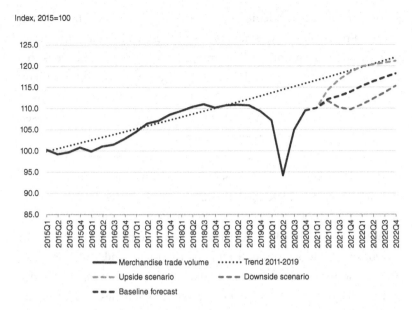

Index, 2015=100

FIGURE 16 Volume of world trade in goods, 2015–2022 (Index, 2015 = 100)
(*Source*: World Trade Organization, 2021)

contraction in exports in 2020, varying from −5.5% for South Korea, −6.9% for Brazil, −9.1% in Japan, −12.5% in Canada, −12.9% in the USA, −14.8% in India and −15.3% in the UK. From the point of view of the world economy, as a result of the pandemic, a process of de-globalisation could be activated, with various effects, such as the isolation of many countries and the re-nationalisation of supply chains, which are now unfolding at the world level.[50] De-globalisation first affects the movements of people. These have been limited due to the closures imposed by the pandemic, but it should be noted that some countries have a feeling of repulsion towards some foreigners, in

[50] In summary, global value chains derive from the breakdown of the production process of an asset into its various component parts, each of which is produced in a different country. This will be discussed more fully later, particularly in Box 3. The effects of the pandemic could be similar to those resulting from the imposition of limitations to the international movement of goods, of the kind of duties, on which see Cappariello et al. (2020). On the negative aspects of these effects see Baldwin and Freeman (2020).

particular towards residents in other EU countries, the United States and, in a particular way, Asia. However, these feelings are not shown towards internal minorities and immigrants. The consequence is that the resumption of trade and international cooperation will also have to take these reflections into account and try to find adequate remedies (Bartoš et al., 2020). Finally, the risk of further trade wars arises, beyond those that have arisen in more recent years.

Some of these effects can be counteracted by appropriate policies of the individual countries concerned, such as monetary policy and capital controls. Such policies are hardly available to the majority of countries, particularly in the least developed countries, which urgently need liquidity to meet international payments. The International Monetary Fund remains the main lender of last resort (García-Herrero and Ribakova, 2020). This institution has responded at least in part to the needs of developing countries and emerging countries since spring 2020, making new funds available. The World Bank acted in a similar way, granting numerous loans to less developed countries (LDCs).

A superior alternative from the point of view of collaboration between countries is the search for a more sensible model of globalisation that focuses on areas of effective convenience, in particular cooperation on public health, environment, production and distribution of essential goods, elimination of tax competition (which reduces public revenues of the various countries or nourishes tax evasion and avoidance), granting of emergency loans to many developing countries, as well as temporary suspension of repayments of their pre-existing debts.

Overall, the future of the world economy depends not only on the action of the virus, but on the responses of public and private operators. In particular, the future of globalisation largely depends on the policies implemented by the United States and China. The European Union will have little impact, being always grappling with its internal problems, which prevent it from deciding on progress towards greater integration of its economic policy instruments and greater incisiveness of its external action. The responses of the single European states have, therefore, assumed a leading role. In the short term essentially two avenues are open to globalisation. The first will confirm the trend of recent years towards certain forms of deglobalisation. However, an alternative route is feasible, tending to emphasize the fields in which globalisation is certainly useful, such as that of protecting health and the environment and reducing tax havens. Cooperation or collaboration in these areas will also contribute to fostering international trade and investment. Further trends of globalisation in the long term will be discussed later in Chapter 4, with reference to its third phase.

More generally, all countries should be aware of the need to adopt – and actually implement – health and other policies capable of addressing not only the pandemic itself, but also the negative distributional effects affecting weaker people and countries. The ordinary resources available to the various international institutions and the extraordinary ones they must equip with for the occasion must be aimed at these purposes: aid to the countries having the most difficulty in controlling the epidemic and to the people and countries most economically affected. 'The international health and financial architecture must be further strengthened, and partly redesigned' as well in order to strengthen the ability to cope with future crises (Berglöf et al., 2020).

1.9   THE SEARCH FOR A VACCINE

Among the policies to be adopted at the world level, a specific discussion deserves those for the research and production of a vaccine. Aside from the difficulties of research, the main obstacle to vaccine development has been due to the fact that the current pharmaceutical legislation – based on the patentability of drugs – involves privatisation and the blocking of knowledge, making it difficult to pool knowledge developed by each research center, which would significantly reduce the time of the research itself (Mazzucato and Torreele, 2020; Stiglitz et al., 2020).

Regarding the possibility of obtaining vaccines capable of fighting the virus in a short time, it is necessary to be very explicit and start, first of all, from experience. Coronavirus is just one of the viruses belonging to a strain that has also hit in the past. In fact, the SARS we suffered from in 2002 came from another strain of the same virus circulating these months. Regarding the possibility that the virus would reproduce in the future in a mutated form, scientists had been very explicit in the past (Florio, 2020).

Large companies in the pharmaceutical industry have been focused for a long time after the outbreak of the pandemic on the production of other types of drugs, which can treat chronic diseases, such as cholesterol, diabetes and hypertension. Therefore, they invest in fields that promise a geographically large, stable or, even better, a market regularly growing over time. They also invested in the development of anti-Coronavirus drugs, as they began to do since March 2020 in the United States, when public funding of over 1 billion dollars was decided and without the conditionality linked to the maximum price constraint wanted by the Democrats. Currently there are about 126 vaccines being tested. Most of them are still in the pre-clinical stage, that is, the one before the tests on people, with only four of them – Pfizer, Moderna, Astra Zeneca, Johnson & Johnson – already being distributed in Western countries, in addition to one in Russia and one in China (see in particular Garde, 2020).

After India and South Africa, US President Biden has supported a move at the World Trade Organization (WTO) for a temporary lifting of patent protections for coronavirus vaccines. By contrast, the EU Commission and Council have not, whereas the EU Parliament was in favour. Still in August 2021 the WTO is discussing the proposal. Considering the EU position, one can understand why this is likely not to be passed.

Looking ahead, it is necessary to replace the action of 'big Pharma' (i.e., of the large pharmaceutical companies) with the activity of an international public entity, possibly at a European level, as mentioned, of the type of CERN. In the United States, a federal research and development institute has been proposed for drug research, together with public companies that materially produce and sell drugs that will be developed at low prices.[51]

I.IO   CONCLUSIONS ON THE EFFECTS OF THE FINANCIAL CRISIS AND THE PANDEMIC

The financial crisis had disruptive effects not only in the United States and other countries, but also – and mainly – in the European Union, where, first of all, it didn't disappear as soon as in the USA. In fact, in the EU it unmasked the imbalances that had been created by the ill-devised nature of its institutions. The financial crisis caused also a crisis of public finances in peripheral countries, since the governments of these countries had to intervene to save their ailing banking sector, threatened by the return to core countries of the financial investments that these had directed to peripheral countries before the crisis.

In addition to the interventions of governments in the peripheral countries, the EU countries tried to cope with the rise of public debt in these countries by prescribing a rule even tougher than the SGP, that is, the fiscal compact, which thus added to financial crisis, due to its deflationary impact.

The pandemic will have effects similar to those of the financial crisis, with multiple consequences, all the more important and

---

[51] In terms of proposals, at least from the point of view of similar future occurrences, Florio (2020) and Florio and Iacovone (2020) have suggested the establishment of an institute at a sufficiently high level such as the European one, which could be called BIOMED EUROPA, with an annual budget between 0.10 and 0.20% of EU GDP, of the same order of magnitude as the National Institutes of Health in the USA (41.7 billion dollars in 2020). This size could have several advantages, in terms of extensive experimentation and production and distribution of drugs at an international scale. It could constitute the largest public biomedical research infrastructure in the world and perhaps induce large private pharmaceutical companies to collaborate. It should also be added that the usefulness of such a structure could go beyond the cure of the current pandemic, extending to the entire chain of viruses similar to the one that is now spreading and, again, in search of other diseases now neglected by private pharmaceutical companies. The Institute could also control the prices of the specialties they produce. A similar scheme has been proposed for the USA by the Democracy Collaborative think tank.

serious the longer it lasts. From this point of view, it is painful to note that its duration depends on the tendency of large pharmaceutical companies not to share the results of their research, to safeguard the possibility of enjoying patent rights. Apart from the suspension – or some attenuation – of these rights, a possible measure aimed at increasing cooperation in the search for antidotes could be offered by the establishment of a common pool of resources among the various countries.

The consequences of the pandemic will be of various kinds, not only of an economic nature, on the levels and distribution of income between people (particularly affected were racial minorities and immigrants) and countries, but also social and political.

At the economic level, the effects will be as profound as ever since the Great Crisis. While an overall limited reduction in GDP was expected earlier in 2020, with a partial recovery in 2021, the violent return of the virus in Europe, the United States and other countries starting at the end of the summer 2020 has certainly worsened the situation. Unfortunately, at present – and until the peak of infections is passed – it is not possible to make reliable forecasts on the extent of the worsening of the economic outlook. One thing is certain: The current deterioration will already cause a reduction in production, employment and international trade and an increase in poverty.

At the social level, first of all, the fraying of the fabric of relationships between people should be noted, which is particularly acute for young people forced into distance learning, perhaps tempered by the acquisition of a greater awareness of the interpersonal effects of their actions. To this end, it is also worth taking up one of the conclusions of the Italian Accademia dei Lincei, according to which 'the technological evolutions in the field of communications and information, which certainly make a contribution to growth, also seem to provide a new tool for social control, which must be regulated in the best way to help fight the epidemic without posing risks to democracy and the rule of law' (Accademia Nazionale dei Lincei,

2020: 4). In addition, it should be noted that the pandemic will affect the structure of international economic and political cooperation, confirming or accentuating the protectionist tendencies that have emerged in recent years. And, apart from the effects on the world economy, even in a more limited context, the pandemic will affect the European economic and political order. The main consequence is that 'it will be shown that this is not the occasion for verifying only the economic effects of a head-on collision, but also of European unity' (Bénassy-Quéré et al., 2020). Finally, it should be noted that the pandemic and the set of measures implemented to curb it or treat its negative effects will affect the relationship between citizens and political power, varying the degree of support not only for the authorities in charge, but also for the public authorities in general. In particular, the epidemic has made evident the shortcomings of Chinese public action and the fragility of some reactions, such as the construction of a hospital in ten days, absolutely insufficient when compared to the spread of infections. Similarly, the shortcomings in the action of Presidents Trump and Bolsonaro were evident. Other important case studies could emerge from considering the reactions of many other countries (Wyplosz, 2020). To these observations we could then add other assessments on the reaction of the economic and social structure of the various countries as well as of the European and international architecture (see, for example, Bénassy-Quéré and Weder di Mauro, 2020b).

2 Stagnation

Stagnation is a recurring theme not only in real life, but also in economic thought. Classical economists had already talked about it. Most of them viewed the 'stationary state' with disfavour, as in this situation the economic system would reproduce itself without growing. This perspective was defended instead by the last of the classics, John Stuart Mill (see Mill, 1887), who favoured a prospect in which men would no longer have to struggle to 'collide' and 'climb over', the former against the others, and there would be room for contemplation of nature and for reflection, a perspective that is certainly full of aesthetically, ecologically and ethically appreciable aspects, but forgets issues of poverty and distribution.[1] The issue remained in the shade until the Great Crisis, at the end of which – as said – a situation of stagnation really emerged, which was analysed by Hansen (1939). The rearmament, before, and the intense development, in the decades following the World War II, again left the subject in the shade (with the exception of Steindl, 1952; see also Steindl, 1979), which was reproposed after 2010, when once again the Great Recession seems to have weakened the factors of development, giving rise to different explanations for this fact (see, e.g., Reinhart and Rogoff, 2009, Summers, 2014).

In the recent decades the reduced trend of GDP growth that had manifested in the past has reappeared, apparently stimulated by the

---

[1] The zeroing of growth or the activation of a *degrowth* process has been resumed in recent decades by scholars of the Club of Rome, by Nicolas Georgescu-Roegen and Serge Latouche (in Italy by Giorgio Ruffolo, Massimo Cacciari and others). Such a prospect, however, would only be acceptable with a drastic redistribution of current wealth, within developed countries and, above all, between these and developing countries. Otherwise, the steady state would favour only those who currently have a privileged position in a society.

financial crisis, but possibly also by other factors, including the deflationary effects of the EU institutions. Countering the secular stagnation requires manifold policies, including <u>unconventional monetary
policies</u> and international coordination.

In this chapter we discuss first the trend of income growth
before and after the crisis (Section 2.1) and the determinants of stagnation (Section 2.2). Next, we deal with the prospects of this phenomenon in Europe and in the USA as well as with the relations between
stagnation and the other 'terrible' three (Section 2.3), finally moving
on to the indication of some possible policies to counter stagnation,
including non-conventional monetary policies and international
coordination (Section 2.4). Section 2.5 concludes the chapter.

2.1   THE TREND OF GROWTH BEFORE AND AFTER THE
CRISES IN THE EUROPEAN UNION AND ABROAD

In recent years, a generalized reduction in income growth rates has
emerged, affecting not only the major developed countries, but also
emerging and developing countries. In fact, not only the Eurozone, but
also the USA and Japan, among the industrialized countries – as well
as the so-called Asian tigers (primarily China, India and other countries in the South East of that continent) and fast-growing countries
scattered in the other continents, Brazil, Russia and South Africa
(which together with China and India form the quintet of the
BRICS) – have strongly reduced their growth rates. Forecasts for the
future are no better than current events.

In past centuries, the reduction in growth rates in the most
advanced countries occurred to some extent after they had passed the
'roaring' years of industrialisation, due to the reduction of the driving
forces deriving from a new discovery or invention, before others
occurred. The relative number of innovations introduced – from the
steam engine to the railways, to the internal combustion engine, to the
plane, to information technology, and so forth – has meant that the
phases of stagnation were considerably limited. After the first Great
Depression that hit developed countries in the last decades of the

nineteenth century, the first concerns arose at the beginning of twentieth century for a reduction in the growth rate. The prospect of stagnation became much more valid after the Great Crisis, which began in 1929 and lasted practically throughout the 1930s. This crisis – and with it the fear of stagnation – was overcome only by the significant increase in public spending for military purposes in Germany, in all other Western countries and elsewhere. After the war, a substantial and long reduction in the growth rate occurred first following the oil crises in the 1970s, and then, further in the same decade with reference to Japan and Europe, for different reasons. In Japan the strong economic growth – of the order of almost 10% per year – enjoyed in the second half of the twentieth century ended abruptly at the start of the 1990s, due to the Plaza Accord of 1985, which had revaluated the yen with respect to the US dollar. This caused a deflation to which monetary authorities reacted by expanding credit. A massive speculative asset price bubble ensued. After 1990, Japan's annual growth rate lowered to little more than a meagre 1%, also due to the Great Recession and some natural catastrophes (an earthquake and a tsunami) and the more recent pandemic. In recent decades, growth has also been very low in Japan. 'Abeconomics', that is, the doctrine imposed by Prime Minister Abe, has sought to revitalize it by using a variety of tools, ranging from quantitative and qualitative easing (see unconventional monetary policy) to traditional fiscal policies and microeconomic reforms (see microeconomic policy). Over the last four to five years the results appeared to be encouraging, mainly in terms of employment, with an unemployment rate in 2019 of 2.3%, as low as in the first half of the 1980s.

In Europe, this was due to the deflationary design of its institutions and to some extent also to the wrong policies that were implemented there. Now, after the financial crisis that began in 2007 and the pandemic, the prospect of secular stagnation is emerging once again.

The dynamics of growth and employment inside and outside the EZ were different, more pronounced outside than within the Eurozone. Various factors have acted for this in the various countries, producing a sort of bifurcation or dualism between them. These factors and the fragility of the EZ institution were not captured by many observers who praised the results achieved by the EMU after ten years, ignoring the existing imbalances – which would soon lead to a deep crisis – and the reasons that could make the situation acceptable only to casual observers, being the result of a kind of drug and, therefore, precarious. The Commission even dared to say that 'after 10 years of existence, the euro is a resounding success' (European Commission, 2008: 3). Wyplosz (2006: 208) stated that researchers, quite critical at the launch of this unique institution, had generally acknowledged later that 'the launch of the euro was a great success', adding, however, that it was still too early to say whether the EMU could suffer from asymmetric shocks, having not been tested (p. 222).

Looking at the growth drivers after 2007, overall investment has been lacking in EMU, and public spending has given the biggest boost to domestic demand, which has been the main driver of growth everywhere, except in Germany (and the Netherlands), where exports – already a critical factor in German growth, following the compression of wages and therefore of prices – have been the most important component, which explains the relative immunity to the crisis of that country. The different inflation rates in the various countries led to a situation in which, as said, the core countries accumulated positive balances of the current account, while the peripheral ones recorded negative balances. The asymmetry imposed by the institutions of the European Monetary Union led to an obligation to adjust the current account placed on the deficit, rather than the surplus, countries[2] and implied a deflationary push and a tendency to

---

[2] In more specific terms, assume only two member countries, Italy and Germany, the first with a current account deficit and the second with a surplus. Italy is obliged to reduce the deficit below 4% of GDP, for example through demand reduction policies, while the obligation to reduce Germany's surplus, through demand expansion policies, is triggered only if the surplus exceeds 6% of GDP. This theoretical obligation for the surplus countries was not followed by the effective observance of the rule, as surpluses of even 8–9% for Germany and 10% and more for the Netherlands were tolerated. The consequence of this has been a deflationary and stagnationist trend impressed on the Union.

stagnate to the entire Union (De Grauwe, 2015). In non-EMU EU countries, the largest component of growth was internal demand (mainly consumption), but no specific role was played by the public sector. The foreign sector has given a stimulus and the exchange rate has been used for this purpose by some countries, such as Poland, the Czech Republic, the United Kingdom and Sweden from 2007 to 2009. This shows how anchoring to a single currency by the peripheral member countries made it hard to exit the crisis : A position outside the EMU would have allowed them to devalue their currency and to support their economy.

The case of the USA is still different. In this country, both before and after the crisis, private consumption – supported in both cases by the strength of the financial market – was the main factor of growth, but also the determining factor of the crisis that erupted in 2007–2008. Exports were boosted by the weakness of the dollar after 2013–2014. Before the crisis, the share of exports in the GDP had remained practically constant. Thus, the only new aspect of the US strategy after the crisis was the role of the foreign sector, complementary to that of the financial sector, which recovered after the crisis. In the second decade of the current century, the economy has always grown, but at lower rates than the previous long-term ones, as seen in Table 1.

As seen in Table 5, in 2020, the economic trends of these countries all worsened due to the onset of the pandemic. As said above, the World Bank estimations for 2020 indicate falls in GDP ranging from 4.7% in Japan to 3.5% in the United States and to 6.6% for the Euro area. Partial recoveries are expected in 2021 for some countries, and perhaps it will take the whole of 2022 to return to levels close to those of 2019.

A fact common to several countries is the deflationary trend impressed by public spending. If in the period 2010–2013 this had grown in the United States, the United Kingdom and the Eurozone by 2% per year, that is, at a rate somewhat below the long-term trend, the level of public spending itself in 2013 would have been higher than the actual one by 10% in the EZ, 15% in the USA and slightly lower in the United Kingdom, with evident expansionary implications. Indeed, GDP would have been higher, for example by 4–5% in Europe (Wren-Lewis, 2015).

2.2 THE GENERAL CAUSES OF STAGNATION

Not initially wanting to discriminate between the various explanations given for it, we can define stagnation in general terms as a situation that implies a reduced rate of GDP growth.

There are two different theories that justify such a trend. The first of these is that of the so-called financial cycle, according to which stagnation reflects an economic phase following the banking crisis that occurs during a financial crisis and has long-lasting negative effects on output. At the end of this phase, growth resumes at the high rates usual before the crisis (see Reinhart and Rogoff, 2009, Reinhart et al., 2015). Juselius et al. (2016) and Borio (2017) present interpretations of the reduced growth rate similar to that of the financial cycle.

The second explanation first of all specifies that the current low growth rate is destined to last for some time and the recovery will not be smooth and fast, contrary to Bernanke's thought (2015a, b). The reduction in the growth rate that this theory deals with refers to the long term, which is why, according to this current of thought, we should speak more precisely of 'secular stagnation'.

Figure 17 shows the downward trend of GDP in advanced economies in the forty-five years after 1971, with the annual rate falling by more than 1 p.p. At the same time, the natural interest rate[3] has lowered even more, reaching values close to zero. Rachel and

---

[3] The natural – or neutral – interest rate is the interest rate associated with a full employment economy and a constant inflation rate. If monetary policy ensures a market interest rate lower than the natural interest rate, the economy is stimulated. Therefore, if the natural interest rate falls below zero, it is difficult for the central bank to offer this stimulus and the economy will stagnate. The importance of a higher target inflation rate for monetary policy is stressed by Dorich et al. (2018).

Percent

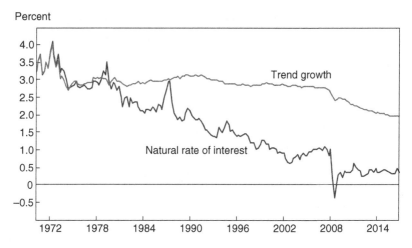

<figure>FIGURE 17 GDP growth rates and neutral interest rates, 1971–2016, advanced economies
(*Source*: Rachel and Summers, 2019)</figure>

Summers (2019) note in this regard that the natural rate would take negative values even of several hundred basis points if it were not for the increase in public debt, which reduces excess savings and keeps market interest rates high.[4]

Figure 18, on the other hand, presents the actual trend of US GDP over the last fifteen years and an estimate of potential output[5] in two different years, 2008 and 2017, showing the fall in the estimate at the second date, which obviously is affected by the trend in the actual GDP (see Summers, 2014).

As said, the initial explanation for secular stagnation was given by Hansen in 1938 (see Hansen, 1939),[6] who doubted that after the

---

[4] Caution in attributing to the secular stagnation the fall in the natural interest rate in a relatively limited period of time, of the order of a few decades, derives from the analysis of Schmelzing (2018), who notes a similar fall over the last eight centuries.

[5] Potential output or product is the product that can be achieved over a period of time with the 'full' use of physical and human resources. The term 'full' indicates a 'physiological' level, corresponding to a system functioning without tensions or bottlenecks (such as to produce inflation), which implies, for example, in a certain time and in a given country a (frictional) unemployment of 4%.

[6] The indication of the existence of a phase of secular stagnation was initially given in 1934 by Hansen and was then reiterated by him in 1938 in his presidential speech at the annual meeting of the American Economic Association. The speech was

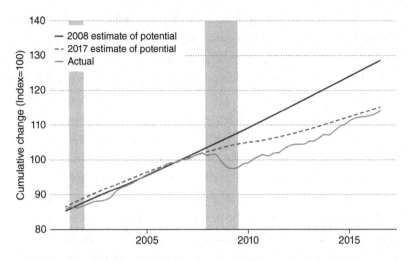

FIGURE 18 Actual GDP and potential GDP growth estimates (%),
2000–2017, USA
(*Source*: Bivens, 2017)
Note: The shaded areas indicate periods of recession.

Great Crisis there would be sufficient investment to fuel growth, due
to the low rate of population growth and, therefore, of the demand for
goods. In fact, Keynes (1930) had already raised the question of
whether the factors underlying consumption would be able to cope
with the increase in productivity.

A further explanation – based on Michał Kalecki's analysis (see
Kalecki, 1954, 1971) – was given by Josef Steindl (see Steindl, 1952),[7]
who attached great importance to the formation of oligopolies,
responsible for a redistribution of profits in favour of dominant firms,
and to the drop in the degree of utilisation of production capacity and,
therefore, the low propensity to invest.[8]

published the following year. This clarification is important, because it was in
1939 that the economies of developed countries began to recover from the Great
Crisis, due to the increase in military spending.

[7] Kalecki influencd Steindl's ideas when both were at the Oxford Institute of Statistics
when they worked together during WWII until 1944. Then Steindl already knew
Kalecki's method and ideas before they were published in English in the works
just cited.

[8] On Steindl's ideas, see recently Hein (2015), who emphasizes that Steindl's
conception allows avoiding some theoretical knots underlying the most recent
analyses of secular stagnation. Anselmann (2020) includes personal income

More recently, it has been said that various factors have emerged over time that imply a situation of secular stagnation. These tend to lower investment levels and increase savings levels, with the consequence of reducing the real interest rate capable of leading to full employment.[9] The result is lower real interest rates capable of ensuring equality between savings and investment, but they can even tend to take negative values. Summers (2014) offers multiple explanations for this. First, lower inflation and perhaps reduced technological progress lower the demand for new capital goods and require less savings. Furthermore, the reduction of the working-age population and the development of electronic commerce (e-commerce) contract the demand for new capital goods for investment, at the same time that there is a reduction in the price of new capital goods associated with an increase in their production capacity and therefore in the savings necessary to purchase them. On the other hand, the increase in inequalities implies a lower average propensity to consume[10] and an increase in savings. The increased uncertainty also reduces the demand for loans and leads to increased savings.[11]

To these factors must be added institutional features – such as the guarantee of security in property rights, the guarantee of legal certainty and civil liberties and in the execution of commercial contracts – that promote investments in physical and human capital that

distribution in a Kalecki-Steindl type model and suggests public intervention policies to correct it.

[9] The propensity to save – i.e., the ratio between savings and income – spiked during the pandemic, passing from 7.5% to 23.5% in the USA.

[10] This is the ratio between consumption and income.

[11] On some of these factors, such as, for example, the change in income distribution, the reduction in investment and structural changes that imply lower labour demand, Blecker (2016) agrees. Aronoff (2016) points to under-consumption as the cause of stagnation. See also Kiefer et al. (2020). On the other hand, Benigno and Fornaro (2015) believe that the low level of demand leads to a reduction in investments in innovation and the low rate of income growth depresses nominal interest rates to the limit of zero. Kobayashi and Ueda (2020) underline the importance of the fear of capital taxation to cope with the high public debt, with specific reference to Japan, where, as is well known, the public debt is particularly high. Therefore, in this analysis, the existence of a high public debt has an effect opposite to that indicated by Rachel and Summers (2019).

contribute to productivity growth (see, among others, Acemoglu et al., 2001, North and Thomas, 1973). The institutional characteristics are also important, in particular with reference to the architecture of the European Union, which – as said – hinders the increase in demand necessary to compensate for stagnation trends (Bergeaud et al., 2018).

The role of longevity and technical progress has been the subject of debate. Thus, Gordon (2012) points to the weakening of technical progress as a possible cause of secular stagnation, but Gordon (2014a, b) changes his previous position on technical progress and instead points out the existence of the following factors to explain the secular stagnation: the reduction of population growth,[12] the slowdown in the growth of education, the increased inequality and the reduction of middle-class incomes, the interaction between information technology and globalisation, the future reduction of public services due to growing indebtedness of the public sector, the growing energy and environmental problems. In agreement with the existence of factors that operate on the supply side in the opposite direction to growth – rather than with the thesis of the technological factors of secular stagnation – is Ramey (2020). Basso and Jimeno (2021) link the reduction of the growth rate and the aging of the population with innovation, arguing that the former favour automation and reduce technological progress. Opposing implications of population aging on innovation and productivity derive from the analysis of Acemoglu and Restrepo (2018) and other works by these authors. Cova et al. (2019) emphasise the role of technology as a factor in slowing development. Popović (2018) indicates the reasons for stagnation in terms of the interaction between supply and demand factors. The first includes the existence of a zero interest rate constraint, which prevents the necessary fall in the real interest rate and the

---

[12] In the same sense goes the lengthening of the average life, which increases the propensity to save in the absence of a parallel increase in the retirement age. The numerous depressing effects of the growth rate, productivity, real interest rate and employment produced by the reduction in population growth are highlighted by Jones (2018).

adjustment of the investment level to that of savings. The supply factors are grafted on to those of demand, as the dynamics of innovation processes are reduced due to the substitution of labour for capital, once the slowdown in growth has led to an increase in unemployment. Finally, Popović notes the link between stagnation and the increase in inequality and globalisation.

Krugman (2014) believes that fears of secular stagnation are based on the following factors: the relevance of the zero limit for nominal interest rates; the secular decline in real interest rates[13] even before the Great Recession; the reduction of debts and the weakening of the rate of population growth. The existence of a high public debt, which tends to channel part of private savings towards investment, only partially compensates for these factors.

As a matter of fact, real interest rates, which are affected by the demand for investment goods and the supply of savings, have fallen to negative levels in the last two decades, despite the increase in public debt (see Figure 19). This is intended as a proof of the validity of the hypothesis of secular stagnation: The difficulties in absorbing savings have probably contributed to limiting the interest rate and the growth rate (Summers, 2020). For the EZ, the real interest rate curve starts at the top and ends at the bottom.

Stiglitz (2017) points to the growth of inequalities and oligopolistic power as factors underlying the stagnation of the US economy. Bivens (2017), Petach and Tavani (2019) and Pariboni et al. (2020) also underline the negative role for growth played by the worsening of distribution, sometimes changing the methodology followed with respect to that of the 'mainstream' secular stagnation theory. Nikiforos (2020) highlights some structural factors – such as the slowdown in productivity, the worsening of distribution, the growth of the oligopolistic sector, and also the excess of indebtedness – that can slow growth, even if not in the long term, thus diverging from the

---

[13] This corresponds to the fall in the natural interest rates already indicated.

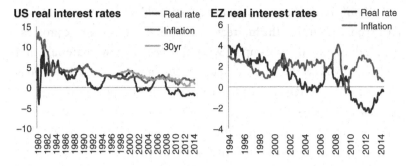

FIGURE 19 Real interest rates and inflation rates (%), 1980–2014, USA and Eurozone

(*Source*: Teulings and Baldwin, 2014b)

Note: For the USA, the real interest rate is calculated as the difference between the overnight interest rate and inflation and is indicated by the curve starting at the bottom in 1980. It is also indicated, since the mid-1990s, the interest rate on securities linked to inflation over thirty years. This rate is less sensitive to cyclical fluctuations and offers a clearer indication of the decline in the real interest rate.

hypothesis of secular stagnation, even if some of the factors indicated by him are common to those indicated by this hypothesis.

Among the structural changes to be highlighted, in addition to those mentioned, the one relating to the production structure must be included (Delli Gatti et al., 2012). The transition from an agricultural economy to an industrial economy was at the root of the stagnation of the 1930s. Similarly, increasing outsourcing may explain the decline in growth we have been witnessing in recent decades in advanced countries. In fact, the growth of <u>productivity</u> in industry implies an expulsion of workers (who can be absorbed slowly by the service sector) and a reduction in purchasing power that led to a fall in demand.

Obviously, reducing equilibrium interest rates to negative levels becomes problematic when inflation is low, as nominal interest rates cannot fall below zero (i.e., they are 'zero lower bound', ZLB), except to a limited extent and in some circumstances.[14]

---

[14] As said, nobody would lend at negative nominal interest rates, i.e., knowing in advance that at the maturity of the loan he will receive a sum lower than the one

Some of the factors cited are questionable. For instance, Mokyr (2014) points out that the indirect positive effects of scientific progress on productivity (for example, with the use of new materials and increasingly powerful tools for data processing) can make direct ones irrelevant. Eichengreen (2014) recalls the similar predictions of the past two centuries about the existence of a secular stagnation, regularly denied by reality. This author also questions the basis of the claim that the change in income distribution would lead to excess savings. He points out in this regard that the savings that are formed at the world level and not only in the most advanced countries are significant. China, for example, puts an excess of consumption on the balance. In fact, the ratio of savings to GDP worldwide has remained constant at around 23–24% in the current century. In this regard, however, it should be noted that the case of China cannot be assimilated to that of long-developed countries such as the United States and the countries of Western Europe. On the other side, Eichengreen et al. (2013) highlight in empirical terms the contribution of demographic and technological factors to the fall in the natural rate of interest and growth.

2.3   PROSPECTS OF STAGNATION IN THE EZ: THE IMPACT OF THE GREAT RECESSION, GROWING INEQUALITIES, GLOBALISATION AND INSTITUTIONS

Crisis, globalisation, inequalities and institutions are important because they influence the determinants of secular stagnation. The Great Recession raised the prospect of stagnation in at least two ways: first, by increasing the burden of debt; second, through dragging effects, that is, hysteresis effects, because profit prospects are reduced and, therefore, future investments are discouraged, with negative

lent, already in nominal terms, without counting any inflation, which would further reduce the value of the sum returned in real terms. An apparent exception to this common-sense rule concerns ordinary credit banks that are willing to deposit with the central bank even at slightly negative interest rates, but this is due to the need to reduce cash custody costs.

Index, 100=2008Q4/2019Q4

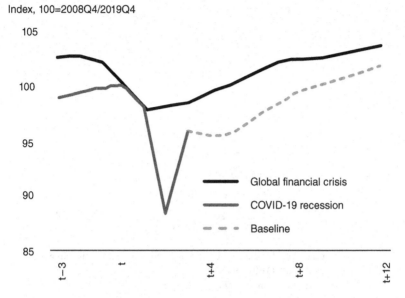

FIGURE 20 Index of the actual GDP trend of advanced countries due to the financial crisis and the pandemic and forecasts for the future
(*Source*: World Bank, 2021b)
Note: The figure shows the actual quarterly GDP trend index from Q1 2007 to Q4 2010 (top line) and Q4 2019 to Q3 2020 (solid bottom line) and the projection for the period until the end of 2022 (dashed line).

effects on potential output. The recovery did not represent a return to previous levels. Starting from 2020, the negative effects of the pandemic were added to the Great Recession, and this phase risks going down in history due to the severity of the crisis, comparable to that of the Great Crisis that began in 1929.[15]

The effects of the crises of this century, compared with those of the Great Crisis, are still modest, but the future developments of the infections will be important. The immediate effects on industrial production of the two recessions of the current century are illustrated in Figure 20. It should be noted that, in fact, these are only the immediate effects ascertained so far. To these will be added other

[15] On the ties between crises and stagnation see Broadberry and Wallis (2017).

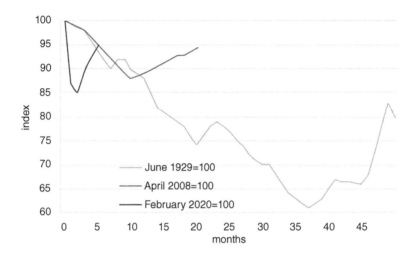

FIGURE 21 World Industrial Production Index: Great Crisis, Great Recession and COVID-19 crisis
(*Source*: De Grauwe and Ji, 2020)

effects deriving from the second phase of the pandemic and, moreover, those produced on the secular stagnation through the processes of hysteresis.

If we refer to different country groups, we can say that emerging market and developing economies (EMDEs) – and, among them especially low-income countries (LICs) where vaccinations remain feebler – are suffering most from the negative effects of the pandemic and will register them not only for the current and the next year, but also – in the case of LICs – for the subsequent years (World Bank, 2021c)

Figure 21, even if it is less updated than the Figure 20 and refers only to industrial production, has the merit of comparing the recent crises with the Great Crisis. The former are clearly less deep than the latter.

As for poverty and inequality, it has already been said that according to the theorists of secular stagnation, these are among the main determinants of the increase in savings compared to investment. However, their impact on long-term growth has been investigated by numerous modern theoretical and empirical studies that reach different conclusions.[16] Some theoretical analyses show positive effects of inequality on growth. Apart from the considerations referred to in the previous Section regarding the effects on overall savings vis-à-vis investment, it should be remembered that inequality would allow some individuals (those belonging to the higher share of income distribution) to acquire a good education and accumulate the minimum necessary to carry out an economic activity (Barro, 2000). Other analyses indicate negative effects that depend on the share of the poorest part of the income earners. In fact, the poor fall ill more easily and accumulate little human capital; moreover, the worsening of income distribution reduces the social consensus that would be necessary to respond to shocks and support growth, thus reducing investment and generating greater political and economic instability. The relationship between inequality and growth may be non-linear, since increases in inequality, when it is at low levels, offer incentives for growth, while beyond a certain point they encourage rent positions and discourage growth. Popović (2018) attributes the increase in the propensity to save and stagnation to the worsening in income distribution. Onaran (2016) believes that the worsening of distribution and the financialisation of the economy contribute to weakening the link between profits and investment: Even in the presence of an increase in the former, capitalists do not make more 'productive' investment, preferring to employ profits in increased financial uses. The net effect of the factors suggested by the various arguments is indeterminate. The results of empirical investigations can further illuminate, but they depend to a significant extent on historical factors and on the set of institutions and economic and social conditions of each country and are therefore subject to change. Laubach and Williams (2016) hold that the deterioration in the distribution of income causes stagnation via a reduction in the natural rate of interest, as there would be a persistent excess of desired savings over investment. According to the

---

[16] For a review see van Treeck (2015).

simulations of Rannenberg (2019), the worsening of distribution, reducing consumption and global demand, increases the demand for government bonds by the rich and thus causes a reduction in the interest rate.

With respect to the debate on the causes of secular stagnation, the institutional aspects and errors of economic policy still need to be considered. Stagnation has appeared in some regions such as Europe and Japan over the past two to three decades. In Japan, the effects of wrong policies and an aging population prevailed. In Europe, as said, there has been the effect of the deflationary approach of the institutions and to some extent of erroneous policies.

In addition to the Great Recession, the crisis resulting from the Coronavirus, and the worsening in income distribution and institutions, the stagnation trend is due to globalisation, which has transmitted crisis and stagnation from the initially most affected countries to others, showing the shortcomings of the existing international organisations. These seem unable to reap the benefits of globalisation and, at the same time, to protect from the evils that can derive from it, through the transmission of shocks and crises. Furthermore, globalisation, while being able to increase growth through multiple routes, can negatively affect it, due to the imbalances associated with financial liberalisation and the fragility of the international financial system, which represent one of the fundamental causes of the global financial crisis and can, therefore, affect growth prospects. Globalisation can also have a negative effect on growth if it implies growing monopolisation. Popović (2018) notes that globalisation has effects similar to those of technology and redistribution, implying a fall in wages, with effects in terms of slowing growth.

Other barriers to growth can arise from: low education, rising public debt, energy shortages and environmental problems. From the point of view of education, Europe, with increasing school attendance rates, is certainly in a rather good position, but in this continent the other factors indicated – and, in addition, the slowdown in productivity that is linked to low investments, the labour market legislation, social security and, more generally, the EU institutions – have a negative influence. Investments have been lower due to the higher returns in the financial sector and global demand stagnation.

2.4 POLICIES TO COUNTER SECULAR STAGNATION

The policies to be implemented against secular stagnation are manifold.

We refer, first of all, to expansionary monetary policies. A difficulty arises from the fact that – as said – the nominal interest rate is ZLB. This constraint is more relevant than previously thought. However, if what matters for the purposes of the investment is the real interest rate, one possibility of reducing this rate is to determine the conditions for an increase in inflation. To monetary policy actions must therefore be added inflationary policies, capable of reducing real interest rates, and finally to control the financial sector (see Summers, 2020, Teulings and Baldwin, 2014b).

A credible promise of high inflation that reduces the real interest rate can indeed produce an economic boom. An effective policy to induce expectations of rising inflation is that of the so-called forward guidance, with which the central bank promises to keep the interest rate low for a certain period of time or until certain publicly announced inflation and/or unemployment rate targets are met (see unconventional monetary policy). Such a policy binds the central bank and creates positive expectations of an increase in inflation, following the stimulus to invest deriving from the awareness that a firm has – thanks to the commitment of the central bank – that it will be able to borrow at an interest rate close to zero for a long time, and not just in the short term, and will benefit from a high rate of inflation. Expectations that the increase in inflation will lower the value of the debt of the firms themselves and of the public sector can also be considered positive factors, reducing in the latter case the need for its consolidation, through painful policies to reduce public spending and/ or an increase in taxation, and restoring flexibility to the public budget, also in an anti-cyclical function. A virtuous circle is then established. The positive expectations about, on the one hand, the maintenance of a low interest rate and, on the other, the possibility of a situation of inflation lead to an increase in investment and aggregate demand, thereby effectively creating the conditions for the increase in inflation, with positive effects on the reduction of the real value of corporate and government debt, that is, of the value of these magnitudes in real terms. Some economists are skeptical about raising inflation rates as a tool to overcome the zero-interest rate constraint and suggest lowering them below zero. But the difficulties of following this suggestion are enormous. Indeed, there would be resistance from many segments of the financial sector and the population. A possible consequence is the accumulation of cash by the population. This accumulation, under certain conditions – for example, when there is some possibility of apparent positive results from the use of cash – could lead to the formation of speculative bubbles. Finally, negative rates would imply a dangerous reduction in loans to businesses and the public sector. As mentioned above, no one would in fact lend their money also having to pay interest to the debtor.

In addition to these policies which tend to act on the short-term factors underlying stagnation, long-term policies are needed, which require structural reforms. These take time to materialize, but in some cases, they can produce immediate positive demand effects, supporting potential income over the longer term. Some structural reforms can have positive or negative effects depending on the circumstances in which they are implemented, such as the cyclical situation or the level of protection in other markets. For example, this can happen due to the reduction of unemployment benefits or of the various provisions for temporary or permanent workers, which can have negative effects in times of crisis. Product market reforms tending to increase competition can reduce employment if there is low labour protection. This indicates substitutability between reforms in product markets and in the labour market.

The public sector also needs structural reforms, as its efficiency should be increased. Also required are the reform of the tax system and the welfare state, the elimination of structural problems in order to increase the rate of change in productivity, the increase in the rate of participation in work, the reduction of inequalities, the strengthening of banking and corporate accounts (Lin, 2016, Pichelmann, 2015). It should be emphasized in particular that the problem of stagnation in productivity has been acute for countries such as Italy since the mid-nineties and must be considered as one of the most pressing ones for this country (Reichlin, 2019). Figure 22 shows the trend in labour productivity growth of the most important countries in the periods 1991–2007 and 2010–2017. In both periods, this is higher in China, India and many other emerging countries and lower not only in more advanced countries,[17] but also in emerging countries such as Brazil, Mexico, Russia and South Africa.

Another field of action is the increase and improvement of physical infrastructure. It is amazing that even countries like Germany and the USA suffer from shortcomings in this area. Therefore. public budget policies are needed to support public investment, even in deficit, especially for countercyclical purposes.[18] The fact that deficit financing can increase the already high levels of public debt may suggest, on the one hand, to proceed with restructuring of this debt[19] and, on the other, may favour forms of financing such as helicopter money (see Buiter et al., 2015). However, it should be remembered that Krugman (2020) proposes to increase public investment on an ongoing basis by financing it in deficit. The deficit will not increase the ratio of

[17] Italy, especially in the period 2010–2017, but also in the previous decade, is at the extreme of developed countries with a low productivity growth.

[18] From this point of view, a high deflationary impact derives from the rules envisaged in the European Union by the SGP and the fiscal compact.

[19] With regard to consolidation and restructuring of public debt, it must be said that they are often pre-eminent objectives of the various countries, which underestimate their short-term costs. These are objectives that should be replaced by that of the weakening of the public debt/GDP ratio obtained through greater investment and more generally through policies of public spending that lead to an increase in the denominator.

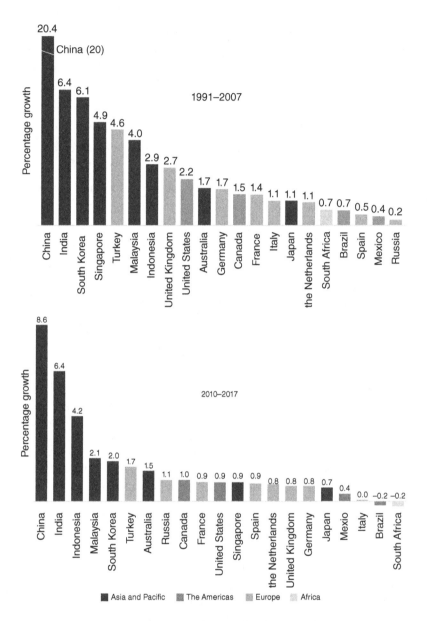

FIGURE 22 Trend in annual labour <u>productivity</u> growth (%), 1991–2007 and 2010–2017, most important countries
(*Source*: Majumdar, 2017)

public debt to income, as its cost is usually less than the rate of growth made possible by public investment.

Other measures must aim at stimulating private investment, by creating a climate of confidence in the private sector. The strengthening of the welfare state can be useful because it keeps the spending power of low-income families high, thus promoting private spending. Connected with the strengthening of the welfare state are policies in favour of a more egalitarian distribution of income and wealth, in order to counteract stagnation tendencies. A similar effect can be obtained by strengthening the educational system, which increases work skills and the fruits of investing in human capital. Moreover, the retirement age must be raised, corresponding to the lengthening of the average age, to reduce excess savings. Also for this purpose, simplified procedures for setting up new businesses (start-ups) and limitations on the action of monopolies can be useful.

The action of the state must then be strengthened precisely in the field of innovation, in order to stimulate technical progress, thus reducing the negative effects of the rents associated with the action of private monopolies in this field (Mazzucato, 2018).

With reference to the indication of the need to increase the optimal inflation rate, it should also be noted that the policy of monetary expansion necessary for this purpose must be adopted together with a set of measures to avoid harmful speculative bubbles. Macroprudential policy for regulation can help in this (Le Garrec and Touzé, 2018).

Other policies that may be particularly useful for Europe concern the exploitation of the spaces available to increase public spending in the surplus countries. Structural reforms can play an essential role in achieving growth, but to this end they need to be formulated in a manner strictly consistent with the characteristics of the country in question and carried out with care (see Terzi and Marrazzo, 2020). If not, they can have a detrimental effect, as has happened in some European countries that have implemented reforms concerning the labour market in particular. These have accentuated the pre-existing imbalances that should have justified them (Hume, 2020).

Policies against secular stagnation must also be evaluated in a broader international perspective. In fact, stagnation in one country also communicates its effects to other countries, through the appreciation (see exchange rate) of the first country's exchange rate, which reduces its demand for goods from other countries, communicating the recessionary impulse to them. Cova et al. (2019) call for expansionary interventions of a fiscal nature coordinated at an international level, tending in particular to incentivize R&D expenses, in order to increase innovations and technical progress.

Posen (2020) calls for international coordination of various policies, in particular monetary, macro-prudential and trade ones. Thus, central banks should increase the amount of their inflation target and the availability of liquidity for the economic system. Macro-prudential policy makers of different countries should grant mutual credit deferrals to small businesses. The protectionist threats, which have increased in recent years, should also cease.

Thus a general problem arises: whether international institutions and alternative policies can be conceived that reduce the prospects of stagnation, also avoiding the risk of financial imbalances and new financial crises. This would in particular require some form of regulation. However, the possibility that low growth rates might be 'the new normal' should be seriously considered also in order to devise the necessary policy attitudes (Jackson, 2019).

2.5 CONCLUSIONS

The past few years have been a period of low income growth that finds little evidence in previous economic history. This low growth can be interpreted as the – temporary – product of the financial cycle, reflecting the effects of the banking crises occurring in the years of the crisis, or as the manifestation of a deeper trend, arising from multiple factors and accentuated by the Great Recession and the COVID-19 crisis, by growing inequalities and globalisation and leading to secular stagna-tion. Such a situation requires numerous policies, ranging from the strengthening of the public budget to the adoption of stimulative monetary policies, even of an <u>unconventional</u> nature, together with 'helicopter money', to raising the retirement age and to numerous other measures of a microeconomic nature, such as limiting the oligopolistic power of large companies.

3   Efficiency, Poverty and Inequalities

Efficiency has various relevant aspects, of a microeconomic (that is, affecting single agents in the economy) or of a macroeconomic nature (that is, that affect aggregate quantities and mainly – among these – total production), static and dynamic. Equity can refer to poverty and various explicit manifestations of inequality. Poverty and inequality negatively affect health, education, social cohesion, political and economic stability. As for economic growth, the effect can be twofold, as we will see. A number of policies can be implemented to reduce the negative effects on efficiency and equity.

In this chapter we deal with all these problems, starting with the appropriate definitions of efficiency and equity. We then continue with the effects of the crisis on them (Section 3.2), subsequently discussing the indicators of poverty and equity, the determinants and effects of inequalities (respectively, Sections 3.3–3.5) and the appropriate policies aimed at reducing them (Section 3.6). Section 3.7 concludes the chapter.

3.1   DEFINITIONS

First of all, we will refer to efficiency, understood in both microeconomic and macroeconomic terms. In the field of microeconomic efficiency, we will not deal with static efficiency, which hardly has practical applications, but with dynamic innovative efficiency, which consists in the ability to introduce new production processes and/or new products. The degree of achievement of environmental objectives must also be considered among the indicators of dynamic efficiency. Static macroeconomic efficiency consists in the ability to fully employ the production factors, in particular the workers who offer themselves in the labour market. Dynamic efficiency in macroeconomic terms is the ability to produce a high rate of income growth. It can be fuelled in particular by R&D and education. We have dealt with this in part in the previous chapters.

The terms *poverty* and *inequalities* have different meanings, but they are related to each other. In fact, it is possible to define a poor person as a person who enjoys an income below a certain value, such as $1.90 per day, as is done internationally. In this case the reference to the income of other people is almost absolutely absent.[1] When we talk about the percentage of people at risk of poverty, we will see that the reference to the income of other people is more evident. Inequality can be measured in various ways, considering analytical indices (share of the total income held by certain fractions of the population, such as the richest or poorest decile – i.e., 10%) or synthetic indices, such as the <u>Gini index (or coefficient)</u>.

3.2 EFFICIENCY AND EQUITY AFTER THE CRISES

In this book we often use data relating not to the last few years for which they are available, but to the last years of the financial crisis, therefore mainly to 2014 and 2015, depending on the incidence of the phenomenon. As for the effects of the pandemic, the data for 2020 and 2021 are only partly available.

3.2.1 Microeconomic Indicators of Dynamic Efficiency

Dynamic efficiency in the period 2008–2017 appears to have increased on average in the EU, but this is to be considered scarcely indicative of long-term trends. Indeed, in 2017 the R&D intensity (i.e., R&D expenses as a percentage of GDP) – which is an indicator of innovative

---

[1] It is true that this level of income is set in such a way as to ensure the survival of one person, but one could observe that reference to the income level of other people is implicit and that the subsistence level is usually raised if the standard of living of these other people is particularly higher. Ultimately, a person lives or survives 'not on bread alone' and often looking at other people's standard of living.

efficiency – for the EU (EMU) increased to 2.06% (2.15%), up 0.3 (0.3) p.p. since 2007, but the increase is due to the effects of the crisis, which reduced the denominator of the intensity. In 2017, the difference with the pre-crisis data was practically the same with the USA (whose R&D intensity was 2.81%), but the position worsened with respect to South Korea, Sweden, Austria and Germany. Apart from the appearance of the positive result, the Europe 2020 target (an R&D intensity of 3%) still appears to be very distant. This result is confirmed by recent studies (see Table 8), which indicate an R&D intensity equal to 2.18% in 2018. The distribution for EU countries of these values is represented – in addition to Table 8 – by Figure 23, which shows the backward position not only of the countries of Central and Eastern Europe, but also of the United Kingdom, with respect to the USA, Japan and South Korea.

Despite the significant lag with respect to this target of Europe 2020, one can hope for a resumption of the efforts of the governments and the private enterprises to increase R&D spending. If this does not happen, as is likely to be the case, the increase in GDP will expose the delay itself of the EU, which has miserably failed the attempt to revitalize its research sector and, in this way, innovation and dynamic efficiency.

Other targets set by Europe 2020 (more precisely, the strategic framework for European cooperation in education and training, i.e., the ET2020 Strategic Framework) that are considered relevant for dynamic efficiency, in its dual meaning of innovative and adaptive efficiency[2] – thus reflecting progress towards an economy based on knowledge and innovation – refer to education and seem to show a more positive trend. The objective of reducing the number of young people aged 18–24 who drop out of school in the EU (EMU) may seem to be nearing completion, given that they decreased in 2018 to

---

[2] Adaptive efficiency is the ability to learn innovations and the new problems that arise with them.

Table 8. *Situation of each member state and the EU with respect to the R&D intensity, 2018*

	R&D intensity 2018	R&D intensity target 2020	R&D intensity compound annual growth [%] 2000–2018[1]	R&D intensity compound annual growth [%] 2010–2018	R&D intensity compound annual growth [%] required to meet the 2020 target 2018–2020
Belgium	2.67	3.00	1.8	3.3	5.9
Bulgaria	0.76	1.50	2.4	3.7	40.9
Czechia[7]	1.90	:[2]	3.0	4.5	:
Denmark	3.02	3.00	1.7	0.4	*Target reached*
Germany[7]	3.12	3.00	1.4	1.7	*Target reached*
Estonia	1.41	3.00	4.9	-1.3	45.9
Ireland	0.99	2.00[3]	-0.5	-5.8	42.2
Greece	1.21	1.30	4.8	9.2	3.5
Spain	1.24	2.00	1.9	-1.1	26.9
France	2.19	3.00	0.5	0.1	17.0
Croatia	0.97	1.40	0.1	3.3	20.4
Italy	1.42	1.53	2.0	2.0	3.6
Cyprus	0.62	0.50	5.8	4.3	*Target reached*
Latvia	0.64	1.50	2.1	0.6	53.2
Lithuania	0.94	1.90	2.7	2.2	42.4
Luxembourg	1.21	2.30–2.60[4]	-1.1	-1.1	42.2
Hungary	1.51	1.80	3.7	2.3	9.2
Malta	0.60	2.00	1.0	-0.2	83.0

Table 8. (*cont.*)

	R&D intensity 2018	R&D intensity target 2020	R&D intensity compound annual growth [%] 2000–2018[1]	R&D intensity compound annual growth [%] 2010–2018	R&D intensity compound annual growth [%] required to meet the 2020 target 2018–2020
the Netherlands	2.14	2.50	0.4	1.8	8.1
Austria	3.14	3.76	2.9	1.8	9.4
Poland	1.21	1.70	3.6	6.7	18.6
Portugal	1.35	2.70–3.30[5]	2.2	−1.6	49.1
Romania	0.50	2.00	1.3	0.1	99.8
Slovenia	1.95	3.00	0.4	−3.0	24.1
Slovakia	0.84	1.20	1.5	4.0	19.6
Finland	2.76	4.00	−0.9	−3.6	20.5
Sweden	3.32	4.00	−0.5	0.6	9.7
EU	2.18	3.00	1.1	1.3	17.2

Source: Rakic et al., 2021

Notes: (1) HR: 2002–2018; EL, LU, SE: 2003–2018; MT: 2004–2018. HU: 2000–2017. (2) CZ: A target (of 1.0%) is available only for the public sector. (3) IE: The national target of 2.5% of GNP has been estimated to equal 2.0% of GDP. (4) LU: A 2020 target of 2.45% was assumed. (5) PT: A 2020 target of 3.0% was (6) DK, EL, FR, IT, LU, HU, MT, NL, PT, RO, SI, SE: Breaks in series occur between 2000 and 2018; when there is a break in series the growth calculation takes into account annual growth before the break in series and annual growth after the break in series. (7) DE: new 2025 target of 3.5%. CZ: new 2030 target of 3.0%. (8) Values in italics are estimated or provisional.

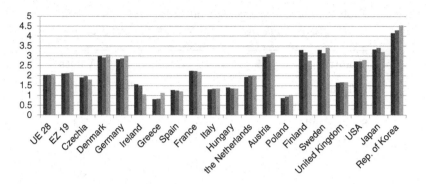

FIGURE 23 R&D/GDP (%), 2013, 2014, 2017, EU, Japan, South Korea, USA
(*Source*: Eurostat)
Note: The histograms indicate, in the order, the various years, 2013, 2014, 2017.

10.6% (11.1%), not far from the 10% target.[3] According to the 2020 report, the ET2020 targets have been only partially achieved. Only nineteen countries have achieved the 10% target of early school leaving. Other countries, notably Spain (17.3%), Malta (16.7%) and Romania (15.3%), have not. The target of 40% of tertiary education attainment of people aged 30–34 has been achieved, again with some exceptions, for example, of Romania and Italy (see European Commission, 2020a).

Some other recent statistics referring to a different class of young people are merciless. In 2019, as many as 12.9% of both young people aged 18–24 and those aged 15–29 in the EU 23 did not attend school, were not employed nor attended training courses. These are the so-called NEETs (Not in education, employment or training) (see Table 9).

At the same time, the share of people aged 30–34 who have completed tertiary education has approached the 40% target for EMU

[3] The countries of Southern Europe seem to have achieved better results, falling to values well below those of the targets, but this may be linked to the greater difficulties in finding a job.

Table 9. *Young people who do not study and do not work (NEET), % of people aged 14 to 29, 2019, various countries*

Country	Values
Iceland	6.1
the Netherlands	6.9
Switzerland	7.3
Norway	8.1
Germany	8.1
Sweden	8.4
Estonia	9.3
United Kingdom	13.3
France	17.3
Italy	25.5
USA	14.2
EU 23 (average)	12.9
OECD (average)	14.3

Source: OECD, 2020b

(39.3%), surpassing it for the EU (40.5%).[4] Again, some countries in Southern Europe (not all) have achieved better results. There is, however, a wide dispersion of values between different countries and one can doubt that the positive character of many indicators will resist the economic recovery, especially for Southern Europe. In fact, this would increase employment and therefore favour prospects for an alternative to school 'parking'. In the past, in fact, it has always happened that the trends in employment and school attendance were opposite not only for the ages considered in Figure 24, but also for children of lower ages.

Yet there are incentives for education and its extension. In addition to a higher probability of employment,[5] there is also the

---

[4] Italy, in which the percentage stood at 26% in 2017, is not included among these.

[5] For the OECD as a whole in 2019 the employment rate of those who had completed only lower secondary education was 61%, compared with 78% for young people with high school graduation and 85% for university graduates; for the EU-23 the percentages were similar.

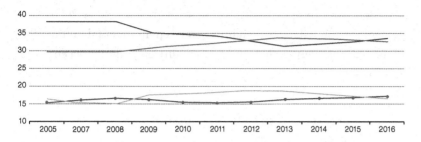

FIGURE 24 Young people aged 20–24 by education and employment
status, 2006–2016, EU
(*Source*: Eurostat)
Note: The line that starts higher indicates 'only employed'. The line just below
indicates those 'only at the studio'. The line that starts even lower refers to those
'not emplyed nor at the studio'. The line with a dot indicates young people
'employed and at studio'.

expectation of enjoying a higher wage. In fact, in the EU of twenty-
three countries, when passing from the first level secondary education
to obtaining a university degree, the remuneration practically doubles
or even increases by more than two times for older employees (in the
OECD the wages of older graduates are more than double, almost
triple) (OECD, 2020c).

At the end of February 2021, the EU member states agreed on a
new common framework for European educational cooperation in the
decade 2021–2030 that is closely aligned with the goals for creating a
European Education Area by 2025.

Even the positive or very positive trend of environmental objectives – in general the 20% reduction of emissions (compared to 1990
levels) – can be linked to the effects of the economic crisis. Indirect
indicators of this are, on the one hand, the negligible improvement in
the share of renewable energy and, on the other, the full achievement
of the objectives in the non-ETS sectors (i.e., those for which the
Emissions Trading System, ETS, does not apply) essentially by the
PIIGS countries, which have suffered most from the crisis. In 2020,
national expenditures on environmental protection of the EU
Member States amounted to €273 billion. Rising on average by over

2% each year, these expenditures increased by 40% since 2006. As a percentage of GDP, expenditure for environmental protection remained relatively stable for the last fifteen years (between 1.8% and 2.0% of GDP).

3.2.2 Macroeconomic Indicators of Static and Dynamic Efficiency

After the crisis, the trend in unemployment and employment rates and other macroeconomic variables has changed significantly compared to the previous situation. Unemployment increased until 2013–2014, but subsequently declined as production resumed (Figure 25). Employment rates also increased, although they remained slightly below the targets (just under 75%) for almost all European countries, but not for Germany and some other Central-Eastern European countries.

Regarding dynamic macroeconomic efficiency indicators, income growth rates are shown in Figure 26.

In the EZ, the negative effects of the crisis began in the banking and financial sector, soon passing on to sovereign debt and then feeding back to the private financial sector of peripheral countries, with an increase in interest rates, a reduction in demand for credit and then a fall in income and higher unemployment. These real effects were subsequently transmitted to the countries of the core through

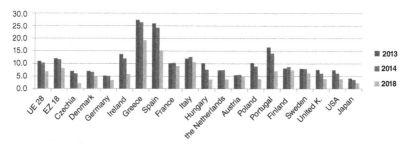

FIGURE 25 Unemployment rates (%), 2013, 2014, 2018, EU
(*Source*: Eurostat)

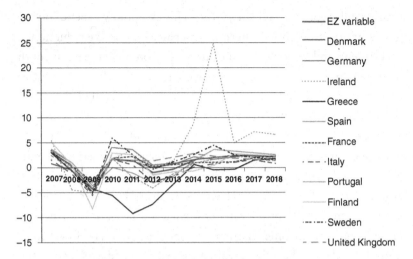

FIGURE 26 GDP growth rates (%), 2007–2018, some European countries
(*Source*: European Commission, https://ec.europa.eu/info/index_en)
Note: Practically, almost all lines have the same trend. The one that shifts to the
bottom in the years 2009–2013 refers to Greece. The one that moves upward since
2013 refers to Ireland.

the channels of trade and confidence and only the expansionary monetary policy of the ECB helped to counter them, both in individual
countries and in the EZ as a whole, as shown by various exercises. The
real negative short-term effects also affected growth, due not only to
hysteresis factors and the effects of current income on potential
income, but also to the weight of sovereign debt and the consolidation
plans implemented to reduce it. The negative effects have hit and will
hit again in the future not only the peripheral countries, but also the
'virtuous' ones of the core, due to the commercial links between
them. Furthermore, they are not limited to the economic sphere, as
they also refer to the thrust of a movement of opinion that had already
begun to manifest itself before the Great Recession, but which has
certainly strengthened subsequently, namely *sovereignism* and
localism.

According to the long-term projections of the OECD, it could
take twenty-five years before European countries regain their pre-

crisis standard of living (OECD, 2012). This essentially depends on the long duration and depth of this crisis, in particular on the reduction of investment (and therefore of innovation), and on the increase in youth unemployment, both factors that have a lasting and long-term effect on human capital, and the consequent effects on the fall of the potential product (Acocella, 2018).

There are no reliable synthetic indicators of sustainable growth, but the environmental objectives indicated above can serve this purpose. Indeed, these are an important determinant of sustainability, although the link with sustainable growth should be subject to further analysis and include other variables, such as the nature of technological progress, income distribution and institutions. However, it should be noted that these variables become <u>endogenous</u> in the long run.

3.2.3 Poverty and Equity Indicators

The crisis has hit hard on poverty and social participation both in the EZ average and in most countries, with the exclusion of Austria, Denmark, France, Germany and Sweden, as shown in Figure 27.

From 2007 to 2017, the percentage of people at risk of poverty – that is, the poverty rate[6] (the main component of the poverty and social exclusion rate – see <u>people at risk of poverty and social exclusion</u>) increased by 0.3 p.p. in the EZ, to 22.1%, but had already reached a maximum value of 23.5% in 2014, reflecting the dynamics of

---

[6] It is defined as the number of poor people belonging to families with an equivalent disposable income (therefore, income net of social transfers) of less than 60% of the national *median* (to be defined in the next footnote). It should be noted that the equivalent income of a family is calculated by applying a scale factor to the net income of the family, in order to take into account the different number of its members and its composition, as the needs of minors and adults differ and economies of scale are realized with the cohabitation of several components. Economies of scale consist in reducing the average cost of production of an asset due to the increase in the scale – that is, the size – of production. The concept applied to the domestic economy means that the average cost of family life generally decreases as the number of family members increases.

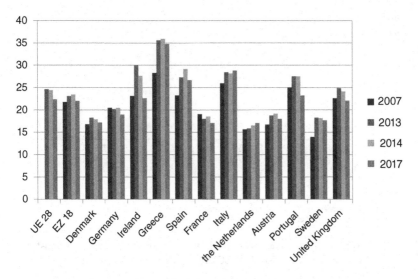

FIGURE 27 People at risk of poverty and social exclusion (%), 2007, 2013, 2014, 2017, various countries, EU 28, EZ 18
(*Source*: Eurostat)
Note: 2007 data are not available for EU 28.

income and employment in the main EU countries. In reality, the slight increase of the indicated rate – in the extreme years of the period now considered – can underestimate the trend of the phenomenon in question. This may be due to the fact that the crisis implies a reduction in median[7] income. In fact, remember that to calculate the poverty rate, the median income is first computed. Then 60% of this value is taken, and those who fail to reach even this figure are considered at risk of poverty. If the median income falls with the average income, it may be that people below 60% of the median income are

---

[7] The median (or median value), for example in the case of income, is the value that separates the higher half from the lower half of the population of income earners, ordered according to their income. The intermediate value is the median income, which therefore separates the inhabitants of a country exactly between half of them who *at least* reach this value of income and another 50% who have a lower income. The average income is instead the income derived by dividing the total income of the population by the number of inhabitants.

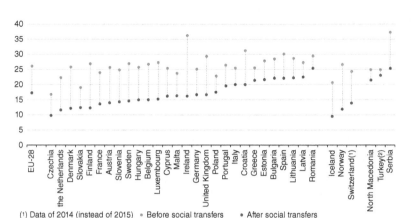

(¹) Data of 2014 (instead of 2015)   • Before social transfers   • After social transfers
(²) Data of 2013 (instead of 2015)

FIGURE 28 People at risk of poverty (%), before and after social transfers (excluding pensions), 2015, EU 28
(*Source*: Eurostat)

fewer than before, but simply because the threshold has been lowered. The underestimation also depends on the fact that the disposable income and not the gross income is taken into account in the calculation of the index.[8] For this purpose, we consider Figure 28, which shows the high incidence of public transfers in the reduction of the poverty rate, equal in 2015 to approximately 9% of the median income for the EU as a whole and such as to reduce the rate of poverty itself from 26.0% to 17.3%. The contribution of transfers is much higher in some countries (not only Scandinavian countries, but also the United Kingdom and other countries) than in Eastern Europe. Of course, in reality the quality of life certainly depends on disposable income. But to support that income requires state intervention, and prolonged intervention can jeopardize the sustainability of public finances.

Over time, poverty rates before and after transfers have moved in different directions. The former remained relatively stable in the

---

[8] For other shortcomings that derive from use of the indicator of the poverty rate see Darvas (2019).

EU between 2010 and 2015, while the latter grew slightly. This may mean either that the values of transfers or their effectiveness have decreased over time. However, given the anti-cyclical nature of transfers, the state can be said to have played a very positive role in offsetting the negative effects of the crisis.

In 2019, the risk of poverty before and after transfers remained at levels similar to those of four years earlier. It should be noted that the gap between the two rates is particularly low for some countries (such as Italy and the other Mediterranean countries). Instead, the component of social transfers is very high, not only in the Nordic countries (Denmark, Finland and Sweden), but also for Ireland and Germany (Table 10).

Globally, the absolute poor fell from 1,086 million in 1981 to 706 million in 2015 and 650 million in 2018, with a percentage incidence on the population that fell at the same time from 42.25% of the world population to just under 10% in 2015 and 8.6% in 2018 (Roser and Ortiz-Ospina, 2019). It is important to underline the notable increase in poverty as an effect of the epidemic (see Figure 29), even if estimates by other authors report slightly different data.

Assuming a fall in GDP according to the estimates already indicated by the IMF, the expected share of people in conditions of absolute poverty in 2020 should have increased by a number of percentage points ranging from 0.8 to 1.5, which is equivalent to an increase of 50–70 million people. These estimates are perfectly in line with those of Figure 29. According to more pessimistic forecasts, in the case of a 20% decline in per capita income, the increase could be about 419 million, which would add to the existing poor (Sumner et al., 2020, UNIDO, 2020).

It is important to note that the impact on poverty and its geographical distribution will not be proportional to the extent of infections in the various countries and areas. Thus, for example, the countries of sub-Saharan Africa are for the moment relatively little affected in terms of the number of confirmed cases of Coronavirus.

Table 10. *People at risk of poverty (%) before and after transfers (excluding pensions), 2020, EU, EZ*

GEO/TIME	2020 before transfers	2020 after transfers
European Union – 27 countries	25.4	17.1
Euro area – 19 countries (since 2015)	25.7	17.3
Belgium	25.6	14.1
Denmark	25.4	12.1
Germany	27.8	18.5
Ireland	31.0[a]	13.1[a]
Greece	23.6	17.7
Spain	27.4	21.0
France	26.0	13.8
Italy	25.2[a]	20.1[a]
Hungary	22.0	12.3
the Netherlands	21.3	13.6
Poland	23.4	14.8
Portugal	21.9	16.2
Finland	25,1	12.2
Sweden	28.1	16.1

Source: Eurostat
[a] values for 2019

But the fact is that many people live there in conditions on the verge of absolute poverty and therefore even a limited impact[9] of the epidemic on economic activity levels is enough to make them fall below that threshold. According to IMF projections, in advanced countries there has been a reduction in income of about 6% in 2020, while in developing and emerging countries, the reduction is of the order of 1%. In sub-Saharan countries, a reduction of this order of magnitude

---

[9] The impact can be direct or indirect, the latter being mainly due to foreign trade, investment and aid or migration.

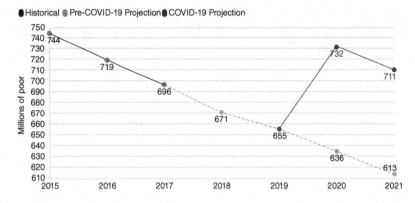

FIGURE 29 The evolution of extreme poverty, 2015–2021, worldwide
(*Source*: Gerszon Mahler et al., 2021)

will be enough to plunge 23 million people below the poverty line. A similar, but smaller, effect has taken place for Asian countries, with an absolute increase in poor by 16 million. Forecasts along these lines had been made by Mahler et al. (2020).

In general, countries responded to the pandemic with large social spending programs, by direct and indirect fiscal support, equivalent to 28% of their GDP. Also emerging and developing economies spent a lot of money, 7% and 2% of GDP, respectively. All the same, in contrast with the more recent trends, the pandemic will accentuate the long-term concentration of poverty especially in African countries that are middle income, fragile and conflict-affected (Kharas and Dooley, 2021).

A more complete picture is offered by Table 11, which indicates the percentage and number of people who in the event of a low income reduction (5%) would be below various absolute poverty thresholds, the minimum – considered so far – of $1.9 a day, and then also the thresholds of $3.2 and $5.5. As can be seen, in both absolute and percentage terms, the most affected region would be that of sub-Saharan Africa, followed by South East Asia, East Asia and the Pacific. European countries and other developed countries (the United States, Canada and others) would be relatively least

Table 11. *People who would find themselves below different absolute poverty thresholds in the event of a reduction in per capita income of 5%: Absolute values and percentages of incidence on the total population, 2018, worldwide*

	$1.9		$3.2		$5.5	
Aggregate	%	Million	%	Million	%	Million
East Asia and Pacific	1.6	33.8	8.8	184.0	27.9	580.0
Europe and Central Asia	1.4	6.7	5.0	24.8	13.2	65.0
Latin America and the Caribbean	4.8	30.5	11.3	72.2	26.0	165.7
Middle East and North Africa	8.0	31.2	21.8	84.4	47.3	183.4
Other high income	0.7	7.4	0.9	10.0	1.4	15.3
South Asia	14.8	259.8	52.3	914.4	83.3	1,457.4
Sub-Saharan Africa	44.2	474.6	69.2	744.0	86.8	932.6
World Total	**11.2**	**844.1**	**27.0**	**2,033.8**	**45.2**	**3,399.5**

Source: Sumner et al., 2020

affected. It should also be noted that as many as 13% of those earning an income of less than $5.5 per day (equal to 65 million) would be below this threshold. In total, more than 800 million people worldwide would have a below-threshold income (Sumner et al., 2020). An increase in the poor of 85 million over the 759 million already in existence in 2018 (making a total of 844 million) is the minimum tribute that humanity should pay – apart from the grief and pain of the infections – as a result of the Coronavirus. As mentioned, the tribute would increase to 419 million in the event of a fall in income not of 5%, but of 20%.

Recent research arrives at a similar conclusion on this topic, as can be seen from Figure 30.

Poverty is important, but inequality must also be considered. Similarly to poverty, inequality can also be measured in various

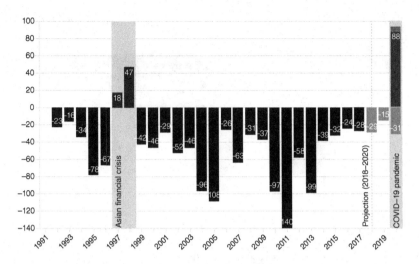

FIGURE 30 Annual change in the number of extreme poor (in millions), 1992–2020, worldwide
(*Source*: Gerszon Mahler et al., 2021)

'spaces', such as consumption, income, wealth, utility, capacity. The most common ones are income and wealth.[10]

Globally, an idea of the distribution of income in various countries is offered by Figure 31, which shows the share of income of the richest 1% of the population for the whole world in 2019 as well as the historical profile of this share in some countries since 1872. As can be seen, some emerging countries, such as South Africa, Brazil and Mexico, show extremely high levels of income concentration. The concentration is much lower in other African countries, such as Algeria, and in Northern Europe (Scandinavian countries). The

---

[10] Income inequality can be related to factors of production (labour, capital, land) or to people (personal distribution) or to geographical distribution. Inequality in wealth can be calculated as gross or net of debt or can refer to specific items of wealth, such as homes, land or financial wealth. Different indices can be calculated for each space and size. For example, personal income distribution can be assessed with the use of synthetic indicators, such as those of Gini (see Gini index) or Theil, or with reference to more detailed values, such as deciles, quartiles or other percentages of income earners.

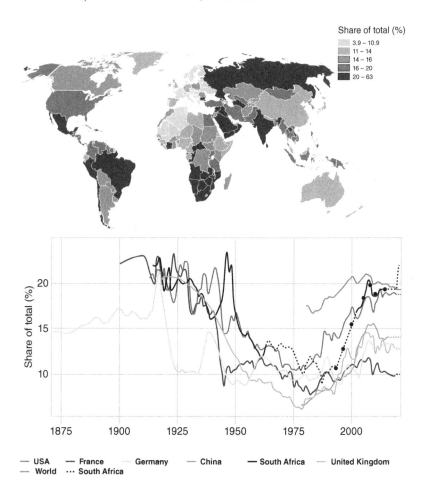

FIGURE 31 Income share of the richest 1% of the population (%),
1871–2019, worldwide and various countries
a) Worldwide
b) Various countries
(*Source*: World Inequality Database, https://wid.world/world/#sptinc_p99p100_z/
US;FR;DE;CN;ZA;GB;WO/last/eu/k/p/yearly/s/false/5.3485/40/curve/false/
country)
Note: Graph b) shows the trend of the share of total income for the richest 1% of the
population in various countries. The data relating to Germany begins in 1871, that
of France in 1900, that of the United States in the 1910s, that of the whole world
in 1980.

Mediterranean countries, Austria, Germany, Ireland and the United Kingdom show low concentrations, whereas for the United States this is near the top. The most relevant aspect of the historical profile offered by part (b) of the Figure is the decline of the share of the top percentile – that is, the top 1% of the income earners[11] – in the last ten to fifteen years.

Regarding country-specific inequality, the results of various studies – referring to different periods, countries and indicators – differ. From 1865 to the years following the World War II, inequality for European countries in terms of the Gini index decreased mainly after the world wars, which had implications that to some extent erased the past and transformed the structure of inequality and society (Piketty, 2013). By using an indicator other than the Gini index, the picture is confirmed and some particular aspects become clearer. More recently, the trend has changed. In the last three decades, inequality has risen a lot in transition countries (mainly the Baltic countries), the UK and some Nordic countries, less so in other countries such as Italy, remaining largely unchanged in Austria, Denmark, France and Germany, particularly after the Great Recession. As Figures 32 and 33 show, in the Anglo-Saxon countries, the income of the richest 1% of the population has grown, especially in the USA, while it has remained largely unchanged in the countries of continental Europe; on the other hand, income inequality increased in the United Kingdom, France and the Scandinavian countries, while it decreased in Spain, Ireland and Italy.[12]

---

[11] To represent the distribution of income in a country, the income earners can be sorted according to income, in ascending sense, and divided into percentages. The first 1% of income earners indicates the percentage of the poorest, the hundredth percentile the 1% of the richest earners. When the text speaks of income percentiles from 30 to 65%, it can be said that they are the middle classes. And, referring to Figure 47 (which will be presented in Chapter 5), the 40th percentile had increased its share of income by 60% in the period 1988–2008 and by about 95% between 1988 and 2011.

[12] On the evolution of income inequality in Europe in the last four decades, see also blanchet et al, (2019).

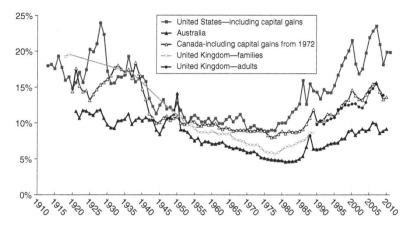

FIGURE 32 Income share of the richest 1% of the population (%),
1910–2010, Anglo-Saxon countries
(*Source*: Alvaredo et al., 2013)

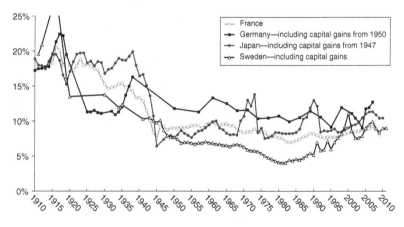

FIGURE 33 Income share of the richest 1% of the population (%),
1910–2010, some countries of continental Europe and Japan
(*Source*: Alvaredo et al., 2013)

3.3 THE CAUSES OF INEQUALITIES

If we refer only to the experience after the World War II, the trend
of inequality was influenced, first of all, by the Keynesian policies
implemented after the war, which reduced unemployment, thus

increasing the income of a substantial part of the population. Redistribution and regulatory policies have had different effects in different countries.

After 1980, inequality was increased in particular by policies of liberalisation of the labour, goods and capital markets and by a reduction in the tax burden on income and wealth (for example, by reducing the inheritance tax) of the richer, particularly accentuated in the Anglo-Saxon countries. It is no coincidence that distribution has worsened a little in continental European countries (in particular, in Scandinavian ones), where redistributive policies have remained largely active. The role of technology is uncertain. Similarly, the globalisation in terms of the movement of goods has contributed to reducing inequalities, while the liberalisation of capital and financialisations have increased capital shares, also creating financial crises. Instead, the expansion of education may have tended to reduce inequalities.

Table 12 shows the trend over time of marginal rates – that is, the tax rates applied on the highest income fraction – in major developed countries.

The pandemic has produced an increase in inequalities, as shown in Figure 34.

Furthermore, the negative effects of the pandemic on unemployment, income distribution and the ratio of public debt to GDP will last for a long time, at least until 2025 (Emmerling et al., 2021).

Wealth has a higher inequality than income. This is due to demographic reasons (wealth is higher for the elderly, who represent a higher share of the population) and to the fact that when net wealth is considered, the gross wealth of many people is reduced, because it is at least partly the result of debt. This happens in particular if we consider – as it normally is – the overall wealth and not only that in terms of certain activities, such as houses. As the number of both the homeless and debtors and the richest have increased, there has been a polarisation of the distribution of wealth.

Table 12. *Marginal income tax rates for some developed countries (%),
1900–2013*

	France	Germany	UK	USA
1900	0	3	0	0
1909	0	3	8	0
1913	0	3	8	7
1918	20	20	53	77
1928	33	40	50	25
1939	53	60	83	79
1941	60	60	98	81
1944	70	60	98	94
1951	60	75	98	91
1964	53	53	89	77
1980	66	56	75	70
1988	57	56	40	28
2000	61	51	40	40
2005	56	42	40	35
2013	53	45	45	40

Source: Pedone (2016)

The worsening in the distribution of income and wealth is
linked to that of the so-called functional distribution of income (i.e.,
the distribution of income among the 'factors' of production), and to a
certain extent this depends precisely on the trend of this type of
distribution, since the returns on capital have increased and those
on labour have decreased.

In fact, from Figure 35 it can be seen that the *corrected* labour
income (wage) share[13] decreased in the 1990s and 2000s in virtually
all countries.

As regards wage labour, there has been a notable deterioration to
the detriment of the poorest workers. Thus, the wages of the top 1%

---

[13] The reference to the correction indicates that account has been taken of the
reduction in the number of dependent workers (who earn wages) compared to the
total number of workers, including the self-employed.

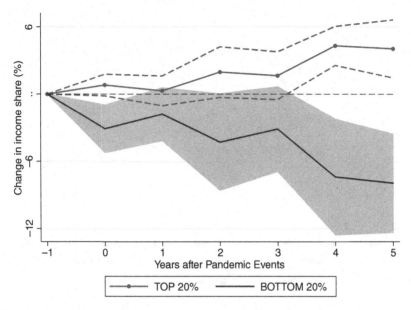

FIGURE 34. Changes in distribution shares following the pandemic, worldwide

(Furceri et al., 2021)

Notes: The horizontal axis indicates the number of years elapsed after the pandemic event; the vertical one, the percentage changes in income shares (in shaded area, all negative, those of the less wealthy 20%; the line with a dot those, all positive, of the wealthiest 20%)

of wage-earning workers in the USA and the UK more than doubled, while the income of the poorest workers fell. This derives from: lower wages of less skilled workers, due to non-typical forms of employment (temporary and precarious employment); reduction in employment during the Great Recession; polarisation of income and capital growth rates. The effect of the latter factor on the personal distribution of income requires an explanation. This is due to the fact that the interest rate (which is the capital growth factor) was higher than the income growth rate. Thus, higher income earners – who have a higher propensity to save, by investing saving in various forms of wealth – find themselves at an advantage over other income earners. In other words, suppose, for example, that everyone's income (high- and

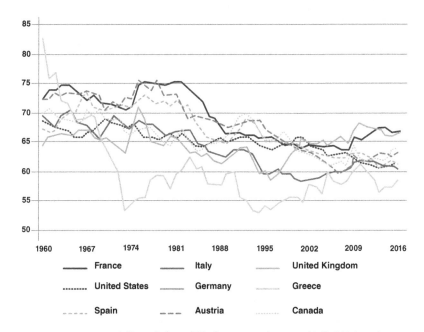

FIGURE 35 Adjusted share (%) of wages on income, 1960–2016, various countries
(*Source*: Canelli and Realfonzo, 2018)
Note: The Greek share of wages shows the lowest profile, while the shares of other countries change more or less in the same way.

low-income earners) initially grows by 5%. In this case, the distances between the most qualified, who earn relatively more than others, and the least qualified, persist and remain unchanged. However, the latter do not save, unlike the former, and therefore their income growth remains equal to 5%. The saving of the most qualified allows them to earn further income and, thus, their wealth increases, for example, by 6%, as the interest rate is supposed to be higher than the rate of growth of income. It can be thought that part of this increase, equal to 5%, is used to keep the ratio between wealth and income unchanged and another part, 1%, increases the distance in terms of income with the less qualified.

In terms of time, it must be said that, in appearance strangely, in the first decades of the postwar period, the improvements in personal income equality were linked to decreasing labour income shares, while more recently the worsening of the former was accompanied by more or less stationary labour income shares. This implies that other sources of income have become more prominent. One of these could be the accumulation of significant financial assets in the period up to 2007. The subsequent crisis, which destroyed financial wealth, could then explain the worsening of personal equality, even with a fairly constant share of earned income, if the destruction affected the major income earners less.

In conclusion, we can say that the crisis has had a significant negative effect on both efficiency and equity. And the clash between equity goals in rich countries and the pursuit of better living standards in other countries has fuelled populism in recent years (Rodrik, 2019).

3.4   THE EFFECTS OF INEQUALITIES

The first reason to deal with inequalities is that they are indicators of equity and this, in addition to having value in itself, is an important factor of social cohesion. Inequalities also affect health, education and both political and economic stability.

From this last point of view, inequalities can imply a low level of aggregate demand, given the lower propensity to consume of rich families. This means that one euro that passes from the income of a poor person to that of a rich person results in a lower level of total consumption.

Inequalities can have dual effects on growth. On the one hand, growth can be positively linked to savings, especially if incentives for innovation and entrepreneurship are increased as an effect of the higher saving, unless wealth generates corruption and parasitism. On the other hand, growth could be reduced because the poor tend to remain trapped in their state of misery, with high fertility rates, low education rates, low levels of health and moral degradation.

Again, inequalities tend to reproduce over time, as they generate a conservative element especially in the attitude of the richest, who normally have the levers of power. Finally, especially when particularly accentuated, they can generate factors of political instability, which reduce growth rates.

The existence of both positive and negative effects does not allow us to draw univocal abstract conclusions on the net effect of inequalities on income growth at the theoretical level. Empirical analysis can help. Data collected by the OECD lead to the conclusion that redistribution in favour of the less well-off strengthens growth in developing countries. Increased growth can produce a reduction in inequality, which – in turn – further strengthens growth. In other words, the reduction of inequalities has positive cumulative effects. In developed countries the relationship tends to be opposite, due to lower levels of inequality. Indeed, empirical studies are to some extent only indicative because many institutional factors and other economic and social conditions influence growth, in addition to income distribution. An example of this are the attitudes of the richest people towards production, which are often the result of historical legacies. History may have shaped elites that are rent-seeking rather than enterprising.

3.5 POLICIES FOR EFFICIENCY AND INEQUALITIES

3.5.1 *Policies for Efficiency*

Let us deal with policies for efficiency first. Incentives are the main instrument for enhancing dynamic efficiency.

The first instrument in favour of dynamic efficiency in general is offered by competition-oriented market policies. In order to foster innovation, proper fiscal or financial incentives can be implemented. As to environmental problems, traditionally, public policy theories have focused on regulation, financial incentives, environmental taxes, voluntary agreements to achieve environmental objectives, such as Ecolabel and Ecoaudit,[14] and information as the main policy tools. Regulation has recently been enriched by the issuance of tradable permits. Environmental regulations have been enforced at the level of many countries since the early 1970s and have resulted in a considerable improvement in the quality of air, water and land. The main

---

[14] Ecolabels and certificates applied to specific products and services inform consumers about their environmental performance. Ecoaudit is a voluntary evaluation made by a firm as to the implications of its production on environment.

international agreements on this matter are those adopted in 2015 at the UN level: the 2030 Agenda for Sustainable Development and the Paris Agreement on Climate Change. The latter entered into force on 4 November 2016 and aims at limiting global warming to well below 2, preferably to 1.5 degrees Celsius, compared to pre-industrial levels. There are environment regulations also at the European level, where in 2005 an Emissions Trading System (ETS) regulating pollution was implemented (Gawel et al., 2014), setting caps for emissions and instituting a trade system of permits to pollute.[15]

3.5.2 Policies for Inequalities

As to policies for inequalities, some of them act on primary distribution, that is, on the distribution before state intervention through the public budget. These policies are both direct actions – which influence wages (for example, through the regulation of the minimum wage and of various forms of wage equality, such as that between men and women) and the promotion of collective bargaining – as well as indirect actions. As to the former, various conventions and a recommendation were passed by the International Labour Office, but they ended in 1981, with no important later action afterwards. During the Great Recession and afterwards in Europe there have been a decreasing bargaining coverage, lower levels of unionisation and decentralisation of wage bargaining. European wage bargaining institutions have become 'more similar to what is the norm outside Europe' (Visser, 2016: 30), leading as a consequence to a rise in inequalities (Jaumotte and Osorio Buitron, 2015). Indirect actions refer to the rights of workers to organize and the promotion of collective bargaining. They can affect inequalities through the promotion of education and vocational training and in general the formation of human capital as well as through measures that tend to encourage people with the lowest income to accept a job.

---

[15] The ETS is a 'cap and trade' system tending to combat climate change (see more at Emissions Trading System).

The importance of the public budget lies not only in the aggregate values of expenditures and taxes, but derives also from their composition. Whereas aggregate values are relevant for business cycle regulation, the composition has effects on secondary distribution. Specific changes in the various items of the budget will thus have an effect on the various categories of citizens. In order not to have negative effects on primary distribution, these measures must be appropriately calibrated. For example, unemployment benefits that are guaranteed for a long time could induce the unemployed person to stay in her state, especially if the job search proves to be difficult and fruitless. To avoid this, they must be temporary and accompanied by measures to improve the professionalism of the unemployed and direct them to activities where vacant jobs exist. The composition of the public budget has also a political relevance, in addition to its economic relevance, as it influences political attitudes of citizens towards the government (Estache and Leipziger, 2016).

It has been said that one of the factors that produces inequalities is the high interest rate compared to the growth rate. Other things being equal, a high interest rate raises the relevance of wealth in a society. Wealth owners' share of income will then increase vis-à-vis other income earners. Creditors will be better off while debtors will see their position worsened. This will give an incentive to save, with the ensuing depressing consequences on the macroeconomic situation. Therefore, one of the policies to adopt in order to boost aggregate demand is the reduction of the interest rate. And these secondary effects on macroeconomic conditions of changing interest rates can be of a relatively high order of magnitude. In fact, lower interest rates – while prima facie hitting wealth owners – can have positive consequences also on them through the incentive offered to aggregate demand and vice versa for higher interest rates.[16]

---

[16] Benoît Cœuré says that 'far from helping savers, higher monetary policy interest rates would only have depressed the economy further' (Cœuré, 2013).

Apart from the value of the interest rate, capital should be taxed progressively. Capital taxation is justified on both equity and efficiency grounds. When trying to implement wealth taxation many practical problems arise that derive from the tax avoidance and tax arbitrage behaviour of wealth owners (Bastani and Waldenström, 2020). Wealth taxation should take place on a global scale or, at least, at the level of unions of countries such as the European Monetary Union. Obviously, such a measure, however desirable, would encounter strong opposition from the richest people or, in any case, from those who would be harmed by it. However, such a measure would also require interventions to combat tax evasion and avoidance for incomes, for example by combatting complacency towards tax havens. These have been identified worldwide, but there are intolerable favourable tax treatments within the European Union itself, as we have already seen. For example, the Netherlands and Luxembourg practice lighter levels of income taxation on a general basis or to be decided on a case-by-case basis. In particular, in the past the then–Luxembourg Prime Minister Juncker, who later became President of the European Commission – the equivalent at this level of executive power in nation states – was responsible for ad hoc agreements with foreign multinational companies in order to induce them to locate themselves in his country (as we have said, the so-called *tax rulings*, i.e., tax regulations). The Netherlands is famously home to multinationals such as FCA, now Stellantis, which controls Fiat, based in Italy and in other European countries.

The European Parliament has carried out inquiries into European tax havens, and it is hoped that action will be taken to eliminate the phenomenon or, at least, to reduce its extent. The need to do so stems from the fact that tax havens[17] not only increase the return on capital (after tax), but also reduce the tax revenues of other countries. In fact,

---

[17] An overview of the lack of cooperation between European national authorities, even in terms of pure exchange of information, is contained in European Parliament (2021).

they induce businesses and even individuals to locate and pay in them the lower tax rates on the income that is produced in the havens themselves and allow multinational companies to reduce the volume of revenues and increase that of costs – thus reducing the profits declared – in the other countries where they operate through the practice of transfer pricing (or, more explicitly, price manipulation of internal transfers to the multinational company).

In July 2021, however, the G20 decided that, starting 2023, a minimum rate of 15% will be applied to the profits of multinationals in various countries, which should significantly reduce transfer pricing and tax regulations.

3.6   CONCLUSIONS

The crises and stagnation have had multiple effects on efficiency and equity. In some cases, the negative effect can be masked by statistics, especially with reference to the effects on efficiency. In fact, with reference, for example, to dynamic efficiency, the effects of the crisis seem not to be negative, as the R&D/GDP ratio has not fallen. But this largely depends on the fact that the drop in the GDP makes the ratio rise, and that the absolute amount of R&D expenses does not fall, as they are rather inflexible. Most indicators of poverty and inequality, instead, show in general the negative effects of the crisis. Also in this case, the true effects are partially absorbed by the impact of the rise in welfare state expenditures, at the cost, possibly, of an aggravation of public finances, which can be unsustainable in the future.

In addition to the effect of the crises and stagnation, inequalities derive from other sources, such as tax evasion and avoidance. Then appropriate policies should be directed not only to fighting the crises and stagnation, but also to removing these distortions through international cooperation.

4 Globalisation

In this chapter we deal with globalisation. Multiple meanings have been attributed to this term. We can briefly define it as the growth on a global scale of the interrelationships between the various national economic and social systems or as an intensification of global interconnectedness (Held et al.,1999) through private economic institutions. Globalisation is different from (increased) competition on the markets for goods and factors of production, even if, in certain phases of the globalisation process, this is an entirely probable outcome, as will be seen later.[1] Indeed, globalisation may not be accompanied by increased competition: The greater interrelationships may also lead to the monopolisation of markets.

The first section of this chapter details the various forms of globalisation. Section 4.2 discusses the various factors that contribute to globalisation. Section 4.3 deals more precisely with those of a political and institutional nature that have been operating after World War II. The object of Section 4.4 is the consequences of globalisation in terms of efficiency, equity and economic policies. Section 4.5 deals with the imbalances of international payments that have arisen in the last decades. The reasons for international coordination are dealt with in Section 4.6, while the two following sections discuss the instability of the multipolar equilibrium that has arisen due to the growth of China and the possibility that a new stage of globalisation will arise. Section 4.9 concludes.

---

[1] The notes contained in Amoroso (1996) are still relevant to the nature of globalisation.

4.1   INTRODUCTION: THE FORMS AND MANIFESTATIONS OF GLOBALISATION

Globalisation is an intensification of global interconnectedness (Held et al., 1999) that manifests itself in the form of movements of people (and of communications and ideas), goods and capital. In addition, it includes interrelationships on environmental and health issues.

International movements of people are of short or long duration. The former are in particular for tourism or short stays for work or care. The latter correspond to international migration, which is to add to migration within a country. Obviously, these flows may involve people with more or less professional training and may have different basic motivations, of a political (often corresponding to persecutions, wars or the like) or health (epidemics) or economic nature (for the need to find work and livelihood). Both in the past and now all these reasons have been or are widely present.

The globalisation of the movement of goods corresponds to the worldwide extension of trade in goods and services. This can be the exchange of raw materials, semi-finished products, final products or their component parts, or exchanges of services, such as the rental or insurance of goods, financial intermediation services, information-technology (IT) services (for example, for processing data) and communication,[2] royalties and licenses for the exploitation of patents and similar, copyright and image rights.

International capital movements are of various types. In fact, there are movements of financial capital under the form of loans at different maturities, short, medium or long. Short-term capital movements often have a high speculative component, which can lead to high returns (or losses), connected in particular with changes in exchange rates. For example, those who expect the dollar to appreciate (see exchange rate) in the short term against the euro will buy

---

[2] The growth of communications and the circulation of information should be considered as an addition to (and within certain limits a substitute for) the physical movements of people, constituting their *virtual* movement.

short-term dollar-denominated loans or securities, to sell them once the dollar has appreciated (see exchange rate). Medium- and long-term capital movements that tend to exploit the higher yields of securities issued abroad are intended to be held for a certain time and are therefore called portfolio investments. They include purchases of shares to an extent that does not give rise to control of the companies that issue them. Instead, the capital movements that lead to the acquisition of controlling interests in pre-existing or newly founded foreign companies are foreign direct investments (FDI). The companies that usually own one or more subsidiaries in various foreign countries are called multinationals or multinational companies or transnational corporations (TNCs). These companies have played an increasing role in economic, financial, human and cultural flows. To cite only one indicator, TNCs are responsible for about 80% of world trade (Ietto-Gillies, 2019, ch. 22, Unctad, 2013).

The increase in international trade in goods, financial capital (short-term capital and portfolio investments) and labour configures a *superficial integration* of the various economies. The increase in FDI – and, consequently, in international production – implies instead a *deep integration*. The reason that leads to define FDI as a case of deep, and not superficial, integration is that they contribute to directly shaping the productive structure not only of the country of destination of the investments, but also of that of origin and of those where the subject who carries them out has some kind of operation, such as sub-contracting. Indeed, multinational companies often design the structure of production in the various centres in an integrated way – as we have said, with the breakdown of the production of individual goods into component parts (*global value chains*, for which see Box 3[3]) – and not as a replica of the operations carried out in one of them.

---

[3] In a synthetic way, these derive from the decomposition of the production process of a good into its different component parts, each of which is manufactured in a different country.

Table 13. *Indicators of globalisation in the nineteenth and twentieth
centuries, % annual changes, unless otherwise indicated*

World	1850–1913	1950–2007	1950–1973	1974–2007
Growth of population	0.8[a]	1.7	1.9	1.6
Growth of GDP (real)	2.1[a]	3.8	5.1	2.9
Growth of per capita GDP	1.3[a]	2.0	3.1	1.2
Growth of commerce (real)	3.8	6.2	8.2	5.0
Migration (net cumulative) to US, Canada, Australia, NZ				
Millions	17.9[a]	50.1	12.7	37.4
Annual rate of changes of the previous row	0.42[a]	0.90	0.55	1.17
Migration (net cumulative) to industrial countries (less Japan)	–	–	–	64.3
Year			1982	2006
World stock of FDI/world GDP (%)	–	–	5.2	25.3

Source: World Trade Organization, 2008
[a] 1870–1913

A more detailed picture of information with reference to the
period after 1850 and up to the beginning of the current century is
offered in Table 13.

The table is important not only for what it tells us, but also for
what it does not say. In fact, there is no information on the period

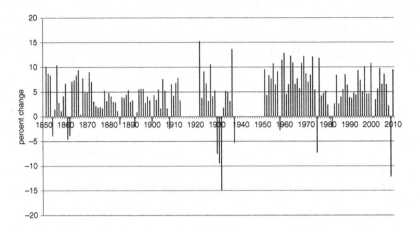

FIGURE 36 Annual changes in the volume of foreign trade (%), 1850–2010, worldwide
(*Source*: Irwin and O'Rourke, 2011)

between the two world wars. This period – and in particular the period of the 1930s – saw a setback for globalisation, due to the effects of the Great Crisis that began in 1929 and to the prevalence of nationalistic attitudes also in the economic field. In many countries this period represents the triumph of autarchy, that is, the containment of economic exchanges within the national sphere. This is implemented, in particular, with limitations on foreign investment, with the imposition of various obstacles to international trade and with the attempt to substitute new nationally produced goods for those previously imported, therefore establishing an autarkic regime. The setback of trade in the 1930s is clearly visible from Figure 36. The setbacks (also impressed by the Great War) of both trade and investment as well as migration can be seen in Figure 37.

The international integration that took place before the Great War could only have specific and limited effects, finding a broad foundation and discipline in the colonial relationship. On the other hand, the number of countries that are part of the global market today is considerably higher than that of pre-1914, although many are still in a marginal position in terms of both participation in the world market

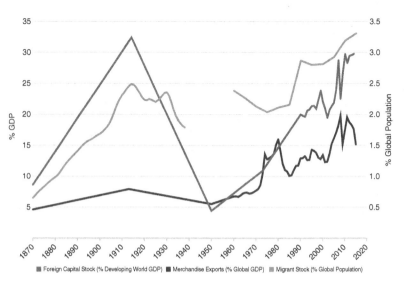

FIGURE 37 Trends in globalisation, 1870–2015, worldwide
(*Source*: Chandy and Seidel, 2016)
Note: The broken curve indicates the stock of foreign capital (expressed as a % of the GDP of developing countries). The curve that rises smoothly and shows cyclical variations since 1970 shows exports of goods as a % of world GDP. Finally, the curve that breaks between 1940 and 1950 indicates the stock of emigrants as a % of the world population.

and degree of development (for example, this is the case of most of the countries of sub-Saharan Africa).

Furthermore, international capital movements (both 'financial' ones and FDI) are now much more relevant than in the period before the World War I, from the point of view not only or not so much of the size, but also and above all of the consequences, in particular on the productive specialisation of the various countries, on competitiveness and on the effectiveness of national economic policies.

Therefore, if even the international economic integration that took place after the World War II represents the re-emergence of a trend that characterised the world economy more than a century ago, the resumption of that trend has taken place with at least partially new characteristics, which justify the use of the term 'second globalisation', the 'first globalization' reflecting the integration process prior to the

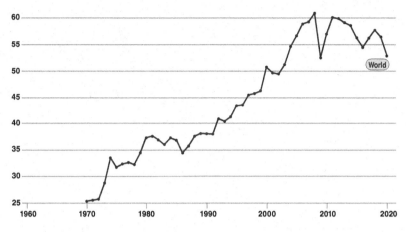

FIGURE 38 Exports/GDP (%), 1970–2020, world total
(*Source*: World Bank, https://data.worldbank.org/indicator/NE.EXP.GNFS.ZS)

Great War. If we take a look at the post–World War II evolution of one of the indicators of globalisation, that of the relationship between exports and GDP, we see the marked character assumed by the phenomenon. This ratio, in fact, increases by more than two times in the few decades that separate us from 1970 (see Figure 38). But also the movements of people and capital take place with slightly different characteristics from those of pre-1914 globalisation.

If we broaden our gaze at the beginning of the twentieth century, the trend in the relationship between exports and GDP appears as in Figure 39, in which the authors – in addition to identifying the main historical facts relevant to globalisation – distinguish a second post-war phase of globalisation from a third phase, while we speak here simply of a second globalisation, reserving the term 'third phase' for a possible near future (see Section 4.8).

4.2 THE FACTORS CONTRIBUTING TO GLOBALISATION: TECHNICAL FACTORS AND ECONOMIC POLICY CHOICES

Globalisation is, therefore, a reality for the markets for goods, services, financial capital and for the movements of 'productive' capital,

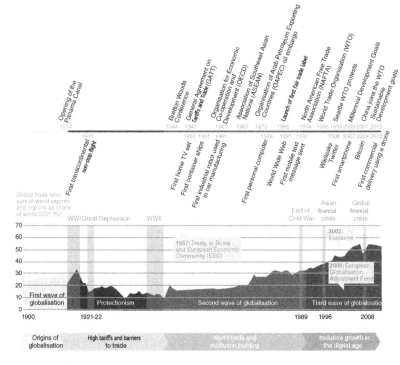

FIGURE 39 The phases of globalisation, 1900–2015
(*Source*: European Commission, 2017)

that is, for the capital directly invested in the production of goods. Technological progress and the choices of economic policymakers contributed to it. We deal with them in this order.

4.2.1 *Technical Progress*

The first factor of growth of globalisation is to be found in technical progress, which in recent decades has led to a significant reduction in the costs of transport and communication and has also made them faster (see Figure 40). The reduction in the costs in question has contributed to attenuating physical distances, making it easier for national economies – characterized by considerable diversity in the endowments of production factors, in distribution variables (in

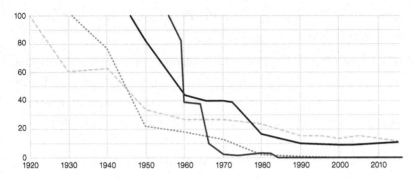

FIGURE 40 Trend over time of transport, communication and data processing costs, 1920–2015
(*Source*: Rodrigue, 2017)
Note: The line starting in 1920 indicates the cost of a three- minute phone call from New York to San Francisco; the one starting in 1931 indicates the cost of a three-minute telephone call from New York to London; the one starting in 1946 indicates the cost of a New York–London return flight ticket; the one starting in 1956 indicates the storage cost per computer of 1 Megabyte.

particular wages), in technologies and preferences – to come into contact with each other.

In particular, the reduction of transport and communication costs makes it possible to:

1 facilitate the specialisation of production and international trade in goods as well as the international movement of factors of production;
2 facilitate the operations of delocalisation of production carried out by multinationals; this effect is connected with the previous one;
3 increase transparency and information about the conditions of sale of an asset, promoting competition.

In addition to the cost reduction, it should be considered that technical progress has also facilitated international exchanges by allowing remote sales, the remote transmission of messages or digital information (in particular with the editing of writings, photographic or cinematic material and the like) and by allowing remote production and/or sales and/or transmission (auditing, document transfer, availability of media, etc.).

4.2.2 The Choices of Economic Policy and the Freedom of Trade

The second factor contributing to globalisation is attributable to the economic policy choices of the various countries and consists, first of all, in the gradual elimination of the obstacles to international trade previously put up by the various governments of the developed countries.

This elimination can be debated, as there are certainly arguments in favour of it, to be considered simultaneously with arguments that can instead justify protectionism. We illustrate them in order.

At the basis of liberalism there is the consideration of the advantage deriving from the international specialisation of production. This is based on the benefits of localising the various activities connected with geographical aspects and various economic variables (such as wages) and made possible by the free circulation of goods.

Among the justifications of protectionism an important place must be assigned to the argument of the defence of 'infant industries'. This is an argument in favour of protectionism initially theorised by the so-called mercantilist current of thought, according to which the wealth of a nation depended on the quantity of available precious metals, created through the surpluses of the balance of payments. From the mid-nineteenth century a further – and more founded – argument was then suggested, which argued that the temporary imposition of protective duties[4] is justified by the attempt to naturalize a foreign industry that in itself is perfectly suited to the conditions of the country in question. Often, in fact, the superiority of one country over another in a branch of production arises only from the fact that this started earlier, thus residing in the acquired skills and experience. The country that protects an infant industry could over time acquire that same ability and experience and thus put itself in a

---

[4] Duties are (indirect) taxes applied to imports from abroad, normally commensurate with the value of the imported goods. They have the purpose of increasing revenues and/or reducing imports and therefore protecting national production.

position to compete with advantage with the country that first started production or even to reach a position of superiority. This is, in particular, the case in which there are economies deriving from processes of learning through experience (*learning by doing*): Their particularity lies in the fact that the economies are not linked to the quantity produced in the unit of time considered, but to the cumulative production over time. This consideration was initially introduced with reference to the air transport industry. It was realized that the number of hours of work necessary for the production of a certain aircraft – which, for simplicity, were taken as a measure of the unit cost – was drastically reduced in the passage from the production of prototypes to mass production and then by the increase in the total quantity produced. This, therefore, took on the meaning of an indicator of accumulated experience.

A final noteworthy argument in favour of protectionism has the nature, so to speak, of legitimate defence against countries that adopt *dumping* policies, that is, sell abroad below cost.

4.3   THE INTERNATIONAL COOPERATIVE INSTITUTIONS BORN AFTER WORLD WAR II

The institutions that governed international and national economic policies after World War II and to a large extent still govern them now are predominantly global in character, although there are also highly developed regional institutions such as the European Union. We focus exclusively on those of a global nature.

4.3.1   *The International Organisations*

4.3.1.1   *Bretton Woods, the IMF and the World Bank*
The international institutions governing the economic aspects were initially conceived even before the end of the conflict. In fact, from the agreements signed in Bretton Woods (United States) in 1944 the International Bank for Reconstruction and Development (IBRD) – commonly known as the World Bank – and the International Monetary Fund (IMF) were born, as institutions aimed at fostering international

cooperation in the economic, social and political fields. Both institutions – together with the WTO (World Trade Organization), which was born more recently and which we will discuss later – constitute specialized institutions of the United Nations. In what follows we refer first to the IMF, then to the World Bank and finally to the WTO.

In order to foster international economic cooperation, the IMF referred to the convertibility of the dollar into gold in force before World War II, which was guaranteed for the central banks of the various countries. The operators of a country could buy foreign currencies (dollars in particular) through their central bank (which could obtain dollars from the United States through the sale of gold or, conversely, in countries with strong dollar reserves, could convert the dollars themselves into gold) to make payments to non-residents. In this way, multilateralism of trade was guaranteed – that is, there was the possibility of equalising the negative balances that a country might have vis-à-vis a second country with any positive balances vis-à-vis a third country, thus overcoming the tendency towards bilateralism (i.e., country-by-country balanced exchanges) that had characterized the period between the two wars and that resulted in a reduction in efficiency, as one country could be forced to accept more expensive sources of supply of some goods, simply in order to equalize trade with the supplier country.

The fixed exchange rate was maintained in the system, at least until 1971. Changes in parities (see exchange rate) were allowed, even if rules had to be observed aimed at avoiding the possibility of such frequent and widespread changes, which were only allowed to overcome serious and persistent imbalances in the balance of payments. To this end, the member countries of the Fund were also induced to adopt some kind of control of capital movements, because the Fund did not grant its assistance to finance imbalances in the balance of payments due to capital exports. Especially after the restoration of external convertibility by European countries in 1958, the rapid movement of capital internationally was made possible. In the 1960s, then, capital movements between the various countries intensified, and the IMF decided to finance them to defend the currencies that were most affected, despite the fact that this was not part of the Fund's statutory tasks.[5] There were also difficulties in imposing rebalancing policies both on persistently deficit countries and on countries with large surpluses and there was an overabundant creation of dollars, which member countries were forced to accept under the obligations inherent in maintaining fixed exchange rates. Apart from this, financing by the Fund assured the country the possibility of coping with the deficit problems of the balance of payments for the time necessary for the adoption and explication of the effectiveness of appropriate economic policies – such as reducing domestic demand and wages and prices – in order to eliminate deficits.

It should be underlined that the burden of adjusting balance-of-payments imbalances was established on both the deficit and the surplus countries. This was in order to avoid the deflationary outcomes that would have derived from a burden imposed only on the former, which could have implied the use of deflationary policies only as a means of rebalancing. It was Keynes, who feared the possibility of a repetition of depressions like that of the 1930s, who insisted on the need of a symmetrical adjustment, which, however, had very few manifestations, due also to the action of the technostructure of the IMF:[6] In fact, the adjustment of the deficit countries clearly prevailed, rather than that of the surplus countries, which rarely revalued their currency or adopted policies of a kind opposite to those of the deficit countries. However, in order to ensure the implementation of the necessary policies to overcome the balance of payments imbalances, the Fund exercised – and still does – a surveillance function on national economic policies.

In addition to the loans granted by the IMF to address temporary balance-of-payments imbalances, long-term financing was (and still

---

[5] Thus, the restrictions on capital movements enshrined in the Fund's Statute were circumvented by the techno-structure of this institution. In practice, almost all advanced countries – especially European ones – have introduced the freedom of all capital movements since the 1980s.

[6] In particular, this happened in 1961, when the IMF granted the UK access to the Fund's reserves to face speculative capital outflows.

is) available. This is granted for specific projects, usually under normal banking conditions, by the World Bank. In any case, the country for some time had to submit to various conditions, which included restrictive demand measures, liberalisation of markets and the like (see the policies provided by the Washington Consensus shortly).

The World Bank has the task of promoting public and private investment in LDCs and regions, in order to allow the improvement of living conditions in these areas. This task is carried out through the financing of the investments themselves and an appropriate technical assistance for their design and execution and, more generally, for the planning of public action.

The financed projects concern both infrastructures and directly productive activities. In more recent years, activities in the fields of education, social infrastructure, food production and environmental protection have been privileged. In the latter field, the Global Environmental Facility has been operating within the World Bank since 1990, tending to assist developing countries in financial terms in carrying out transnational environmental improvement projects.

The guidelines of the World Bank in favouring the fields of investments to be financed and in setting the conditions for financing have changed over time.

In the 1970s the causal link between poverty and growth initially sustained was overturned: to alleviate poverty, growth was promoted with laissez-faire policies aimed at increasing the role of the market. The countries that received the funds were induced to 'adjust' their economies, in particular by:

- removing constraints and 'distortions' present on the goods markets, the labour market and internal financial markets;
- privatising large shares of the public sector of the economy and drastically reducing public deficits;
- liberalising the movement of goods and capital;
- adopting freely floating exchange rates;
- avoiding large fiscal deficits with respect to gross domestic product.

Particular emphasis was placed on adapting the internal conditions of the markets to international ones, that is, on the integration of the economic system into the international sphere.

This set of measures goes by the name of the Washington Consensus. This term is intended to indicate an identity of positions between the United States Treasury, the World Bank and the IMF, all three institutions located in Washington.

Contrary to its original aims, which tended to place the burden of external rebalancing not only on deficit countries but also on those with surpluses in the foreign accounts, the Fund imposed the adoption of severe cuts in public deficits and other deflationary measures only to deficit countries. Thus, an asymmetry was configured in reality in the Fund's behaviour, which has had the effect of imparting a deflationary tendency to the world economy.

In the opinion of various economists, the policies suggested or imposed by the World Bank (and the IMF) on various countries – including Chile, Mexico, Turkey, Eastern European countries and South Korea – have often been costly beyond measure in terms not only of equity, but also of excessive and prolonged reduction in the rate of growth of income and employment. Certainly, privatisation and liberalisation, often carried out in the absence of real markets (as, in particular, in the case of Eastern European countries), and the abrupt exposure of economies that were often vulnerable to conditioning and shocks of international markets, particularly financial ones, have led to severe situations of crisis, accentuating the costs of adjustment. The policies of the World Bank and to some extent also those of the IMF tending to favour privatisation and liberalisation have recently been questioned by their own governing bodies.

4.3.1.2   *The GATT, the Negotiating Rounds and the WTO*

The institutions devised at the end of World War II at Bretton Woods to ensure international economic cooperation, in addition to the IMF and the World Bank, also included the International Trade Organisation. The first two have already been dealt with. The third organisation, which aimed at ensuring cooperation in the field of trade policies, should have been established as a UN agency, but was never created, due to the failure of the United States and other countries to adhere to the 1948 international agreement (Charter of Havana) from which it derived[7].

Instead of the International Trade Organisation, an international agreement operated, which should have been provisional, but lasted until 1 January 1995. This was the General Agreement on Tariffs and Trade (GATT), signed in Geneva in 1947.

The sectors of interest for GATT action gradually expanded and new problems were also introduced in the last negotiation session, the Uruguay Round.

The GATT encountered difficulties in pursuing its objectives, due to the need to obtain unanimous agreement of the countries concerned, in the event of a conflict produced, for example, by the introduction of obstacles to trade by a country. However, its action can be considered positive, as it allowed a gradual return to the principles of multilateralism, after the widespread use in the period between the two world wars of discriminatory trade practices, such as *trade balancing* for each country pair, rather than at the multilateral level.

The Uruguay Round was the last multilateral session of negotiations organized by the GATT. It started in 1986, mainly under pressure from the USA and Japan. It was, in particular, the United States that urged a new round of negotiations to face the negative consequences of the appreciation (see exchange rate) of the dollar and improve its competitive position on world markets (especially those of South East Asia, for industrial products and for services, and European ones for agricultural products).

On 1 January 1995, the World Trade Organization (WTO), created with the Marrakesh Agreement, at the conclusion of the

---

[7] The formal reason why no trade agreement was negotiated at Bretton Woods, deferring it to a later conference, was that Bretton Woods was attended by representatives of finance ministries, not of trade ministries.

Uruguay Round, began to operate. It constitutes 'the seat of multilateral trade negotiations and of confrontation between states regarding the implementation of the trade agreements reached' and therefore assumes the role of the organisation envisaged at Bretton Woods.

The WTO has replaced the GATT, but retains its principles and many rules. Therefore, it aims to ensure the application of the already existing rules of multilateral cooperation in the field of trade in goods and services, as well as to promote free trade in the sectors still protected (in particular, agriculture, textiles, services) and to remove trade barriers stemming from member country policies in related areas.

The WTO has a more pronounced institutional character than that of the GATT, presenting, unlike this, a stable structure and providing for the almost automatic resolution of conflicts between the various members in matters of trade, which is entrusted to one of its bodies (the Dispute Settlement Body). Among other things, its competences include conciliation or arbitration procedures and the possibility of imposing trade sanctions against the condemned country that does not comply with the decision itself.

In the first years of its activity, the WTO continued the action of the GATT, strengthening it in the new matters of interest to the GATT itself and discussed in the Uruguay Round. At the Fourth Ministerial Conference (held in Doha in November , under pressure from many developing countries, a Declaration was approved on: (1)Trade-Related Aspects of Intellectual Property Rights (TRIPS), which establishes standards for the protection of rights and tools for the application and execution of agreements through national legislation and for the resolution of disputes; in particular, the protection of patents in all areas of technology is envisaged for a period of twenty years; (2) public health, which introduces some flexibility in the application of intellectual property rights to this matter, such as the possibility of authorizing in certain circumstances member countries to produce patented medicines without the approval of the patent holder (*compulsory license*); the derogation has been used by various developed countries to overcome the monopoly of companies from other advanced countries, in some way helping developing countries in the fight against AIDS and other diseases. The Conference then launched a new series of negotiations (called the Doha Round) for the liberalisation of world trade, in particular in the field of agricultural products and textiles as well as services. Negotiations are also planned on direct investment policy, procurement and the defence of intellectual property. These negotiations remained essentially blocked until December 2013, when an agreement was reached on the 'Bali package', the result of the ninth Ministerial Conference. The agreement aims to: reform customs practices and formalities; reduce duties and agricultural subsidies as well as eliminate import quotas, in favour of developing countries.

4.3.1.3   Other International Organisations

Among the subsidiary bodies of the United Nations, we should mention: the FAO (Food and Agricultural Organisation), the United Nations Organisation for Food and Agriculture, with the aim of contributing to increasing levels of nutrition, increasing agricultural productivity, improving the living conditions of rural populations and contributing to economic growth; the ILO (International Labour Organisation), which promotes social justice and internationally recognized human rights, with particular reference to those relating to work; the UNCTAD (United Nations Conference on Trade and Development) and the UNDP (United Nations Development Program), in particular in relation to issues of interest to developing countries; the UNESCO (United Nations Educational, Scientific and Cultural Organization), to promote education, science and culture; the UNEP (United Nations Environment Program), to promote the improvement of the environment.

4.3.2   The Inspiring Principles and Practical Applications

As for the inspiring principles of the IMF, it can also be said that the World Bank expressed a 'temperate' liberalism, moderated by Keynesian thought.

Liberalism was undoubtedly the guiding principle of the solutions adopted at the time at the international level. It is found in the liberalisation of trade in goods and in the multilateral approach mentioned above. However, as we have said, it is a principle tempered by Keynesian thought, which grafted on to this liberal basis a series of public policy interventions, mainly tending to ensure the maintenance of full employment and the coordination of economic policies. This was behind the required symmetry in policies for rebalancing balance of payments, established with reference to both deficit and surplus countries: The deflationary policies adopted in the former to reduce their deficit would have been less severe if opposite, expansionary policies had been implemented in the surplus countries.

For the same reason, the liberalisation of capital movements was subject to limitations, as will be seen better below. In fact, it could have been translated into a further reason for asymmetry, difficult to cure. Moreover, such arguments could actually be referred *not only to international financial markets, but also – more generally – to all short-term financial markets.*

For them, first of all, Keynes's criticism was based on the fact that speculation acts as in a *beauty contest* in which not the one who indicates the most beautiful faces wins, but the one who can better understand the prevailing preferences of the participants in the competition thinking about their idea of beauty about the face itself. Obviously, as said, higher order arguments such as *'everyone thinks others think, etc.'* are likely. More recently, the enormous size of international capital movements (compared to the limited foreign exchange reserves available in the various countries and the funding available from multilateral organisations), the high speed of movements, the occurrence of 'herd' effects – which repeat and amplify the mechanisms in action in the beauty contest – increase the probability of self-fulfilling expectations, having little or no relationship with the trend of fundamentals.

As for the historical antecedents, it must be said that the comparison between the results in terms of growth of both GDP and international trade obtained in the period of the first globalisation and the effects of the protectionist policies adopted in the period between the two world wars proved to be valuable. While these policies had greatly limited the growth of international trade, the liberalisation before the Great War had been a harbinger of growth in trade.

For both the IMF and other international institutions (and in particular for those dealing with the barriers that can be used by the various countries), the need for bodies ensuring international coordination derives from the need to avoid a 'race to the bottom' by the various countries. In a world in which, on the one hand, the competitive pressure has increased as a result of the progress of transport and communications and, on the other, the action of international organisations has been successful to break down the classic tariff and non-tariff barriers, a country may tend to strengthen its competitive position by resorting to more permissive policies on the environment, anti-monopoly policy, policies towards foreign direct investment and multinational companies, social protection policies. For example, in order to attract more investment from abroad, a country reduces taxes for foreign companies, forcing others to do the same. More generally, similar things can happen for every possible subject of regulation. Such an attitude can be strengthened by the backward conditions in which the country may find itself. Permissive policies of the kind indicated allow a country to acquire advantages in the short term, even if at the expenses of possible disadvantages for itself and others in the longer term. It is evident that the permissive policies adopted by some countries may be followed by similar policies by the others, tending to restore the initial conditions. The race to the bottom between various national governments, while not solving the problems of the most backward countries, would risk downgrading public intervention to levels and methods that would prevent effective control of the markets or their 'replacement'. The need for international coordination is undoubted.

4.4   THE CONSEQUENCES OF GLOBALISATION

The consequences of globalisation are numerous, since it can be assimilated to a change in the rules of the game, which, therefore, implies a necessary change in the results for the various operators, at least if they continue to adopt the old strategies. The effects of globalisation are therefore very complex. As we know, every economic phenomenon can be evaluated in terms of efficiency and equity, both from a short and a long-term point of view.

4.4.1 The Effects in Terms of Efficiency

Many *short-term* results of globalisation depend on its consequences in terms of competitiveness. Others are related to the interdependence of the economy of the various countries. Let's deal with the two issues in order.

It can hardly be refuted that globalisation usually leads, at least in the short to medium term, to increased competition. The ensuing increase in efficiency in any case generates advantages in terms of stimulating innovation and growth of production for the various economic systems as a whole. In fact, with appropriate conditions, innovation implies the possibility of producing a greater quantity of goods with the resources available. Growth in production is not, however, a necessary result. Among the conditions to be met is the existence of policies that do not depress demand.

In a long-term context, which appears to be the most appropriate to the phenomenon in question, the consequences of globalisation in terms of efficiency are above all those of an increase in the growth rate of the world economy (see Figure 41). The higher growth seems particularly evident in the higher growth rates of the 2000s, even if these somewhat reduced since 2007. This result stems from the fact that globalisation manifests itself through increased specialisation (which parallels the increase in trade and FDI). Among other things, specialisation allows better exploitation of economies of scale and therefore translates into a reduction in costs and an increase in the growth capacity of the world economy.

However, it is precisely the exploitation of economies of scale that leads to the increase of large companies and economic concentration. Therefore, in the long run, the fiercest competition that arises in the

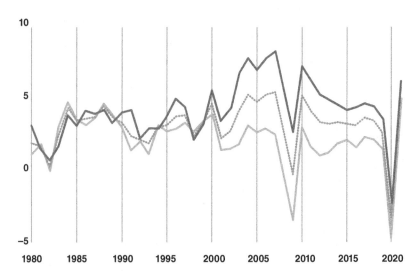

FIGURE 41 Annual GDP growth rates, 1980–2018, worldwide, emerging
and developed countries
(*Source*: International Monetary Fund database, www.imf.org/en/Data)
Note: The top curve refers to developing countries and emerging countries, the
bottom one to advanced countries and the intermediate one to the whole world.

initial stages of globalisation can give way to a phase of monopolisation
of the markets by some companies, not necessarily the most efficient
ones: the extension of markets is accompanied by the extension of the
size of companies, as a result of their internal or external growth, and
larger companies adopt forms of cartelisation through agreements
between them that hinder competition and protect their profits. In the
broader market (the global market) there may be an economic concentration or a degree of monopoly no less than those previously existing at
the national level. This can have a negative effect on growth.

   To similar conclusions about the different effects in the short
and long term of the international opening on the degree of competition come scholars who, correctly, identify in the fixed costs of adver-
tising and R&D – rather than in the price – the tools with which
competition takes place in many sectors. In these sectors, any expansion of the market tends to result in an increase in costs themselves,
rather than in a reduction in prices.

BOX 2 **Deindustrialisation**

A particular aspect of the growing specialisation concerns the deindustrialisation of developed countries, that is, the sharp fall in the share of manufacturing employment in the total that has occurred in these countries in the last four to five decades.

Some economists have attributed deindustrialisation to the globalisation of markets and production. As a matter of fact, there has been a growth of exports of manufactured goods by developing countries due to the autonomous growth of some of them and, at the same time, to a tendency on the part of all developed countries to

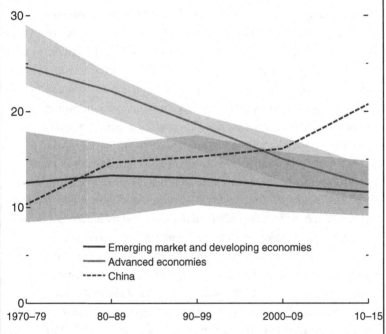

FIGURE B2 *Share of manufacturing employment in the total employment, 1970–2015, advanced economies, emerging economies, China*

(Source: International Monetary Fund, 2018)

Note: The continuous line that is always decreasing refers to advanced economies, whereas the similar line that initially rises and after 1980 declines refers to emerging markets and developing countries.

BOX 2 **(cont.)**

relocate part of their manufacturing production to developing countries, through investments in these countries or agreements of subcontracting and the like.

This growth of exports of manufactured goods from developing countries could then explain the (relative) loss of employment in the manufacturing sector of industrialized countries. However, deindustrialisation (measured in terms of income produced or employment in the sector of industry) could also be explained with reference to demand and technological factors. First of all, as the average income per inhabitant of a country increases, the share of services on the total GDP increases, because there is a tendency to demand more services than physical goods. On the technological level, it is well known that productivity growth in many services (the major exception being the so-called knowledge-based services, such as accountancy; publishing and editing; digital products; media) is lower than in industry, which implies that given increases in demand for those services require a higher increase in employment than increases in demand for industrial goods. The result is a trend towards a reduction in the share of industrial employment on the total.

The empirical investigations carried out so far have not made it possible to resolve the controversy that has arisen between those who attribute deindustrialisation to globalisation and those who provide an explanation based on the indicated demand and technological factors. The prevailing opinion considers deindustrialisation as a normal feature of growth in advanced countries, even if it can sometimes occur in ways that manifest difficulties in the process of adjustment or productive reconversion, due to the slowness of the process itself because of the obstacles it encounters (low growth rate, institutional rigidities, barriers to entry into the service sector, etc.). The difficulties of adjustment, which can result in increases in the unemployment rate, can also be exacerbated by increased competition from developing countries. However, this plays a marginal role in the explanation of deindustrialisation and could not be attributed the role of the main cause of the increase in unemployment experienced by many industrialized countries in the recent years.

4.4.2   The Effects in Terms of Equity

The distributive consequences of globalisation concern the distribution of its benefits and costs among the various countries, in addition to the distribution within each country among the various forms of income and within each category of income, such as between wages of skilled and unskilled workers. We deal with them, starting from the consequences within a country.

4.4.3   The Consequences within a Country

If – and for as long as – there is increased competition, the prices of productive goods and labour tend to level down, compressing the rents enjoyed by various operators (firms and workers) in the sectors with a monopoly position. If economies of scale are enjoyed and competition exists over the long term, consumers will benefit even more. Obviously, if all subjects are advantaged as consumers by paying lower prices to procure goods and services, some of them, particularly those whose monopolistic rents are shrinking, will be damaged accordingly. The opposite result occurs in the phase of an increasing degree of monopoly.

Therefore, globalisation benefits some people and disadvantages others. From another point of view, the most advantaged – or least disadvantaged – tend to be those who operate in the sectors least exposed to strong international competition. This concerns in particular many operators in the service sector (e.g., commercial distribution, professional services), as often foreign operators cannot provide services, unless these decide to establish an operational branch in the country concerned. Among the advantaged, or less disadvantaged, there are also highly skilled workers, for whom foreign competition is less pressing than for unskilled workers. It is therefore understandable that the countries, sectors and operators most exposed to competition may suffer more or benefit less.

As said, the category of operators that has been identified as most exposed to the disadvantages of globalisation is that of unskilled workers in industrialized countries, who suffer from direct competition (due to immigration from developing countries or the relocation, often implemented through FDI, of production with a high intensity of low-skilled labour) as well as indirect competition (through the import of goods with a high intensity of low-skilled labour). We have already mentioned the effects of greater direct competition. Indirect effects occur through the prices of goods and factors. The increased availability of goods with a high content of low-skilled labour, exported from developing countries, succeeds in lowering the relative price of these products and, as a result, the relative price of the factor of which those products are intensive, that is, low-qualified labour.

This may help explain the significant increase in the wage gaps between skilled and unskilled work observed in some developed countries, especially the United States and the United Kingdom. However, according to many economists, the main explanation for the widening of these wage differentials is to be attributed to technical progress, which has increased the demand for skilled labour, relative to that for unskilled labour.

Poverty in absolute terms (or *extreme poverty*) has tended to decrease. The number of people who do not enjoy an acceptable minimum standard of living has indeed decreased. Prior to 2016, this minimum standard was set at an income of $1.25 per day. On the basis of this standard, the United Nations calculated that in 2015 about 836 million people lived below this threshold, while there were 1.2 billion in 2010. According to the new minimum standard measure setting it at an income of $ 1.90 per day, the absolute poor in 2019 were between 703 and 729 million.[8] The vast majority of the poor (96%) reside in the South East Asia, sub-Saharan Africa, the West Indies and the Pacific.

[8] As we have seen in Chapter 3, data for absolute poverty derived from other sources are somewhat different. Furthermore, there are no data that allow meaningful time comparisons with the new standard line set at $1.90 per day.

A total of 422 million people live below the global poverty line in Africa. They represent about 60% of the world's poorest people. A large share of the poor are resident in India. The reduction of extreme poverty and hunger was the first of the Millennium Development Goals set by the United Nations in 2000, which aimed at halving poverty by 2015. As we have seen, this has not been fully achieved, despite a substantial reduction. By 2030 the United Nations has set forth the goal of poverty eradication.

4.4.4 The Consequences of Globalisation from the Point of View of the Distribution of Advantages among the Various Countries

On this point it can be said above all that it is true that some countries are emerging from their condition of backwardness also thanks to the liberalisation of trade and the creation of a world market. A reduction in globalisation would likely harm far more people than those favoured. Some authors, however, also emphasize the fact that the growth of trade and international movements of capital not only has not contributed to curbing the process of marginalisation that has characterized part of the least developed countries in recent decades, but, sometimes, could have strengthened it, for numerous reasons: the fall of the tariff barriers erected by some of them to protect their fragile internal productive structure; the fall of the tariff preferences adopted towards them by some industrialised countries; the increase in the prices of agricultural products exported by many developing countries, deriving from the cancellation of the subsidies previously granted to these products by many industrialised countries (as part of the provisions provided for in favour of the former colonies), which has reduced the demand for them in these countries. All these changes produced by a high degree of globalisation have reduced the demand for the goods of these countries. According to Rogoff (2020a) it is certainly necessary to rectify the course of globalisation, strengthening the social safety net in advanced countries and extending it to emerging economies, but the way forward is that of continuing the interpenetration between the different areas, that is, of the globalisation process.

More generally, there are differing views on inequalities. Inequalities between countries may have received positive or negative impulses from globalisation. For example, Piketty (2013) blames globalisation for the increase in income and wealth inequalities. MacEwan (1996) had argued in the same sense. Instead, Rogoff (2020a) refutes this statement, which appears to him correct only with reference to developed countries, but not to most of the LDCs. He points out that it is in fact true that trade competition has reduced the incomes of unskilled workers, as we have said, and that financial globalisation, on the one hand, has increased the profits of multinationals and, on the other, has caused damage to others, small- and medium-sized savers, especially during the financial crisis. However, outside the developed countries, where 86% of the world population lives, billions of people have been able to escape from poverty, thanks to globalisation.

4.4.5   The Consequences of Globalisation for Economic Policies

For the purposes of economic policies are important not only the effects of globalisation on efficiency and equity, as said in the previous sub-sections, but also other effects, linked precisely to increased interdependence. First of all, some effects are due to the increased international division of labour. If this involves breaking down the labour process for producing a good across countries (through 'global value chains', for which see Box 3), the traditional effects of exchange rate variations may not manifest themselves or may take place to an attenuated extent. The devaluation of a currency, which normally implies an increase in the competitiveness of that country, and therefore more exports and fewer imports for the country that devalues, may not have these effects or have them to a lesser extent. If, for example, to produce a car in country A, locally produced engines, transmissions produced in country B, and other components produced in countries C, D and so forth, are used, the devaluation of the currency of country A will not imply an appreciable increase or an increase at all in automobile exports. It could instead imply their invariance or decrease, if at the same time the currency of one or more other countries in which other component parts are produced are revalued.

BOX 3   **Global Value Chains**

It is important to understand the nature of these value chains. Until a few decades ago, the specialisation of production between the various countries passed through large sectors (for example, mainly agriculture in Country A, industry in Country B) or, within each of these, for example, wine production in Country A and wheat production in Country B, or car manufactures in one country and washing machine manufactures in another country. Subsequently, due to the reduction of transport and communication costs and other obstacles to international trade and with the progress of globalisation, a further form of specialisation of production has spread, in which the production of, for example, cars derives from assembly in country X of different parts produced in countries Y, Z and so forth. For example, Apple's iPhone is imported from China, where however no more than 5% of its value is produced, the remainder being entrusted to many hundreds of suppliers abroad (including the Italian STMicroelectronics).

The specialisation of the various countries in the production of the various parts depends on the economies of scale, the intensity, the type and the cost of labour required for the production of each part, as well as the transport costs to the country where the final assembly will take place. Thus, for example, the production of engines or braking systems will take place in large plants located in advanced countries, if it requires economies of scale and has low non-qualified labour intensity and a high qualified labour content. This occurs despite the higher hourly cost of labour, due precisely to the high qualification required. Conversely, wheel rim production may require less skilled

BOX 3 **(cont.)**

labour and may therefore be relocated to a country that does not have highly skilled work and where labour costs are low.

The possibility of delocalising industrial production with these very convenient methods leads to a reduction in the share of employment in many advanced countries, as well as in the agricultural sector, in the manufacturing industry (with a reduction in low-skilled work, which probably exceeds the increase in highly skilled workers), to the benefit of the service sector, for example, financial, marketing, thus contributing to deindustrialisation.

Figure B3 shows this shift in employment in EU countries over the period from 1995 to 2008.

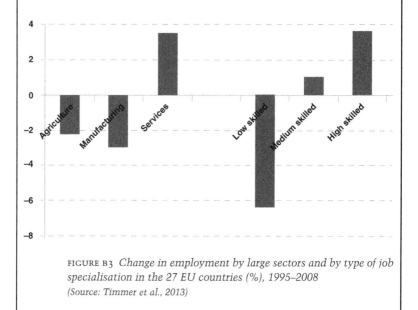

FIGURE B3 *Change in employment by large sectors and by type of job specialisation in the 27 EU countries (%), 1995–2008*
(Source: Timmer et al., 2013)

Still other effects are related to the increased exposure to external shocks. This exposure can be of two types: real (that is, concerning non-financial products and services, such as tourism or trade) or financial. Let's deal with them in that order.

Since national economies are more interdependent in terms of production, any reduction in economic activity in one of them, whatever the cause, is more easily transmitted to other economies, precisely through the international ties that unite them: thus, for example, a fall in global demand in Germany has negative repercussions that are all the more serious in Italy the greater the share of Italian production exported to Germany.

Globalisation can also entail some disadvantages in terms of reduced decision-making autonomy in a non-large country, whose economic conditions cannot significantly differ from those prevailing in other countries: Exposure to the world market limits the deviant behaviour of private and public operators of the country in question.

For example, in a context of globalisation, the consequences of a policy of income expansion by Italy would be extremely negative on its balance of payments, in a period in which income trends in other countries are stagnating, due to the substantial increase of the net Italian imports that would result. Similar – but in this case, it is a question of financial and not of real interdependence – is the effect of a policy of the European Central Bank tending to lower interest rates in Europe, when interest rates in the rest of the world remain unchanged. This would cause a deficit in the European balance of payments, due to the outflow of capital towards foreign countries that would result.

Furthermore, structural policies that impose limitations on the action of economic operators (in particular, businesses) in a country – for example, regulations for environmental or anti-monopoly or consumer protection purposes, heavier tax regimes – risk incentivising these operators to locate elsewhere, in countries where fewer restrictions are imposed, beyond what would happen for a process of 'normal' productive specialisation. On the other hand, a country is exposed to the negative consequences of the lax economic policies of other countries which tend to favour the localisation of consumers and businesses in those countries.

In general, in the short term each national government finds limits in implementing policy measures aimed at expanding demand or structural measures that increase the short-term costs of operators located in the country in question, even if capable of producing positive effects in the longer term.

Financial markets play the most important role in transmitting the effects of both asymmetric shocks that occur autonomously in a country and of a country's 'abnormal' policies, since, as is well known, they tend to accentuate and accelerate the reaction of operators and have an essential role in the formation of expectations. A case of considerable interest arose with reference to the financial crisis that broke out in 2007 in the USA and immediately transmitted to the United Kingdom and the rest of Europe by virtue of the credit and debt relationships between banks and other US and European financial institutions.

4.5 THE IMBALANCES OF INTERNATIONAL PAYMENTS IN RECENT DECADES

Despite the considerable tensions that emerged since the 1970s and the absence of a well-thought-out and substantial reform, the international payments system was able to operate without further traumatic disruptions after that of August 1971 – when, as said, the dollar's convertibility into gold was abandoned – but has come under severe strain at various stages. The growing international imbalances that have emerged in the last three to four decades are, on the one hand, specific to relations between certain groups of countries and, on the other, concern all countries. These imbalances are, first, indicative of the different trends in the development of the various countries. In addition, they constitute the premise for the financial crises of recent decades.

Current account imbalances – which we allude to – may or may not be entirely appropriate. The first is the case of emerging countries, which need to buy investment goods – and, not infrequently, raw materials – abroad to build their industrial apparatus and still do not have the possibility of producing enough or producing sufficiently competitive goods at all. Inappropriate current account imbalances are those resulting from distortions in the country's economic system and, potentially, in some cases from excessively risky situations.

The distortions can be caused by low wages and an excess of savings within the country, which lead to insufficient demand and, therefore, to low imports while tending to stimulate exports, with the consequence of a current account surplus. The policy followed is often a 'policy that harms the neighbour', that is, deriving from a *beggar-your-neighbour* strategy. Germany exemplifies this surplus situation. The reverse case of deficit can lead to risky situations. It is exemplified by the peripheral countries of the EU, in which a current account deficit was associated to a strong capital inflow, starting around the mid-1990s. This produced speculative bubbles and the growth of domestic demand, with a consequent further increase in imports and current account deficit. As said in Chapter 1, when the financial crisis broke out, capital inflows in peripheral countries ceased and their repatriation began, with the consequence of causing the illiquidity of the banks and the prolongation of the financial crisis.

The coexistence of similar strong imbalances of opposite nature is not new worldwide. In the interwar period, the United States and France enjoyed significant current account surpluses, while Germany and the United Kingdom suffered from high deficits and the inability to find a shared solution to the problem accentuated the Great Crisis of 1929.

Over the past four decades, current account imbalances have grown globally, particularly in the 1990s and later until the Great Recession. At the outbreak of this, the total of surpluses and deficits went from 2 to 2.5% of the total world GDP in the early 1980s to about 3.5% in 2000 and 5.5% in 2006, to then settle down again at 3.5% in 2017 (see Figure 42).

The imbalances of recent years have grown especially among the more advanced countries. In particular, the surplus of Germany and China has increased, as well as that of the Netherlands, Sweden, Korea and Singapore. Certainly in some cases, as already mentioned

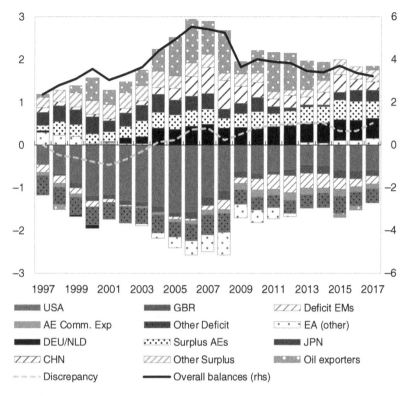

FIGURE 42 Current account balances in % of world GDP, 1997–2017
(*Source*: International Monetary Fund database)
Note: Negative balances are indicated at the bottom, positive balances are at the top.
Both are in % of world GDP and are measured on the left-hand scale. Negative
balances should be equal in absolute value to positive ones. Then the difference in
values depends on errors and omissions. The solid line at the top indicates on the
right-hand scale the sum of the absolute values of the negative and positive
balances, again as a % of world GDP.

for Germany, but also for China, the surplus derived from a policy
tending to damage the neighbour. Conversely, the USA, UK, Brazil,
Indonesia, South Africa and Turkey have increased their deficit.
While the case of the deficit of the first two countries derives from
policies different from, but to some extent harmful to, other

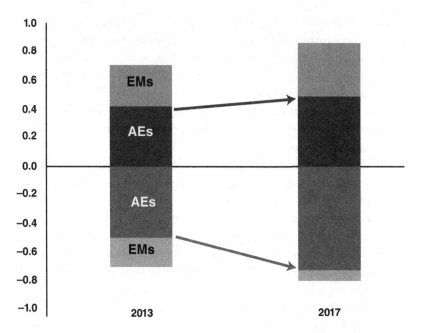

FIGURE 43 Excessive global imbalances as a % of world <u>GDP</u>, 2013–2017, emerging economies (EMs) and advanced countries (AEs)
(*Source*: International Monetary Fund database)

countries,[9] that of the emerging countries configures, as mentioned, the typical consequences of a development strategy (see Figure 43).

The recent financial and currency crises have provided a wealth of information useful for domestic and international economic policy. They indicate, first of all, the need to adopt certain rules of conduct for the various countries, which ensure:

1 the elimination of deficits by restrictive fiscal and monetary policies and the adoption of structural policies for the reform of labour and product markets, with particular regard to those that increase labour <u>productivity</u>;

___

[9] With particular reference to the United States, there is a broad consensus that imbalances are not sustainable. The problem is of this kind: Can American operators continue to borrow from abroad? Of course, this depends on the willingness of the rest of the world to acquire dollars while continuing to finance the United States. To solve this problem, President Trump had started a trade war, particularly with China, but also with Europe.

2 the elimination of surpluses through expansionary <u>macroeconomic policies</u> as well as structural policies aimed at reducing excessive savings;

3 international coordination leading to the adoption of more incisive regulatory and surveillance policies on the internal financial and credit market, with the more widespread application of the standards regarding the capital adequacy requirements of banks, prudential control and information requirements for the public formulated by the Basel Committee on Banking Supervision;[10]

4 the study of cases in which it is not convenient to resort to a <u>fixed exchange rate</u> regime: Although useful for gaining credibility in the initial stages of a return from periods of high inflation, <u>fixed exchange rates</u> are in the long run difficult to sustain for countries characterized by weakness in terms of the real and/or financial economy;

5 the reduction of the complete liberalisation of international capital movements, in particular by limiting short-term ones, which have a potential speculative character;

6 the reassessment of the role that international organisations, in particular the IMF, can play.

4.6 THE REASONS FOR INTERNATIONAL COORDINATION

International coordination can be defined as a situation in which each country manoeuvres the policy instruments at its disposal in order to achieve not only its own objectives, but also those of the rest of the world.

The need for coordination can arise when there is interdependence between the various economies. In this case, the uncoordinated action of the various countries usually leads to sub-optimal results.

Economic interdependence between the various economies finds expression in the globalisation of markets and production. In an era of globalisation, what happens in one country, as a result of the action of private or public operators, has repercussions in other

---

[10] On the new rules established by the Bank for International Settlements, which go by the name of Basel III, see Bank for International Settlements (2017). Changes to these rules were approved in 2017, which go by the name of Basel IV and will come into force in 2022.

countries that can be positive or negative. Therefore, these constitute forms of externalities (*spillover*) or external economies and diseconomies, that is, effects, positive or negative, caused by the action of a subject on other subjects, without the former, respectively, receiving or paying a compensation.

1 In some cases, the concepts of external economies and diseconomies and public goods are directly applicable, as occurs for pollution or for the dissemination of knowledge through some means of communication or for defence.

Global or international public goods have recently assumed particular importance in relation to the phenomenon of globalisation. These are public goods whose benefits extend beyond national borders, affecting citizens of different countries, at the limit the whole of humanity: peace, the environment, biodiversity, health, scientific and technical knowledge, financial stability, the existence of common technical standards, such as accounting rules, measurement systems and technical standards (think, in this case, of power sockets). The negative effects of the lack of (or scarce) production of global public goods are more difficult to remedy than in the case of national public goods, as the main operator that tends to avoid such negative effects in a national context, that is, the State, can act itself as a free rider – that is, as a 'freeloader' or parasite – with respect to global public goods. In other terms, one can say that there is no international public body that can remedy to the lack of global public goods.

For example, the positions taken by some countries to refuse accession to international treaties that provide for limitations on pollution factors can be explained in this key: Evading the adoption of the (certainly expensive) measures that make the necessary improvements possible, these countries benefit from the positive effects on the climate produced by the limitations adopted by others. After the ratification by Nicaragua and Syria, the United States had remained the only country in the world that was playing this role. Indeed, the Trump administration had decided not to ratify the Paris Climate Agreement. However, in February 2021 the new US president, Joe Biden, has declared that his country officially rejoins the Paris accord.

In the absence of a supranational authority, international coordination of the public actions of various countries can offer limited results. In this situation, the study and coordination of international institutions, such as the United Nations, is precious. This, however, clashes with the impossibility, on the one hand, of requiring states to respect the agreements reached at this level and, on the other, of directly providing global public goods by any international institution, due to financial issues.

2 In other cases the effects of external economies and diseconomies and public goods can be better represented in *macroeconomic terms*, and it is these that we will deal essentially with in this section. Let's see how they can originate.

Let's assume the existence, in a fixed exchange rate regime, of only two countries, France and Italy, which have roughly the same economic size, have only one policy instrument (public spending) and tend to increase income, while safeguarding their balance of payments equilibrium.

If a country, say France, expands its GDP a lot, it can cause a reduction or even a deficit in its balance of payments. And similarly for Italy. Therefore, the two countries are induced to slow down their expansionary policies. But if Italy adopts expansionary policies at the same time as France, it is likely that the balance of payments of neither of the two countries worsens. This shows that international coordination ensures better macroeconomic outcomes than independently adopted policies.

The transmission of the effects of one country's policy to the other can be negative rather than positive, as in the example presented now; that is, instead of having a positive 'external' or macroeconomic effect, there is a negative 'externality' (see external diseconomies) or a negative macroeconomic effect: the action of the country considered is then configured as a beggar-my-neighbour policy. Exchange rate depreciations and protectionist policies are examples of this in some cases. In some other cases, however – as noted above – devaluation or protectionism, used in conjunction with other policy measures, may not translate into beggar-my-neighbour policies. Financial stability is an example of international public good that can be conceived in macroeconomic terms.

3. A further reason in favour of coordinating the policies of the various countries lies precisely in avoiding competition between governments such as to reduce the degree of achievement of common objectives, with the possibility of a race to the bottom, implying losses for all countries. This occurs in the most disparate fields, ranging from environmental policies to anti-monopoly policies, from policies of labour protection to fiscal ones. In the tax field, countries that practice 'soft' policies are configured as real tax havens. Some of them are part of the European Union itself (e.g., Luxembourg, Ireland, the Netherlands), as already said.

Generally speaking, international coordination, as will be specified later, normally allows better results to be achieved *for all countries*, in terms of a given objective. It is not certain, however, that *every country* receives an advantage from the coordination and, even if it does, that it finds the coordination itself convenient, as the defection from, or *non-participation* in, the agreement could lead to a better result, in absence of 'retaliation' from other countries.

In the light of these considerations, it can be concluded that international coordination tends to be favoured by the presence of both an effective system of sanctions for the countries that decide to act as free riders and an adequate compensation mechanism in terms of other objectives for the countries that, despite being damaged with respect to a given objective, adhere to multilateral agreements, respecting them.

Obviously, cooperation in these matters implies that the problem of safeguarding starting positions is addressed, in particular, for countries that are in a disadvantaged position and which could even see this position worsened. To meet these requirements, exceptions, delays, safeguard clauses, and the like, are often introduced in international agreements for the weaker countries.

The real problem, however, is that these favourable conditions are often insufficient to allow the LDCs to overcome their condition. Other measures are indeed essential to attack the underlying reasons for underdevelopment and which often go beyond the capabilities of individual developing countries.

As for the modalities, coordination can take place through ad hoc consultations (for example, a negotiation only on the level of duties and not on other aspects of international relations) or through the adoption of rules that give rise to institutionalized cooperation (e.g., with an agreement aimed at keeping fixed exchange rates, also with the contribution of specially created bodies).

This second mode of cooperation normally establishes rules or regimes that make it possible to at least partially avoid the inefficiencies deriving from unilateral solutions, thus providing a certain and lasting form of cooperation. The gold standard in force until 1914 for all countries (except for the USA, for which the convertibility of the national currency into gold lasted until August 1971), the Bretton Woods system, the European Monetary System (EMS), the rules established in Maastricht for participation in the third phase of the EMU project are examples of such type of coordination. Unlike the last case, in the first cases precise policy prescriptions were not provided, but a common objective was agreed upon – exchange rate stability – from which, as mentioned, beneficial consequences were expected on the functioning of the various economic systems (for example, in order to avoid policies of the kind that harm the neighbour, i.e. beggar-my-neighbour) and the achievement of which required quite stringent policies.

There are reasons that would lead to preference for institutionalised cooperation over an ad hoc cooperation: For example, the latter is more easily exposed to pressure from various power groups. In addition, the need to repeat ad hoc negotiations before any concerted action makes it inefficient, all the more so the greater the problems of political instability, with the connected turnover of negotiators.

On the other hand, the awareness of the existence of rules that are difficult to renegotiate in institutionalized cooperation (and, therefore, in the abstract to be respected for an indefinite or long time) can accentuate the difficulty of this type of cooperation. Furthermore, ad hoc (and therefore discretionary) interventions may be necessary whenever countries are faced with events not foreseen by the rules of institutional-ized cooperation or, in any case, with facts that would require a behav-iour of the policy makers different from that envisaged by the rules; to this end, however, institutionalized cooperation often provides excep-tions – or safeguard clauses – with respect to the usual rules. Finally, the rules of institutionalized cooperation require periodic revisions that cannot be avoided simply in order to avoid slow and difficult negoti-ations: In the absence of such revisions, the discretion and flexibility required by the changing historical context would be entrusted to the action of the technocrats of the institutions, with distorting effects. As said, an example of such distortions concerns the decision to allow access to the resources of the International Monetary Fund for deficits arising from exports of capital: As said, access was first denied and then granted by the bodies of the Fund, without the statute having been changed in the meantime, with significant practical consequences.

In general, the effectiveness of international cooperation is entrusted to the presence of rules and public bodies capable of covering in geographical terms the global space in which private institutions (markets, firms) now operate. In other words, it is a question of matching global private institutions with a world government – or at least a gov-ernment at a 'regional' (supranational) level, such as the European Union – capable of dealing with the failures of the former in terms of efficiency and equity, precisely at a global or regional level. The problems of political representation, especially at a global level, are enormous, but this seems to be the way to go. Otherwise, the well-known issues that arise at the national level will reproduce at a new and wider level.

4.7 RECENT CHANGES OF COURSE AND THE DANGERS FOR THE WORLD ECONOMIC EQUILIBRIUM

4.7.1 The Growth of China and the Instability of the Multipolar Equilibrium

China's vigorous growth in recent decades at rates of the order of magnitude of 10% and more – which in recent years has lost its pace only in relative terms (i.e., only when compared to that experienced previously by the same country), while remaining much higher than that of other countries – has led a new player to excel in terms of overall income, as well as of foreign exchange reserves, with ambitious plans for further progress. In this country, the number of the absolute poor (i.e., those earning less than $1.90 per day at purchasing power parity in 2011) was reduced from 835 million in 1981 to 6 million in 2019, representing a percentage of the population which fell at the same time from 84% to less than 1% (.51%). However, higher incomes have also grown and therefore inequalities have not decreased, but increased. In some cases, even the wages paid are higher in China than in some European countries, those of Eastern Europe.

In terms of technology, China is now a leader in many sectors. In many cases, the primacy has been achieved thanks to a skilful imitation of the technologies adopted in cutting-edge countries, as well as the imposition of special rules for foreign direct investments in the country. For example, full ownership of the share capital by foreign investors is prohibited in some sectors, and access to the Chinese market was – and perhaps still is, despite the ban resulting from the country's entry into the WTO – traded for transfer of technology. In addition, China has encouraged multinational companies to set up R&D centres in China, which implies the emergence of positive externalities for the country, in particular through the training of highly qualified personnel.

The increased importance of the Chinese economy and the recent financial crisis have accentuated the requests for reform in the architecture of the International Monetary Fund. Following these requests, the G20 decided, in November 2010, to increase the Fund's shares allocated to emerging countries. Since November 2015, the yuan, together with the US dollar, the euro, the yen and the British pound, has been one of the reserve currencies that make up the Special Drawing Rights, with a weight of 10%. The decision of the Fund will have no other practical effect than that of admitting the renminbi, that is, the yuan, in the determination of the value of a notional currency such as the Special Drawing Rights (whose value is given by that of the basket of currencies that compose it), which was created for loans from the Fund to governments and to make payments or intervene in the foreign exchange market by selling its holdings against convertible currencies. Countries that accept these rights, usually those in surplus position, increase their availability of reserves and will be able to use the rights themselves to pay off any future deficit positions, benefitting, however, from the interest.

The decision to admit the renminbi in the determination of the value of these rights constitutes an important signal at the political level, as it puts an end to the *'exorbitant privilege'* of the dollar, denounced at the time by French President Charles De Gaulle. The Chinese think similarly to De Gaulle: Some countries, on the path of losing economic primacy, cling to the privilege of their currency. At the economic level, this recognition of the importance of the Chinese currency also implies that China will try to keep the value of the yuan stable, avoiding devaluations of its currency in order to compensate for the slowdown in growth.

Apart from this, in the longer run there may be the fear that the multipolar equilibrium situation is unstable, as similar situations have been in the past, for example when the pound and the dollar were at the centre of the system. Unlike in the past, due to cultural and political factors, the conditions that allowed a painless or almost painless transition from multipolar equilibrium to an equilibrium in which a single currency is dominant may not exist today.

Favourable conditions include progress in China's protection of intellectual property rights. There have in fact been many patent registrations in recent years, with China now holding 20% of international patents, immediately following the United States, which owns 23%. But what is most impressive is that China's growth rate of registrations has been in double digits for several years. In 2019 China filed more patent applications than the USA.

On the other hand, it must be acknowledged that China is still the holder of silent violations of international agreements that have resulted in European appeals to the WTO and US retaliation, actually followed by a second round of Chinese counter-retaliation, first, and American, after. In fact, for technology transfers from the EU, China imposes particular rules on industrial property rights and other intellectual property rights, which are different from those it applies to technology transfers between Chinese companies. This takes place by discriminating against holders of foreign intellectual property rights as well as limiting the ability of foreign parties to protect some intellectual property rights in China, thus violating the WTO obligations. Officially in retaliation for Chinese violations of international agreements – but in reality as part of a neo-protectionist policy – in 2018 the United States introduced tariffs of 25% on 818 Chinese industrial and technological products, ranging from cars to electronic products, medical equipment and aircraft parts, worth $34 billion in imports. Beijing's response was to trigger similar sanctions on 545 US products, ranging from agricultural goods to vehicles. In these behaviours, therefore, we can almost see the outbreak of a real trade war. Partly in defence of China is the consideration of the fact that a country that is just emerging from a state of backwardness has more justifications than a country at the forefront of the world economy in adopting measures to restrict the action of foreign companies. However, the acceptance by the Chinese of international rules that provide for such cases implies compliance with the rules themselves.

The Trump administration also followed a policy that seriously threatened compliance with global and regional international agreements and undermined the existing structure and equilibrium. In September 2020, the WTO ruled that the United States had violated international rules by having imposed high additional tariffs on goods for more than $380 billion against China since March 2018.

In terms of threats to the current equilibrium in international relations, to the actions of the United States towards China mentioned above must be added the threat (thankfully returned) of the

USA to introduce duties against Europe and the denunciation of the regional agreements entered into by the United States that led to the renegotiation of the duties initially established within the NAFTA (North American Free Trade Agreement), with Canada and Mexico. This Agreement has been substituted since April 2020 by the USMCA Agreement between the same countries.

Towards the WTO, the Trump administration tried to justify what was actually a violation of the Organisation's rules – that is, the use of discriminatory tariffs on steel and aluminum – with the argument that they are goods of importance for national security, even if that could hit some 'friendly' countries such as Canada and Japan and would undermine the global trading system. In reality, Trump's decision in some measure can not only have negative effects in these two countries, but also backfire on the United States, as products subject to tariffs enter different value chains, from which also goods produced in the United States originate, which leads to an increase in the prices of these goods.

Another action by which the Trump administration had weakened the WTO is that which attempted to block the activity of this organisation's Dispute Settlement Body by failing to renew its members.

4.7.2   Problems of Global Equilibrium in the Absence of a Global Government: Rodrik's Trilemma

A Turkish economist, Dani Rodrik, highlighted the mutual incompatibility between deep international integration, national sovereignty and democracy. This is the trilemma taking its name from the economist, which is illustrated in Figure 44.

According to this trilemma, two of these conditions can be satisfied at the same time, but not the third. For example, globalisation and the nation state imply giving up democracy, because national sovereignty would interfere with the consequences of international integration, which requires following the guidelines of the markets.

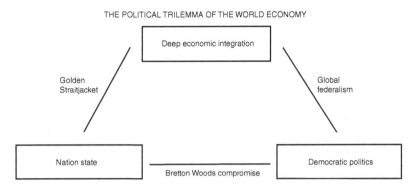

FIGURE 44 The political trilemma of the world economy
(*Source*: Rodrik, 2011)

The acceptance of the democracy–nation state binomial prevents full international economic integration, because that binomial would lead to results not pleasing to the markets, due to the fact that the state would direct the economy in a different direction from markets. So it was in the world of Bretton Woods, where capital movements were limited, to leave room for freedom for nation states.

Finally, international integration and democracy at the international level would imply the non-existence of the nation state, because it would be necessary to accept the guidelines of the international bodies.

International integration, democracy at the international level and the nation state are anyway the three poles between which the world economy and its political structure oscillate. The various countries have chosen paths that are halfway between acceptance and rejection of the various poles. Thus, for example, while remaining at the level of the nation state and accepting democracy, some of them have opened up to forms of international integration as deep as that of the EMU or less deep, as for the G20. Others, on the other hand, refused such rather intense forms of integration, remaining only within the ambit of less active organisations and often putting themselves at odds with the decisions of other member countries, such as Hungary, which, although part of the EU does not comply with the Dublin Regulation.

4.7.3 The Current Position and Perspectives of International Relations

As mentioned, the institutions born at the end of World War II were inspired to a well-tempered liberalism, but this principle was later disregarded in practice, in particular by the *IMF*, leaving space instead for an exasperated liberalism, which found its maximum expression in the Washington Consensus.

Bretton Woods institutions, as they have evolved, have led to positive results in terms of international integration and income growth rates, but are also responsible for financial and currency crises, some of which are closely related to the demands made on countries in need of loans to liberalise capital movements. The World Bank is also responsible for the policy followed for a certain period of time to encourage the growth of the recipient country, on the assumption that this would lead to an automatic improvement in the living conditions of the poorest classes of the population. Numerous criticisms have been addressed to this extreme liberalism, many of which have been accepted by international organisations.

If until a few years ago the history of post-war international economic relations had offered a period – indeed limited – of temperate liberalism followed by a longer period of almost complete liberalisation, in the most recent years we are witnessing a new change of direction, with at least two countries, China and the United States, engaged in more or less open trade wars, in various ways (Acocella, 2019).[11]

The growth of China threatens the current equilibrium situation based largely on US hegemony, and a multipolar equilibrium is looming, in which this country is joined by China. The bipolarity of the balance and the trade struggle between China and the United States, which is a manifestation of it, as said, can generate instability and dangers for the world economic balance.

---

[11] On the recent relations between China and the United States see also Bordo and Levy (2019), in addition to Sub-section 4.7.1.

Thus, the solution of tempered liberalism at an international level desired by many to avoid the instability highlighted by Rodrik's trilemma – which already today shows strong cracks, with the government of almost all international bodies firmly in the hands of the USA and, in part, of Europe – may receive further blows in the future and prove unworkable. Further obstacles may derive from the spread of hesitations towards the transfer of power at supra-national levels and of broad waves of populism[12] in many advanced countries, especially in Europe, and from the widespread manifestations of episodes of protectionism, primarily by the United States and China.

The future, therefore, does not look rosy at all and the probability of a return to the situations of commercial war that were typical of the interwar period is significant.

From the well-tempered liberalism expressed by the international bodies founded at the end of World War II, we have moved on to a pushed liberalism and perhaps the current spread of protectionism could be the product, certainly excessive, of that extreme liberalism. The populist waves that afflict Europe, heralds of similar closures, can find a similar foundation.

It would be desirable, but at the present time difficult to predict, that the world stops on the path that leads to a trade war and closure of borders and reconstructs the climate that led to temperate liberalism.[13]

Instead, a third phase of globalisation may emerge, made possible by teleworking and telerobotics, which would make it possible to operate remotely and provide various types of work, that is, hybrid work, both intellectual and manual, through 'virtual' emigration. Their impact on various countries, in particular on emerging economies, including through the possible boost to global value chains, is uncertain (see World Trade Organization, 2019).

---

[12] On the roots of populism see Rodrik (2019).

[13] Very wise indications on the ways in which globalisation (and its benefits) can be saved from the breakdowns produced by its to the bitter end supporters can be found in Rodrik (2007).

4.8 TOWARDS A III OR IV STAGE OF GLOBALISATION?

Post-war globalisation presents two faces. On the one hand, most European countries and the United States have controlled free flows of people, by imposing regulations and bans on entry of foreign immigrants. These movements have then been much smaller than those of the decades around the beginning of the twentieth century. As to the attitudes of nation states and international institutions with respect to other aspects of globalisation (i.e., movements of goods and capital), a *laissez-faire* attitude has prevailed, except in the very recent years with reference to the USA and China. The various countries have assumed a different attitude towards other aspects of global problems, that is, environment and climate change issues. Only recently, with the Paris Agreement of 2015, have they agreed on the need to reduce pollution and have imposed a limited reduction of it.

Considering these attitudes on the whole, we can say that only some aspects of globalisation have been governed. Therefore, this is a *negative* aspect of the current situation that makes globalisation to become one of the '*terrible four*' we have alluded to before, whereas it could produce *positive* effects in case it were controlled.

Globalisation has been the object of criticism from those who want fair trade more than free trade, such as Joseph Stiglitz and the ordinary people that have found expression in the no global movement, contrary to free trade and the organisations that regulate it, which would represent a threat to social rights and respect for the environment.

Moreover, the de-globalisation tendencies that had already arisen before the pandemic have strengthened, being certainly accelerated by it (see also Razin, 2021). A blow to globalisation had already resulted from the recognition of the damages produced by excessive international movements of capital, but the various countries had not imposed restrictions on them. On the other hand, the flows of goods – particularly those relating to merchandises – stagnated after 2008, while trade in services increased (see Figure 45) since the beginning

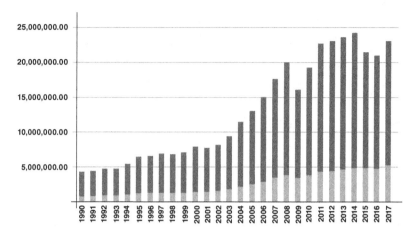

FIGURE 45. World exports of goods and services, 1990–2017, in millions of dollars

(*Source*: Janiri and Sala, 2019)

Note: The upper part of rectangles indicates exports of merchandises; the lower part is for exports of services.

of the financial crisis. Now, the pandemic has further undermined one of the three pillars of globalisation, namely international production, hitting the connective tissue constituted by the global value chains, or the production chains of goods that cross borders and countries, from one end of the world to the other, of which has been said in Box 3.

The international fragmentation of production between various countries expressed by global value chains can have different effects in a situation of vast pandemic. On the one hand, it has been shown that firms with greater market power and larger global value chains have better resisted the impact of the pandemic (Hyun et al., 2020). On the other hand, chains can cause problems to other firms during a pandemic. In fact, the suspension of international traffic that follows the limitations introduced by the various countries (which are certainly more binding than those that can be decided in a single country) can impair the production of the final good, causing a negative supply shock. Consider that in the period January–February 2020 alone, China reduced its exports of data processing tools by more than 30%

and imports of the same products by more than 45% (Seric et al., 2020). Even if in the long term and in the absence of the problems created by the epidemic, the re-nationalisation of chains is less advantageous from an economic point of view, due to the loss of the long-term advantages deriving from relations with foreign suppliers (see Giovannetti et al., 2020), in the presence of the pandemic it would certainly reduce the drop in production. This is why many – such as, for example, the French Minister of Economy and Finance, Bruno Le Maire – are asking the European authorities to ensure sovereign and independent supplies (see Le Maire, 2020).

Moreover, Ricci (2020) notes that 'the epidemic has vividly shown large companies that this network is also beyond their control. They realized that, in many cases, they have no idea about who supplies that particular component, where the hell it is and whether, at this point, it will continue to supply material or not'. And in the future, catastrophes other than an epidemic, such as a tsunami (or even trade wars) can have similar effects.

Both American and Chinese firms are adapting to simplify these chains, but it is the European ones that have resorted to them to a greater extent, covering about 70% of the value of the products that are exported and therefore require now more profound adjustments.

All this will lead to a further slowdown in the international integration process, in addition to that which has already occurred in terms of global flows of capital and goods, and this slowdown has been defined by the English weekly *The Economist* with the term *'slowbalisation'* ('slowing of globalisation' or *'de-globalisation'*)[14].

In any case, the goal should be pursued of a multilateral attitude tending to implement sustainable development goals (Unctad, 2020). To this end, efforts should be made to promote growth through appropriate investments, not only in environmental matters, but also in the implementation of the latest technologies (industry 4.0 – i.e., the

---

[14] On slowbalisation – in addition to *The Economist* (2019) – see the recent article by Irwin (2020) and the empirical and analytical review by Kandila et al. (2020).

fourth industrial revolution enlarging automation of traditional manufacturing and industrial practices – artificial intelligence, machine learning, etc.), in order to facilitate sustainable development. In addition, the current globalisation should be made more inclusive as to the countries involved and a countervailing power with respect to that of specific countries and the multinational companies by various operators should be developed: national and – even more – international public institutions and some private ones, such as those of workers (Ietto Gillies, 2020). In other terms, liberalisation should be balanced with a proper regulation.

4.9 CONCLUSIONS

Apart from some parentheses, globalisation has proceeded over time, due to various factors, of a technical nature and of an economic policy kind. Among the latter, a cooperative international political-institutional environment plays a decisive role, which can help explain the sustained pace of globalisation after World War II. The consequences of globalisation on efficiency can be different in the short run, when they are generally positive, and in the long run, when they can be negative if globalisation leads to an increased degree of monopoly. As to equity, the effects in single countries are beneficial for some people and negative for others. A similar impact can derive from globalisation on different countries. However, it should be recalled that ungoverned globalisation can lead to economic imbalances, which raises the need for some kind of international coordination. In the recent decades this has proceeded with beneficial effects, but in the last few years notable oppositions have grown, in particular by China and the United States, leading to tariff wars and the like.

5 Pulling the Strings of Our Arguments

Mutual Relations between the Terrible Four

Many issues arise, if one looks at our findings in the previous chapters of the book. They first regard the relationships between each of the phenomena examined there in terms of the various channels tying these phenomena and, in some cases, the direction of causality between them – for example, the links between crisis and distribution. In fact, crises can affect distribution, while inequality has an effect on crises. There are also links between crises and globalisation. The former can negatively affect the latter, insofar as they cut global value chains, leading to the re-nationalisation of many activities. Globalisation, in turn, can affect distribution in single countries and at the world level. More specifically, globalisation can have negative effects on distribution. Stagnation can have effects similar to crises. Various links are then established between the various issues. This means that the indicated issues must be treated in an integrated way. In any case, the problem arises whether there are enough instruments to solve them.

In the following section we deal with the nature of the interrelationships between the various issues. Section 5.2 investigates the problem of the number of instruments to face the various targets.

5.1 THE INTERRELATIONSHIPS BETWEEN THE VARIOUS ISSUES

Let us deal first with the effects of crises on distribution, beginning with the effects on single countries.

An empirical investigation referred to twenty-four countries shows that banking crises have increased income inequality in the pre–World War I and post–World War II periods, even if not in the Interwar period. Currency crises increased top incomes up to World War II, but decreased them after this war in the years 1950–2012. Banking crises have influenced distribution through the availability of credit to production and the cost of credit to households, whereas currency crises have had an influence on the terms of trade (Baeten, 2016) and, thus, on the distribution of income between countries. According to Bodea et al. (2019), the effects of crises on distribution operate in the long-run.

The crisis – and globalisation[1] – in most cases have exacerbated the problems of poverty and inequality between countries, the effect much depending on the way we measure inequality. Figure 46 shows the trend of worldwide inequality – measured in terms of Gini coefficients – according to different interpretations (inequality between the average incomes of the various countries weighted and unweighted for the population of each country or inequality between the incomes of the various people in the world measured in the same way it is done among people within a country).

The emergence of some countries in the foreground on the economic scene, first of all China and India, especially in the current millennium, has produced a significant increase in their average income, although in many cases the differences between the less well-off and the better off have increased inside them. Therefore, worldwide inequality, after having increased continuously since 1950, has shrunk in this century, if it is measured in terms of average incomes in the various countries, without weighing the countries themselves with their population (this corresponds to the 'Concept 1' of Figure 46). The same result is not obtained if we consider the differences between countries by weighing the countries themselves with their population (what corresponds to 'Concept 2' in the figure). In fact, if measured in this way, inequality has continuously reduced.

---

[1] To be true, it is difficult – but not impossible – to disentangle the effects of these two factors.

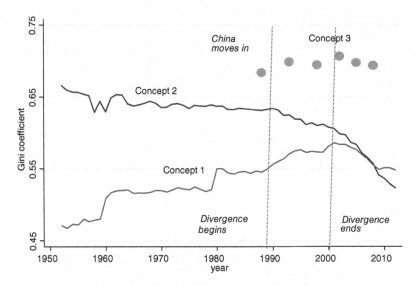

FIGURE 46 International and global inequality, 1950–2010
(*Source*: Milanovic, 2013)
Note 1: An increase in the Gini coefficient indicates an increase in inequality and vice versa for the case of a reduction.
Note 2: Concept 1 refers to inequality between average incomes of various countries not weighted by the population of each. Concept 2 refers to the inequality between average incomes of various countries weighted by the population of each. Concept 3 measures inequality between all individuals on the planet in a way similar to that with which inequality is measured within a country, referring to the income of every person (or family) in the world.

As was to be expected, the worldwide inequality considering the income of each inhabitant regardless of the country of origin is higher and has a fluctuating trend over the last twenty to thirty years up to 2010 ('Concept 3').

In the last ten years, inequality has continued to decrease according to the first two concepts, but more recently, with respect to the effects of the pandemic on inequality, international income inequality has decreased with Concept 1, while increasing if weighted by population (Deaton, 2021).

If, instead of underlining in synthetic terms the trend over time of inequalities, we try to examine the variation of the inequalities

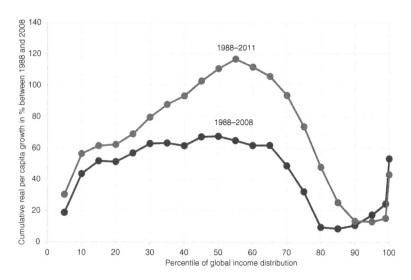

FIGURE 47 Percentage gain of real income at different points of the
distribution, worldwide
(*Source*: Milanovic, 2016)

themselves for the various subjects over time and, in particular, as a
result of the economic crisis, we can see how what has been called
the 'elephant' has changed over time. Figure 47 shows the profile of
the elephant before the financial crisis: in the twenty years following
1988, the income earners who had benefitted most were those
included in the percentiles from 30% to 65% (in short, the middle
classes), with gains equal to or greater than 60%. The higher-level
income earners had instead lost ground (with gains even lower than
10%). Only the last percentile still had gains close to 60%. The
reason for this is relatively easy to explain. In fact, the two decades
following 1988 are those in which income growth has increased
exponentially in some emerging countries, especially China and
India, whose population now largely constitutes the world's middle
class. The crisis that broke out in 2007–2008 had the effect of
accentuating these trends, increasing the incomes of the middle
classes (with earnings reaching 120%) and limiting those of the
wealthiest classes, with the last percentile earning 'only' just over

40% more.[2] Indeed, the crisis has hit the most the European countries and the United States, where the income earners with the highest incomes live.

If one looks at the effects of the crisis on poverty and distribution in single countries, as we largely have done until now, they are certainly negative. If one looks, instead, at the income distribution at the world level, he can find – as seen in Figure 47 – that it has not worsened, from some points of view, that is, if it is measured as for a single country. It is true that the share of the highest income earners has risen, but the share of middle classes has increased much more. It is also true that this depends on the differential growth rate of developed and emerging economies – which has been higher for the latter than for the former – but the origin of this can be imputed to globalisation. One can, however, say that this is only the initial effect of globalisation. In fact, longer-term effects can be negative, due to increasing monopolisation. Thus, this was the (initial) effect of globalisation, while – as said – the financial crisis had no clear negative influence on this distribution.

As mentioned, the crisis has also led to rethinking the extension of production internationally, making us reflect on the opportunity to re-nationalize global value chains and on the possibility of a process of de-globalisation.

In addition to the effects of crises on inequality, there are also effects in the opposite direction. In fact, one can argue that rising inequality has a negative macroeconomic effect, as it creates downwards pressure on aggregate demand. In addition, increasing inequality can originate a crisis due to the higher propensity to speculate and to hold riskier financial assets of richer households (Stockhammer, 2015).

---

[2] However, it should be noted that Kharas and Seidel (2018) downsize these results, showing that sampling data covering all realities would result in a much more modest increase in the incomes of major income earners, equal to about 13%.

Rajan (2010) argues that US consumers with low incomes have reduced their saving and increased their debt since the early 1980s. This contributed to creating a credit bubble, which eventually burst in the second half of the first decade of the 2000s, leading to the financial crisis that soon spread to Europe. Rajan adds that inequality had an influence on the crisis mediated by politics, which raised housing subsidies. Acemoglu and Robinson (2006), instead, think that it was politics that influenced both expansion of financial lending (thanks to lobbying of the financial sector) to the poorer segments of the population and inequality, thus fostering top incomes growth.

Crises and stagnation have an apparently positive effect on efficiency through the environment, but available evidence partially contrasts this opinion. In fact, stagnation has produced a deterioration in biodiversity in terrestrial and marine ecosystems at the global level, while there have been improvements in some air pollutant emissions in middle- and high-income countries. A transition to a sustainable socio-environmental system requires concerted policy efforts (Cantone et al., 2021).

As for the relationship between globalisation and stagnation, from some points of view it is quite clear that the formation of international oligopolies can contribute to stagnation by reducing the competitive pressure, which is the driving force behind product-ivity growth. From some other points of view, de-localisation can have positive effects on the growth of the countries of origin for the products that are de-localised (Bernard et al, 2020), and is likely to have a similar effect on the destination country. At a more general level too, one has to distinguish the effects of globalisation on employment and those on the value added of manufacturing in developed countries: While those on employment of rising imports from emerging countries are negative, those on the manufacturing value added are positive (Fort et al., 2018).

As said, stagnation has effects similar to those of the crisis on poverty and inequality. The consequences of inequality on growth can indeed be very different. In some emerging countries, as in China, rising inequality has been associated with rising growth, but it must be recognised that it was structural transformations that produced growth and, as a consequence of this, inequality (see, e.g., Unctad, 2012). In other countries, mostly developed ones, inequality implies an increase in savings and a fall in investment, with consequent weakening of growth (see the literature cited in Section 2.2). As to the effect of the crisis on globalisation, we can say that it is negative, since it threatens global value chains, thus inducing firms to re-nationalise at least some segments of these chains. In addition, crises might upturn existing governments and open the way for a more inward-looking attitude, thus reducing international economic relationships. It must be said, however, that the opposite can be also true, that is, a crisis can lead to a new government with a more outward-looking attitude. As to the effects of globalisation on crises, usually the former can amplify the effects of the latter, by transmitting the negative impulse of a crisis in one country to all the other countries having economic ties with it. A typical example is that of the financial crises, which spread very quickly from one country to another, such as in the case of the financial crisis that started in mid-2007 in the United States and propagated to the whole world by 2008.

Stagnation is fostered by a deep and prolonged crisis, as we have been arguing in the previous pages. As said, it can have effects similar to the crisis on distribution.

Various links are then established between the various issues we have dealt with in the previous chapters. The problems indicated are also linked to each other by the fact that all raise the question of the public action necessary to counter them. Briefly, we can say that it is now time to abandon the liberalism that for too long (has not) guided public action and find a balance between the forces of the market and public action (Johnson, 2019).

5.2 ECONOMIC POLICY AS A LAME DUCK?

As we have seen, there are currently a number of hard problems to be faced by economic policy. But, together with these hard problems a number of new instruments have been devised that are available to policymakers. Blanchard et al. (2010: 10) say that defining a new macroeconomic policy framework is a very difficult task, more than before, but not a desperate one. 'The bad news is that the crisis has made clear that macroeconomic policy must have many targets; the good news is that it has also reminded us that we have in fact many instruments, from "exotic" monetary policy to fiscal instruments, to regulatory instruments. It will take some time, and substantial research, to decide which instruments to allocate to which targets, between monetary, fiscal and financial policies.'

Thus, the bad news aspect is due to the fact that many issues have arisen with evidence at the same time. The Great Recession and the Covid pandemic, secular stagnation, rising inequality and globalisation are the (partly) new issues that have arisen in recent decades. To be true, they had already manifested in the past, but seemed to be dormant or to have been tamed for a while. This was the case of the financial crises, with the ensuing stagnation, whose main occurrence dates back to the Great Depression of the 1930s. Globalisation and rising inequalities within both developed and less developed countries – even if inequality between them decreased after World War II – seemed to have been under control for a while (say, until the 1970s), but re-emerged in the following decades.

Thus the emergence of so many problems has raised questions as to the ability of economic policy to adequately deal with them. Monetary and fiscal policy were the classic tools to deal with economic issues like those indicated. However, availability of only two such tools was not enough to solve so many problems at a time. In fact, a number of policy tools equal to that of policy objectives is required for reaching fixed policy targets (*golden rule of economic policy*).

In addition, insurgence of constraints has practically implied dropping some policy tools: In the case of fiscal policy, they are due to fiscal constraints, such as the limit to the budget deficit; for monetary policy they are due to the impossibility or difficulty of lowering the nominal policy interest rate below zero, thus remaining stuck at the ZLB. This prevents the current short-term interest rate and the expected future short-term rates – on which long-term interest rate depends – from reaching the level that would be required by the market for profitable investment.[3] The alternative to dropping some policy tool has been confining its use within strict boundaries, which is tantamount to the impossibility of respecting the golden rule and the need to resort to a 'second-best' prospect. The implications for managing public policy have thus been negative, as the set of tools available for a lasting exit from the crisis has been impoverished.

In order to enlarge the number of existing policy instruments, monetary policy has searched for unconventional tools[4] to add to the usual interventions in the short-term market, with the intention of lowering long-term interest rates – which influence investment and thus recovery and growth – and is particularly difficult to do in conditions of ZLB. In addition, a number of new instruments have been introduced that can face the new issues, at least in theory. These are a series of unconventional monetary policy measures such as 'quantitative easing' and 'forward guidance' – putting emphasis on monetary action in the long-term section of financial assets as well as announcements on the future path of policy – and possibly recourse to 'helicopter money'. Due to the mixed nature of some unconventional policies and the helicopter money, response to the crisis has also blurred the distinction between monetary and fiscal policy to the point that this may appear to have vanished. Also microeconomic prudential rules have been adapted to face systemic risks, giving rise to macro-prudential policies. These new policies as well as the double nature of some monetary policies make the case for coordinating all

---

[3] As said, since 2014 the ECB and the central banks of other non-EMU countries (e.g., Denmark, Sweden, Switzerland and Japan) have introduced the practice of negative interest rates for bank deposits with the central banks themselves in order to encourage banks to increase lending. The action, however, has been almost ineffective, and the enduring deflation has really hindered the effort to expand the economy.

[4] They are called 'exotic' instruments by Blanchard et al. (2010: 10).

macroeconomic policies, balancing their extent and timing, also to ensure proper functioning of democratic institutions. In addition, the need arises to reflect on the adequacy of the low inflation targets inherited from previous decades, which are set at too low a level for the monetary policy to relieve the economy at a sustained pace and reduce soaring public debt. Finally, new rules of fiscal policies have been introduced, such as: (1) the so-called *golden rule of deficit financing*, prescribing that current revenues must balance only current spending over the cycle and borrowing is permitted to fund public investment or (2) debt target rules, instead of budget rules.

Then, new instruments can face new issues, at least in theory. In practice, there are a number of constraints limiting the possibility to use these new instruments to deal with the new issues that have arisen in the last decades.

New limits have arisen especially due to political constraints. First, they refer to the use of some tools. In fact, the crisis has overburdened public finances in most countries and soaring public debt has constrained expansionary fiscal policy. The limits to increases in public debt derive from: the implied excessive burden thrown on future generations; the risks related to the stability of the system, possibly emphasised by the operation of financial markets; and, finally, the constraint related to high levels of public debt on the potential for fiscal policy to deal with the next negative shocks and secular stagnation. The attitude of governments has therefore changed, and they have set or confirmed limits to public debt or both to it and the public deficit. The United States has confirmed existing constraints to rising debt in absolute terms by only slightly adjusting the ceiling. In the European Monetary Union (EMU) the fiscal compact has set limits more stringent than the SGP to both deficit and debt as a ratio to the GDP.

Conclusions

In this book we have dealt with the major problems of our time: the crises, stagnation, inefficiency and inequality, globalisation. The problems facing us – and the next generations – are largely ancient problems, but they have grown worse recently. In the previous pages we have analysed these problems both in isolation and in their inter-relations. In fact, they are strictly interrelated one to another and are certainly to be faced by public action considering these interrelations.

The financial crisis that has hit in particular Europe has been followed by the pandemic, increasing the prospect of a secular stagnation and negatively influencing efficiency and equity. Globalisation, which has proceeded over time, due to various factors of a technical nature and of an economic policy kind, has positive and negative consequences on efficiency and equity, in single countries and at a world level. All these economic problems are relevant and their relevance is increased by: (1) the fact that, as said, the problems facing us – and the next generations – are largely ancient problems but have been aggravated recently; (2) the 'golden rule' of public action requires availability of a number of policy tools at least equal to that of targets.

It is true that, facing the multiplication and aggravation of the problems there has been an increase in the number of instruments, due to the inventiveness of the economists, which has provided a number of new tools, ranging from macro-prudential policy to unconventional monetary policies. These have partly remedied the reduction in the effectiveness of some traditional instruments, which has decreased due to the duration and depth of the crisis, but also to the constraint of the ZLB, which blocks policy interest rates at a zero level, as negative interest rates are not conceivable (or are limited to very specific circumstances). However, it is also true that, at the same time, the use of some policy tools is limited not only by further economic constraints – due to the consideration of the possible reaction of markets – but also by political constraints, which only partly express the existence of these limitations due to markets. This implies that economic policy appears as a 'lame duck'.

Glossary

Asset-backed security (ABS). A security whose payments for principal and interests depend on (i.e., are 'backed' by) the value of a specified pool of underlying assets. These, in turn, are a group of small and often illiquid assets that cannot be sold individually, such as mortgages, credit card debt, student loans and auto loans. They are pooled in order to allow the risk of investing in the underlying assets to be diversified (and thus reduced) and are to be sold to general investors, a process called *securitisation*.

Capital (or financial) account. It is a part of the balance of payments recording the movements of short-, medium- and long-term capital, which are mainly divided into:

- direct investments (purchases or sales of shares and equity investments such as to ensure control of companies located abroad);
- portfolio investments (purchase or sales of shares and equity investments without control of the company participated, purchase of bonds and government securities);
- other investments (public and private loans; short-, medium- and long-term trade credits; bank capital and investments of other short-term assets).

Current account. It is the part of the balance of payments that substantially includes exports and imports of goods, that is, goods, including services (e.g., freight, insurance, tourism income), and income from labour and capital employed abroad as well as unilateral transfers (contributions or public and private donations to/ from international bodies). All these items are in the nature of current transactions. Within this account, transactions involving goods alone give rise to the *trade balance* (by extension, this term is often used, even if improperly, to include services as well); the other items are called 'invisible items'.

ECB. This is the European Central Bank, which has the exclusive right to: authorize the issuance of banknotes within the European Monetary Union; carry out foreign exchange transactions for the purpose of influencing the exchange rate of the euro with other currencies and counteract excessive or erratic fluctuations; hold and manage the official reserves of the Member States; promote the smooth functioning of payment systems.

Its primary objective is to maintain price stability, defined as an annual increase in the medium term below, but close to, 2% of the consumer price index for member countries. Without prejudice to this objective, the Bank must support all the Union's economic policies, for example in favour of employment.

The ECB is independent of the EU bodies and therefore cannot receive guidelines or be influenced by governments and other European institutions. Furthermore, it can choose the operations capable of securing its objective and is prohibited from opening credit lines to public institutions of the EU or to member countries. The purchase of public securities is allowed only on the secondary market, that is, it must be of securities already in existence.

Emissions Trading System. In 2005, an Emissions Trading System (ETS) regulating pollution was implemented in the EU, setting caps for emissions and instituting a trade system of permits to pollute. This is the key EU tool for reducing greenhouse gas emissions (mainly carbon dioxide), limiting emissions from heavy energy-using installations operating in the EU countries and covering around 45% of the EU's greenhouse gas emissions. The ETS is a 'cap and trade' system tending to combat climate change. A cap – tending to be lowered over time in order to reduce total emissions – is set on the total amount of certain greenhouse gases that can be emitted. Companies receive emission allowances within their cap. In case their emission is lower than the cap, they can sell the permission – for the part they didn't use – to the other firms that cannot respect their cap. The limit on the total number of allowances available – properly determined according to an assessment of current emissions – ensures that they have a value. The ETS sectors include power and heat generation, combustion plants, oil refineries, coke ovens, iron and steel plants and factories making cement, glass, lime, bricks, ceramics. The emission cap can in fact be changed. If it is set at a lower level, the consequence is that a rather high carbon price results, implying a high value of the externalities created by emissions and a high stimulus to carbon-use saving and its replacement by renewable energies.

Endogenous. Something that happens having an internal cause or origin. With reference to the determinants of the level of income (see GDP), consumption is endogenous (as it depends on the level of income itself), whereas investment, government spending and exports are exogenous. With reference, instead, to growth, one can say that economic growth is primarily the result of technical progress, which in turn depends on improvements in productivity, tied directly to investments in human capital and innovation from governments and private-sector institutions. If one thinks instead that technical progress depends not on this activity, but on factors independent from it and completely autonomous (as in the case of casual discoveries), technical progress is of an exogenous nature.

ESM. The European Stability Mechanism is also known as the 'Bailout Fund'. It is a European institution in existence since 2012 that aims to ensure financial assistance to Member States in difficulty, with a maximum lending capacity of €500 billion. The assistance is subject to strict conditionality, linked to the non-existence of excessive public deficits. Since 2019, a reform tending to exacerbate this conditionality is under discussion, but the epidemic and the consequent increase in the needs of member states have led to the suspension of the reform and, indeed, do favour the granting of loans exempt from many conditions, except that the funds are earmarked for healthcare costs.

Europe 2020. The agenda set by the EU for growth and employment in the decade 2010–2020 aimed at achieving objectives in the following five areas: employment (with more than 75% of people between 20 and 64 years occupied); a percentage higher than 3% of GDP to be invested in R&D; a 20% reduction compared to 1990 in greenhouse gas emissions together with a 20% increase in the share of renewable sources in final energy consumption and a 20% increase in energy efficiency. In terms of school attendance, the share of early school leavers had to be reduced to under 10%, and at least 40% of 30-to-34 year olds should have completed tertiary or equivalent education. As to poverty and social exclusion, there should have been at least 20 million fewer people at risk of poverty or social exclusion. A rather complete assessment of the degree to which the targets have been fulfilled shows that the employment and R&D targets have not been met, whereas the tertiary education one has been reached and the greenhouse gas emissions and the early leavers values were close to their targets in the EU as a whole. Obviously, the situation differs widely between the various countries.

Exchange rate. The price of a foreign currency in terms of the national currency, for example, $1.25/1 euro, or 0.8 euro/$1. This price can be fixed – or practically so, when it revolves around the so-called parity (or central rate) between the two currencies, for example when the exchange rate between dollars and euros can vary by 1–2% more or less around $1.25/1 euro – and then you have *fixed exchange rates*. It is flexible if it can vary without such limits (*flexible exchange rates*). When fixed exchange rates exist, parities can be changed, implying that – after their change – exchange rate fluctuations must revolve around the new parities. Generally speaking, we can say for simplicity (in the doctrine there are subtler semantic distinctions) that, when the quantity of foreign currency (say, the dollar) increases per each unit of national currency (the euro), there is a *devaluation* or a *depreciation* of the dollar and a *revaluation* or *appreciation* of the euro.

Exogenous. An entity that is (or can be considered) as being independent of another one. With reference to the determinants of the level of income, investment, government spending and exports are exogenous as they do not depend on that level, whereas consumption is endogenous. With reference, instead, to growth, one can say that an exogenous factor of it is technological progress, which is almost independent of economic forces. In the exogenous growth model, economic growth in the long run depends on exogenous technical progress, and not on other economic variables.

External economies and diseconomies (or externalities). Respectively, any positive (negative) effect caused on operators other than the one who incurred the cost of producing (or who consumed) the good to which the external economy is connected. A famous example of external economy is the production of fruit by a farmer, which benefits the beekeeper placed nearby, because the bees feed on pollen and nectar, without the beekeeper incurring the cost of producing the fruit. As a matter of fact, the beekeeper's activity also generates external economies (in favour of the fruit grower), as bees pollinate the orchards. This is indeed a case of production of crossed external economies. A classic example of external diseconomies is the smoke of factories, but that of house chimneys is also of the same type.

Fallacy of the composition. This is the mistake that is made at the macroeconomic level (i.e., at the level of the entire economy), if the implications derived at the level of individuals are also referred to the entire economy. If each family increases its propensity to save, at the level of the entire economic system there is not a higher amount of savings, but a smaller one. In fact, by virtue of the savings paradox, the level of income that will be produced in that economic system as a whole will be lower and, correspondingly, the level of savings will also be lower than that desired by individuals.

Fiscal policy. It is the manoeuvre of the expenses and/or revenues of a public body, that is, the manoeuvre of the public budget, which can lead to a balance that is negative (i.e., with a deficit), zero (a balance) or positive (surplus).

GDP (Gross Domestic Product). The aggregate market value of all new goods produced over a certain period of time (usually a year) within an economic system. It is called *gross* because the part of the value of pre-existing durable goods (for example, plants) that is reduced due to deterioration and physical consumption as a consequence of production, has not been subtracted from this value. GDP can be considered equal, on the one hand, to the total remuneration paid to the so-called factors of production (labour, capital, land) and, on the other, to the overall demand for goods expressed in the system, for consumption and investment (private and public) and for net exports (i.e., exports less imports) in that period.

Gini index or coefficient. It is a measure of the inequality of a distribution. It is often used as a concentration index to measure inequality in the distribution of income or wealth. It assumes values between 0 and 1. Low values of the coefficient indicate a fairly homogeneous distribution, with the value 0 corresponding to perfect equidistribution. This happens in a situation in which everyone receives exactly the same income; high values of the coefficient indicate a more unequal distribution, with the value 1 corresponding to the maximum concentration, that is, the situation in which one person receives all the income of the country while all the others have zero income.

Golden rule of public finance. It is the rule according to which the objective of pursuing a balance of the public budget must be limited to current expenditures and revenues only, offering the possibility of financing public investment in deficit. The request to adopt the golden rule tends to allow public investment to be made rather than being reduced. This would indeed happen in the case a rule were adopted asking for a balance of the whole budget, as in this case the need to reduce public expenditures in order to ensure the balance of the whole budget would be met by cutting public investment, which is more easily compressible than current expenditures. In fact, it is possible (or easier) to stop the construction of a new public work (thus reducing investment expenditures), but not to stop the payment of salaries to public employees (which are consumption expenditures).

Helicopter money. Simply in order to show some effects of monetary policy, Milton Friedman coined the parable of distributing money to everyone through a helicopter flying over people, or of directly transferring money to people's checking accounts. This would have the consequence of increasing their spending power (and, according to him, raising prices).

Macroeconomic policy. It is the manoeuvre of macroeconomic instruments, which are those that directly leverage *aggregate* quantities (the variables that make up GDP, i.e., public and private consumption, public and private investment, net exports). Macroeconomic policy is implemented through various instruments: monetary policy, which via the interest rate acts essentially on private investment and, to some extent, on private consumption; macroprudential policy, which deals with financial instability; fiscal policy, for example, with changes in public spending (consumption and public investment) and/or in taxes, which influence consumption and investment; exchange rate policy (devaluation or revaluation), which affects exports and imports; incomes policy, which sets both the remuneration of production factors, establishing wage changes with respect to productivity, and prices, thus affecting private consumption and investment.

Macroprudential policy. The policy that deals with financial instability (or systemic instability), that is, a situation in which the economic system may find itself due to a set of choices of operators that lead to a phase of euphoria followed by a crisis, initially mainly in the financial sector and then spreading to the real sector. In the initial phase of euphoria, a speculative bubble is created, with a considerable and self-sustaining increase in the prices of financial assets (mainly shares) and of real assets (in particular, real estate). The 'bursting' of the bubble leads in succession to: a similarly pronounced and self-sustaining fall in the prices of these assets; inability to make payments by financial or other operators; decline in deposits; bankruptcy of banks and businesses; possible distrust of banks and bank runs; fall in economic activity and employment and possibly also in the general level of prices of goods. The one just described is the sequence of instability that has manifested itself on two occasions in the last ninety years, first during the so-called Great Crisis that began in 1929 and then during the financial crisis that began in 2007, which is mentioned several times in the main text.

At the heart of financial instability are the choices of the banking system. Macroprudential regulation has precisely the objective of coping with underlining externalities (due to the ripple effect that insolvencies can have) and increasing resistance to systemic risk. In many cases, it consists of the same instruments as the microprudential one, that is, credit limits applied to specific sectors or to the entire economic system, or deposit insurance. To act in a systemic way, macroprudential regulation must have countercyclical effects, which can be achieved by introducing requirements (for example, of capital) that are different according to the state of the economy and the likelihood of bubbles forming in activities. The requirements are therefore higher in periods of expansion, lower during contractions. The nature of the related rules can be discretionary or automatic. This second is the case in which requirements are linked to some indicators of economic activity, precisely in order to reduce the cyclical trend. Capital requirements are the main tool of these policies.

Market failures. We speak of market failure when it is judged that the market fails to ensure a good social position, leading to an inefficient and/or unfair situation. We talk about inefficiency if all those goods that could be produced with the available resources are not produced. An example of this inefficiency is given by the lack of exploitation of a plant or of the human resources available, which may be the effect of a monopoly position that leads to rationing the quantity offered. A further interesting case of such market failures is given by external economies and diseconomies (for example, damage caused by pollution) and by public goods, which are the goods that are not convenient for the single individual to produce due to the <u>external economies</u> that arise from them. The benefit that he receives is less than their production cost. The typical case is that of the lighthouse: For a single sailor, it is not profitable to build a lighthouse, as he does not receive all the possible benefits produced by it. The subject appointed to produce these goods is then the public body, for which the problem does not arise, since the public body looks to the benefits of the whole community. The inequity of income distribution also constitutes a market failure.

All these cases of market failure are highlighted by an analysis of the positions and choices of *individual* operators, and therefore we speak of them as *microeconomic failures*. If, on the other hand, we look at the values of some variables in aggregate terms (i.e., for the total economy), there are several cases of *macroeconomic failures*: unemployment, inflation, financial system instability, insufficient growth, imbalance of the balance of payments. Unemployment (involuntary) is a clear case of inefficiency, because the full potential of the human resources available to work in a certain system is not used. Inflation can constitute a case of inefficiency, because - if it is high - it does not allow reliable calculations of economic convenience (thus generating inefficient choices) and can involve costs in particular for some people, for example those who enjoy fixed incomes, who suffer a loss of their purchasing power (thus generating inequality). Financial system instability takes place when the financial system cannot provide crucial services to households and businesses and the system risks being incapable of withstanding shocks and financial imbalances. Low growth means that an economic system generates less than the possible increases in income in each period, although the situation may correspond to the full use of all economic resources. For example, this happens if there is little innovation in a system, which would allow it, say, to produce more with the same resources through the use of more efficient production techniques. Finally, the balance of payments can give rise to a macroeconomic failure if, for example, foreign currency revenues (say, in dollars) are less than foreign currency outlays. To cope with the excess payments abroad, it is therefore necessary to draw on the available foreign exchange reserves. In anticipation of their exhaustion, it will be necessary to increase revenues and reduce currency outlays, which is normally done through the *devaluation* of the national currency (see exchange rate). This, on the one hand implies an increase in exports; on the other, it decreases imports, due to the fact that they have become more expensive. If these are difficult to compress, because they are, for example, raw materials, the increase in their price will imply an inflationary trend. The imbalance in the balance of payments can therefore lead to a macroeconomic failure.

Microeconomic policy. This is the policy aimed at influencing the quantities relating to individual operators or their categories. Among the instruments of microeconomic policies we should mention: the attribution of property rights, for example with reference to the participants in the activity of a corporate enterprise (in particular, for the role of owners and managers); the various forms of anti-monopoly policy (e.g., regulation, recourse to public enterprises); environmental policies; industrial policies, which tend to facilitate the adaptation of firms to change or to introduce change itself, thereby strengthening the growth capacity of the system; policies of personal (or family) income redistribution; policies of regional and sectoral redistribution.

Monetary policy. The set of tools with which the central bank aims to influence interest rate on short-term loans (but see also unconventional monetary policy, tending to influence long-term interest rates). The goal is to increase it, in order to curb demand and inflation, or to reduce it, tending to stimulate demand. The instruments used are different and range from the manoeuvre of the official discount rate (practiced by the central bank to banks that want to obtain liquidity in exchange for transfer of part of the bills in their possession) to open market operations (with which the central bank buys or sells short-term securities, thus, respectively, increasing or decreasing the liquidity of the system) and, finally, to the compulsory reserve manoeuvre (that is, to the change in the percentage of bank deposits that the central bank requires to be deposited with itself).

Multiplier. When an <u>exogenous</u> component of aggregate demand, such as investments (public or private) and/or exports, increases, the resulting increase in income is not equal to the increase in these items of overall demand in the economy (see <u>GDP</u>), but is usually higher. For example, an increase of 100 in the investment will cause an increase in demand equal to a multiple of 100. In fact, an investment of 100 will result in an increase in compensations to the factors of production, which in part are consumed, the more so the greater the propensity of people to consume. In turn, the increase in consumption will cause a new increase in factor compensations and a further increase in consumption, and so forth. At the end of the multiplicative process, <u>GDP</u> will be increased, for example, by 200, with a multiplier of 2 of the initial investment.

If we consider, as is normal, a country open to international trade, the multiplier will be smaller. In fact, the initial 100 increase in compensations translates only in part into an increase in consumption of domestic goods – and therefore in domestic demand. A part of the demand is addressed instead to the rest of the world, due to the increase in imports from foreign countries, that is, exports from these countries, and, therefore, translates into an increase in *their* GDP. A joint effort – say, by all European countries – to increase investment reduces the extent of the leakage in the increase of <u>GDP</u>. In fact, in the case of investments only in Italy, the part of the demand that would turn inwards (and which increases the aggregate demand in Italy) would be accompanied by a part of imports increasing exports from Germany and a part increasing, for example, exports from the USA, increasing aggregate demand in these countries. If, instead, of a purely Italian investment there were also a German investment, these investments would stimulate demand in Italy to a higher extent than that of a purely Italian investment, because it is true that the higher Italian investment translates in part into imports from Germany, but the increase in German <u>GDP</u>

deriving from German investment would partly lead to more imports from Italy. There would therefore be a sort of 'cross-fertilisation', with an increase in the multiplicative effect, even if this effect is not as great as it would be in the theoretical case of a Europe closed to the rest of the world or in the case when all countries in the world increase their investment.

Parity. This (also called *central rate*) is the value around which, under a fixed exchange rate regime, some minor fluctuations, for example 1%, in the exchange rate are allowed.

People at risk of poverty and social exclusion. This is a three-component indicator. The first component takes into account people who are at risk of poverty from the point of view of the income that they receive. This category includes all those people who are part of families who are unable to reach at least a certain income threshold. To calculate this threshold, the median income is first calculated. Then 60% of this value is calculated, and those people who fail to reach this figure are considered at risk of poverty. To complicate matters is the fact that the computations are repeated for all families according to the number of their members, following the idea that as a family is more numerous, the amount necessary to support each of its components decreases. People at risk of poverty among Italians exceed 20%, that is, one in five people, while in the European Union they are one in six.

The second indicator to add to the first one takes into account people who are in a situation of 'severe material deprivation'. In this case it is not their income that is taken into account, but the situation in which people live: if they live in houses that are adequately heated, if they can afford a washing machine, a car, a telephone, if they can pay bills and eat adequate meals. This is the smallest component of the poverty indicator, fortunately, but also the one in which the differences between one country and another are stronger. The average of this indicator is 7% for the EU population, or one person in about 14. However, in Bulgaria 30% of the inhabitants are in severe material deprivation, while in Sweden the value drops to 1.1% and in Italy it exceeds 10%, which means that in Italy there are people in this situation almost ten times more numerous - as a percentage of the total - than in Sweden.

The third component of the synthetic index calculated by Eurostat is that of people living in families with low work intensity, which means that people of working age in that family have actually worked very little. More specifically, it means that in that family those who are between 18 and 59 years old (but excluding those who study and who are under 24) have worked on average 20% or less of what they could have. That is, they worked less than one day a week, excluding Saturdays and Sundays. This is how 9.3% of EU citizens and 11.8% of Italians live.

Productivity. Productivity means efficiency of production. It is measured by various indicators according to the input one wants to refer to. Then, with respect to some raw material, productivity is measured as the ratio of the quantity of an output to the quantity of that raw material, to indicate the efficiency with which the raw material is used in the production process. The main reference is, however, to the labour input. This is the case, for example, of the GDP per person employed, that is, GDP divided by total employment in the economy.

Public goods. These are goods *non-rival* in consumption – as the consumption of these goods by an individual does not imply that other individuals cannot consume them at the same time (as in the case of a work of art) – and whose consumption by subjects who did not contribute to producing it *cannot be excluded*. The typical case of a public good is that of a lighthouse, a non-rival and not-excludable good. These characteristics mean that there is little propensity to produce these goods by private individuals.

Savings paradox. This is the situation that arises at the level of the entire economy when each person increases his propensity to save, that is, reduces his propensity to consume. In this case, instead of having greater savings capable of financing investments, the value of the multiplier is reduced and therefore at each couple of investment expenditure and foreign demand (i.e., of the exogenous expenditure) corresponds a lower value of total income and then of total savings. In other words, a rise in the propensity to save, which means a reduction of the propensity to consume, implies a reduction in the value of the multiplier. Then, to a given value of exogenous expenditure (i.e., of investment and foreign demand) will correspond a lower value of GDP.

Social capital. We use the term *social capital* in the meaning of the set of aspects of social life, such as relational networks, norms and mutual trust, which allow members of a community to act together more effectively in achieving shared goals. It is these informal norms that determine the actual behaviour of social groups and individuals. A high level of social capital derives from the existence of mutual trust and a sense of identity of shared values, which ensure the observance not only of legal norms, but also of informal norms of common sense, cooperation and reciprocity of behaviour. On the contrary, the scarcity of social capital determines not only the non-existence of these informal rules, but also often the non-compliance with legal rules.

State failures. The action of the state, like that of private individuals, may not ensure an excellent result for society. This depends, for example, on the inefficiency of the action of the bureaucrats and/or of the persons in charge of elected positions, who act not to satisfy the needs of the community, interpreted in some way (in the case of politicians) or according to laws (in the case of bureaucrats), but to reduce their own workload or insure benefits and the like.

Tax havens. These are the countries that have introduced tax treatments lower than the average of other countries, especially those belonging to the same union. Within the EU, tax havens are: Belgium, Cyprus, Ireland, Estonia, Hungary, Luxembourg, Malta, the Netherlands. Outside the EU they are: Switzerland, Bermuda, the Caribbean, Puerto Rico, Hong Kong, Singapore. It is no coincidence that some of the major companies in Italy and other countries have established their parent company in some of these paradises, such as in the Netherlands. The advantage is that, with proper transfer pricing, multinationals can concentrate their profits in these centers, where tax rates are lower.

Transfer pricing. This is the determination of prices relating to the transfer of goods and services within multinationals. These transfers refer to intermediate goods or specific services that are often, but not always, actually provided by a subsidiary (or parent company) to another of a multinational company. Given the specificity of these goods or services, it is difficult or impossible in many cases to compare the transfer prices practised by multinationals to the prices charged on the market for the same or similar goods or services and, therefore, the parent company of the multinational company can choose them in a way to vary its revenues and costs and those of the various subsidiaries and, thus (given the different tax rates existing in the various countries), the total fiscal charge for the company. For example, by increasing the price of a service – actual or imputed – it provides to a subsidiary, the parent company will increase its profit and reduce that of the subsidiary, in the case that the corporate income tax rate in the country where it is located is lower than that of the country in which the subsidiary is located, thus reducing the total tax paid by the company. This is why the parent company of a multinational is usually located in a tax haven or in a country that adopts the 'tax rulings' mentioned in the text.

Unconventional monetary policy. In times of a particularly severe recession, the conventional monetary policy manoeuvre, which consists in influencing market *short-term* interest rates, is not sufficient, for various reasons. The main one has to do with the fact that the reduction in the short-term interest rate obtained by this manoeuvre is not transmitted to the long-term interest rate on which investment depends.

One of the reasons for that is that it may not be sufficient to lower the market short term rate enough, because it meets the limit of the zero interest rate (*zero lower bound*, ZLB). A bank normally borrows from the central bank if it can lend to businesses (or consumers). But, if businesses and consumers do not ask for loans (or, as they say in the jargon, if the 'horse does not drink'), the bank has convenience to deposit with the Central Bank the available liquidity (in order to avoid the cost of holding cash, due to possible theft), certainly as long as the latter is willing to pay a positive interest. One of the possible actions for the Central Bank in order to stimulate economic activity is to set an interest rate sufficiently low – even negative - on bank deposits with it, but banks will certainly be discouraged to re-deposit the funds they receive and cannot lend, if the negative interest rate set by the Central Bank is too low.

Thus, a situation arises where short-term market interest rates are stuck at zero and there is excess liquidity. Precisely because short-term rates cannot become negative in general (apart from the case referred to), economic recovery is not stimulated. On the other hand, future rates could even be expected to increase, and this would not ensure that the interest rate is low enough in the long-term section of the market. In short, investment is hindered by current and expected rates: given the poor return expected from the investment itself, interest rates even equal to zero or relatively low immediately (but not necessarily so in the future) are not enough to stimulate it.

In these conditions, in order to cope with the financial crisis, in addition to normal monetary policy operations, *non-conventional operations* are necessary, which guarantee sufficiently low (even if not negative) levels of interest rates directly on long-term securities (and loans): instead of open market operations on short-term securities, similar operations are carried out on long-term securities (for example, on ten-year Treasury bills). These are the *'quantitative easing'* operations. The same result can be obtained by firmly and credibly reporting to the market the intentions of the monetary authorities for future actions. To this end, to influence expectations, central banks have frequently announced their willingness to maintain low (or zero) interest rates for a certain period of time or until unemployment and/or inflation rates have reached certain predetermined values, corresponding to the desired objectives. The Central Bank therefore provides in this case a 'guide for the future' (*forward guidance*).

References

Accademia Nazionale dei Lincei (2020). La crisi Covid e la possibile svolta per l'Unione Europea. https://bit.ly/2CAeV0R.

Acemoglu D., S. Johnson and J. A. Robinson (2001). The colonial origins of comparative development: An empirical investigation, *The American Economic Review*, 91(5): 1369–1401.

Acemoglu, D., and P. Restrepo (2018). Demographics and automation. NBER W. P. No. 24421, March.

Acemoglu, D., and J. A. Robinson (2006). *Economic Origins of Dictatorship and Democracy*. Cambridge: Cambridge University Press.

Acocella, N. (2015). A tale of two cities: The evolution of the crisis and exit policies in Washington and Frankfurt. In B. Dallago and J. McGowan, eds. *Crises in Europe in the Transatlantic Context: Economic and Political Appraisals*. London: Routledge.

Acocella, N. (2018). *Rediscovering Economic Policy as a Discipline*. Cambridge: Cambridge University Press.

Acocella, N. (2019). 1948–2018: From the free-trade vision to protectionist attitudes. *Economia internazionale/International Economics*, 72(4): 367–392.

Acocella, N. (2020a). *Caccia all'untore: L'economia al tempo del Coronavirus*. Rome: Castelvecchi.

Acocella, N. (2020b). *The European Monetary Union: Europe at the Crossroads*. Cambridge: Cambridge University Press.

Acocella, N. (2020c). *La globalizzazione e l'equilibrio economico mondiale: Le cause, le istituzioni, i pericolic*. Rome: Carocci.

Alfano, V., and S. Ercolano (2020). Capitale sociale bonding e bridging alla prova del lockdown: Un'analisi delle regioni italiane. *Realtà economica del mezzogiorno*, 24(3): 437–454.

Alvaredo, F., A. B. Atkinson, T. Piketty and E. Saez (2013). The top 1 percent in international and historical perspective, *Journal of Economic Perspectives*, 27(3): 3–20.

Amoroso, B. (1996). *Della globalizzazione*. Barletta: La Meridiana.

Angeloni, I. (2020). *Beyond the Pandemic: Reviving Europe's Banking Union*. London: CEPR Press.

Anselmann, C. (2020). *Secular Stagnation Theories: A Historical and Contemporary Analysis with a Focus on the Distribution of Income.* Heidelberg: Springer.

Aronoff, D. (2016). *A Theory of Accumulation and Secular Stagnation: A Malthusian Approach to Understanding a Contemporary Malaise.* New York: Palgrave Macmillan.

Aum, S., S. Y. (Tim) Lee and Y. Shin (2020). COVID-19 doesn't need lockdowns to destroy jobs: The effect of local outbreaks in Korea. NBER W. P. No. 27264, May.

Badré, B., and M. Lemoine (2020). Europe's Covid crossroads. Project Syndicate, 18 May.

Baeten, L. (2016). The effects of financial crises on income inequality: Evidence in the long run of history. Erasmus School of Economics, August.

Baldwin, P. (2021). *Fighting the First Wave.* Cambridge: Cambridge University Press.

Baldwin, R. (2016). *The Great Convergence: Information Technology and the New Globalization.* Cambridge, MA.: Harvard University Press.

Baldwin, R., and R. Freeman (2020). Trade conflict in the age of Covid-19. VOX CEPR Policy Portal, 22 May.

Baldwin, R., and B. Weder di Mauro, eds. (2020). *Economics in the Time of COVID-19.* London: CEPR Press.

Banca d'Italia (2020). Relazione annuale 2019. Roma, 29 May, chapter 15. L'epidemia di Covid-19 e l'economia.

Bank for International Settlements (2017). Basel III: Finalising post-crisis reforms. Basel Committee on Banking Supervision, December. www.bis.org.

Barnes, S., and E. Casey (2020). Insights into post-COVID-19 fiscal policies. VOX CEPR Policy Portal, 9 June.

Barro, R. J. (2000). Inequality and growth in a panel of countries. *Journal of Economic Growth*, 5: 5–32. https://doi.org/10.1023/A:1009850119329.

Bartoš, V., M. Bauer, J. Cahliková and J. Chytilová (2020). Covid-19 crisis fuels hostility against foreigners. CESifo W. P. 8309/2020, May.

Bartscher, A. K., S. Seitz, S. Siegloch, M. Slotwinski and N. Wehrhöfer (2020). Social capital and the spread of Covid-19: Insights from European countries. CESifo W. P. 8346/2020, June.

Basso, H. S., and J. F. Jimeno (2021). From secular stagnation to robocalypse? Implications of demographic and technological changes. *Journal of Monetary Economics*, 117(C): 833–847.

Bastani, S., and D. Waldenström (2020). How should capital be taxed? *Journal of Economic Surveys*, 34(4): 812–846.

Battistini, N., and G. Stoevsky (2020). Alternative scenarios for the impact of the COVID-19 pandemic on economic activity in the Euro Area. European Central Bank, Economic Bulletin, Issue 3.

Battiston, P., and S. Gamba (2020). COVID-19: RO is lower where outbreak is larger. University of Milan Bicocca, Department of Economics, Management and Statistics W. P. No. 438, 21 April. Online at Ssrn.com. https://bit.ly/2DEUKiL.

Baumeister, C., D. Leiva-León and E. Sims (2021). Tracking weekly state-level economic conditions. CAMA W. P. 55, July.

Becchetti L., G. Conzo, P. Conzo and F. Salustri (2020). Understanding the heterogeneity of adverse COVID-19 outcomes: The role of poor quality of air and lockdown decisions, 10 April. Ssrn.com (https://bit.ly/2DOy9Ax).

Bénassy-Quéré A., R. Marimon, J. Pisani-Ferry, L. Reichlin, D. Schoenmaker and B. Weder di Mauro (2020). COVID-19: Europe needs a catastrophe relief plan. CEPR Policy Portal, 11 March.

Bénassy-Quéré, A., and B. Weder di Mauro, eds. (2020a). Europe in the Time of Covid-19. A CEPR Press VoxEU.org eBook, CEPR Press.

Bénassy-Quéré, A., and B. Weder di Mauro (2020b). Europe in the time of Covid-19: A new crash test and a new opportunity. In A. Bénassy-Quéré and B. Weder di Mauro, eds. Europe in the Time of Covid-19. A CEPR Press VoxEU.org eBook, CEPR Press.

Benigno, G., and L. Fornaro (2017). Stagnation traps. ECB Working Paper Series, No 2038, March.

Bergeaud, A., G. Cette and R. Lecat (2018). Long-term growth and productivity trends: Secular stagnation or temporary slowdown? Revue de l'OFCE 2/3 (157): 37–54.

Berglöf, E., G. Brown, H. Clark and N. Okonjo-Iweala (2020). What the G20 should do now. VOX CEPR Policy Portal, 2 June.

Bernanke, B. S. (2015a). Why are interest rates so low? Ben Bernanke's Blog, Brookings, 30 March.

Bernanke, B. S. (2015b). Why are interest rates so low? Part 2: Secular stagnation. Ben Bernanke's Blog, Brookings, 31 March.

Bernard, A. B., T. C. Fort, V. Smeets and F. Warzynski (2020). Heterogeneous globalization: Offshoring and reorganization. NBER W. P. 26854, March. www.nber.org/papers/w26854.

Bivens, J. (2017). Inequality Is Slowing US Economic Growth: Faster Wage Growth for Low- and Middle-Wage Workers Is the Solution. Washington, DC: Economic Policy Institute, 12 December.

Blanchard, O., T. Philippon and J. Pisani-Ferry (2020). A new policy toolkit is needed as countries exit COVID-19 lockdowns, Policy Contribution 12/2020, Bruegel.

Blanchet, T., L. Chancel and A. Gethin (2019). Forty years of inequality in Europe: Evidence from distributional national accounts. VOX CEPR Policy Portal, 22 April.

Blecker, R. A. (2016). The U.S. economy since the crisis: Slow growth and secular stagnation. *European Journal of Economics and Economic Policies: Intervention*, 13(2): 203–214.

Bodea, C., C. Houle and H. Kim (2019). Do financial crises increase income inequality? Conference Paper, November.

Boot, A., E. Carletti, H.-H. Kotz, J. P. Krahnen, L. Pelizzon and M. Subrahmanyam (2020). Corona and financial stability 4.0: Implementing a European pandemic equity fund. VOX CEPR Policy Portal, 25 April.

Bordo, M., and M. Levy (2019). Tariffs and monetary policy: A toxic mix. VOX, CEPR Policy Portal, 18 October. https://voxeu.org/.

Borio, C. (2017). Secular stagnation or financial cycle drag? National Association for Business Economics. 33rd Economic Policy Conference, Washington, DC, 5–7 March.

Brinca, P., J. B. Duarte and M. Faria-e-Castro (2020). *Measuring Sectoral Supply and Demand Shocks during COVID-19. Covid Economics: Vetted and Real-Time Papers, Issue 20*. London: CEPR Press.

Broadberry, S., and J. Wallis (2017). Growing, shrinking, and long-run economic performance. VOX CEPR, 5 July. https://voxeu.org/article/growing-shrinking-and-long-run-economic-performance.

Buiter, W., E. Rahbari and J. Seydl (2015). Secular stagnation: The time for one-armed policy is over. VOX, CEPR Policy Portal, 5 June. https://voxeu.org).

Canelli, R., and R. Realfonzo (2018). Quota salari e regime di accumulazione in Italia. Economia e politica, 09 February 2018.

Cantone, B., A. S. Antonarakis and A. Antoniades (2021). The great stagnation and environmental sustainability: A multidimensional perspective, *Sustainable Development*, 29(3): 485–503.

Capelle-Blancard, G., and A. Desroziers (2020). The stock market and the economy: Insights from the COVID-19 crisis. VOX CEPR Policy Portal, 19 June.

Cappariello, R., S. Franco-Bedoya, V. Gunnella and G. Ottaviano (2020). Rising protectionism and global value chains: Quantifying the general equilibrium effects. Bank of Italy, Temi di discussione. W. P. 1263, February.

Caselli, M., A. Fracasso and S. Scicchitano (2020). From the lockdown to the new normal: An analysis of the limitations to individual mobility in Italy following the Covid-19 crisis. Global Labor Organization Discussion Paper Series 683, October 13.

Centra, M., M. Filippi and R. Quaranta (2020). Covid-19: Misure di contenimento dell'epidemia e impatto sull'occupazione. Inappolicy Brief, no. 17, April.

Chandy, L., and B. Seidel (2016). Is globalization's second wave going to break? *Global Economy and Development*, No. 4, October.

Cinquegrana, G., G. de Luca, P. Mazzocchi, F. Pastore, C. Quintano and A. Rocca (2020). L'emergenza socio-economica: La digitalizzazione come chiave di lettura. Mimeo.

Ciocca, P. (2020). Viviamo una crisi peggiore e diversa da quella del 2008. Il manifesto, 21 May.

Claeys, G. (2020). The ECB in the COVID-19 Crisis: Whatever it takes, within its mandate. Monetary Dialogue Papers, Study for the Committee on Economic and Monetary Affairs, Policy Department for Economic, Scientific and Quality of Life Policies, European Parliament, Luxembourg, June.

Claeys, G., and G. B. Wolff (2020). Is the COVID-19 crisis an opportunity to boost the euro as a global currency? Policy Contribution 11/2020, Bruegel.

Clancy, E. (2020). Behind the spin on the EU's Recovery Plan, 'la Tribune', 29 May, or Emma Clancy: Behind the spin on the EU's Recovery Plan, Braveneweurope. com, 6 June. https://bit.ly/38ZOvSo.

Cochrane, J. H. (2020). A fiscal theory of monetary policy with partially repaid long-term debt. NBER W. P. No. 26745, February.

Codogno, L., and P. Van den Noord (2020). Assessing next generation EU. https://blogs.lse.ac.uk/europpblog/2020/10/07/assessing-next-generation-eu/

Cœuré, B. (2013). The economic consequences of low interest rates. Public lecture, International Center for Monetary and Banking Studies, Geneva, 9 October.

Conticini, E., B. Frediani and D. Caro (2020). Can atmospheric pollution be considered a co-factor in extremely high level of SARS-CoV-2 lethality in Northern Italy? Environmental Pollution, Sciencedirect.com. https://bit.ly/2DIiPoU.

Costa, P. (2020). Recovery Fund: I tre errori da non compiere, se vogliamo diffondere l'innovazione. Micromega, 28 October. http://temi.repubblica.it/micromega-online/recovery-fund-i-tre-errori-da-non-compiere-se-vogliamo-diffondere-l-innovazione/.

Cova, P., A. Notarpietro, P. Pagano and M. Pisani (2019). Secular stagnation, R&D, public investment, and monetary policy: A global-model perspective. *Macroeconomic Dynamics*. https://doi.org/10.1017/S136510051900066XPublished online by Cambridge University Press, 30 September 2019.

Darvas, Z. (2019). Why is it so hard to reach the EU's poverty target? *Social Indicators Research*, 141: 1081–1105. https://doi.org/10.1007/s11205-018-1872-9.

Darvas, Z. (2020). Next Generation EU: 75% of grants will have to wait until 2023. Bruegel.org, 10 June. https://bit.ly/2WnYImE.

Darvas, Z. (2021). The nonsense of Next Generation EU net balance calculations. Policy Contribution 03/2021. Bruegel.

Deaton, A. (2021). COVID-19 and global income inequality. *LSE Public Policy Review*, 1(4):1. http://doi.org/10.31389/lseppr.26.

De Grauwe, P. (2015). Secular stagnation in the Eurozone. Project Syndicate, 30 January.

De Grauwe, P., and S. Diessner (2020). What price to pay for monetary financing of budget deficits in the Euro Area. VOX CEPR Policy Portal, 18 June.

De Grauwe, P., and Y. Ji (2020). A tale of three depressions. VOX CEPR Policy Portal, 24 September.

De Grauwe, P., and W. Moesen (2009). Gains for all: A proposal for a common euro bond. *Intereconomics*, 44(3). https://doi.org/10.1007/s10272-009-028.

Deb, P., D. Furceri, J. Ostry and N. Tawk (2020). The effects of containment measures on the COVID-19 pandemic. *Covid Economics: Vetted and Real-Time Papers*, 19: 53–86.

Delli Gatti, D., M. Gallegati, B. Greenwald, A. Russo and J. Stiglitz (2012). Mobility constraints, productivity trends, and extended crises, *Journal of Economic Behavior & Organization*. 83: 375–393.

Didier, T., F. Huneeus, M. Larrain and S. L. Schmukler (2020). Financing firms in hibernation during the COVID-19 pandemic. Cowles Foundation D. P. No. 2233, 7 May.

Dorich, J., N. L. St-Pierre, V. Lepetyuk and R. R. Mendes (2018). Could a higher inflation target enhance macroeconomic stability? *Canadian Journal of Economics/Revue canadienne d'économique*, 51(3): 1029–1055.

Durante R., L. Guiso and G. Gulino (2020). Asocial capital: Civic culture and social distancing during Covid-19. Cepr DP 14820.

ECB (2021a). ECB staff macroeconomic projections for the euro area. September.

ECB (2021b). *Economic Bulletin*. Issue 4.

Economic Commission (2008). 10 years of Economic and Monetary Union: A resounding success but testing times ahead. Downloads/10_years_of_Economic_and_Monetary_Union__a_resounding_success_but_testing_times_ahead.pdf.

The Economist (2019). Slowbalisation: The future of global commerce. 24 January

Eichengreen, B. (2014). Secular stagnation: A review of the issues, in C. Teulings and R. Baldwin, eds. *Secular Stagnation: Facts, Causes and Cures*, A VoxEU. orgBook. CEPR Press.

Eichengreen, B., D. Park and K. Shin (2013). Growth slowdowns redux: New evidence on the middle-income trap. NBER W. P. No. 18673.

Eisenschmidt, J., D. Kedan, M. Schmitz, R. Adalid and P. Papsdorf (2017). The Eurosystem's asset purchase programme and TARGET balances. ECB Occasional Paper Series 196, September.

Emmerling, J., D. Furceri, F. L. Monteiro, P. Loungani, J. D. Ostry, P. Pizzuto and M. Tavoni (2021). Will the economic impact of COVID-19 persist? Prognosis from 21st century pandemics. IMF W. P. 21/119, April.

Estache, A., and D. Leipziger (2016). Overview: Fiscal policy, distribution, and the middle class. Brookings Institutions, 7

European Commission (2017). Reflection paper on harnessing globalization, 10 May. https://ec.europa.eu/info/sites/info/files/reflection-paper-globalisation_en.pdf.

European Commission (2020a). Education and Training Monitor Report 2020: European countries did not meet the ET2020 targets in education, 8 December.

European Commission (2020b). Europe's moment: Repair and prepare for the Next Generation. Brussels, 27.5, COM (2020) 456 final.

European Commission (2020c). SURE: Supporting Member States to help protect people in work and jobs. SURE Factsheet, 2 April.

European Parliament (2021). Draft report on the implementation of the EU requirements for exchange of tax information: Progress, lessons learned and obstacles to overcome, 2020/2046 (INI), 12.3.2021.

Fang, C. (2021). *Economics of the Pandemic: Weathering the Storm and Restoring Growth*. London: Routledge.

Fisher, K. A., M. W. Tenforde, L. R. Feldstein et al. (2020). Community and close contact exposures associated with COVID-19 among symptomatic adults ≥18 years in 11 outpatient health care facilities – United States, July, US Dept. of Health and Human Services/Centers for Disease Control and Prevention MMWR, September 11, 69 (36): 1253–1264.

Florio M. (2020). Biomed Europa: Dopo il coronavirus, una infrastruttura pubblica per superare l'oligopolio farmaceutico. Forumdisuguaglianzediversita.org, 29 March. https://bit.ly/2C7Y1qF.

Florio, M., and L. Iacovone (2020). Pandemie e ricerca farmaceutica: La proposta di una infrastruttura pubblica europea (parte seconda). Menabò di Etica ed Economia, n. 127/2020, 16 May.

Fornaro, L., and M. Wolf (2020). Coronavirus and macroeconomic policy. VOX CEPR Policy Portal, 10 March.

Fort, T. C., J. R. Pierce and P. K. Schott (2018). New perspectives on the decline of US manufacturing employment. *Journal of Economic Perspectives*, 32(2): 47–72.

Furceri, D., P. Loungani, J. D. Ostry and P. Pizzuto (2021). Will COVID-19 affect inequality? Evidence from past pandemics. IMF W. P. 21/127, April.

Galí, J. (2020). Helicopter money: The time is now. In A. Bénassy-Quéré and B. Weder di Mauro, eds., *Europe in the Time of Covid-19*. A CEPR Press VoxEU. org eBook, CEPR Press.

García-Herrero, A., and E. Ribakova (2020). COVID-19's reality shock for external-funding dependent emerging economies. Policy Contribution 10/2020, Bruegel.

Garde, D. (2020). STAT's Covid-19 drugs and vaccines tracker. Statnews.com, 26 May. https://bit.ly/2OvO09c.

Garicano, L. (2020). Towards a European Reconstruction Fund. VOX CEPR Policy Portal, 5 May.

Gawel, E., S. Strunz and P. Lehmann (2014). A public choice view on the climate and energy policy mix in the EU: How do the emissions trading scheme and support for renewable energies interact? *Energy Policy*, 64(S): 175–82.

Gerszon Mahler, D., N. Yonzan, C. Lakner, R. A. Castaneda Aguilar and H. Wu (2021). Updated estimates of the impact of COVID-19 on global poverty: Turning the corner on the pandemic in 2021? 24 June.

Giavazzi, F., and G. Tabellini (2020). Eurobond perpetui contro il Covid-19. LaVoce. info 27 March. https://bit.ly/3evnR4N.

Giovannetti, G., E. Marvasi and G. Vannelli (2020). The exposure of Italy along the Global Value Chain in a Covid-19 world. Mimeo.

Giovannini, A., S. Hauptmeier, N. Leiner-Killinger and V. Valenta (2020). The fiscal implications of the EU's recovery package. *ECB Economic Bulletin*, Issue 6.

Giuntella, O., K. Hyde, S. Saccardo and S. Sadoff (2021). Lifestyle and mental health disruptions during Covid-19, *Proceeding of the National Academy of Sciences, USA*, 118(9):e2016632118. https://doi.org/10.1073/pnas.2016632118.

Gobbi G., F. Palazzo and A. Segura (2020). Le misure di sostegno finanziario alle imprese Post-Covid-19 e le loro implicazioni di medio termine. Banca d'Italia, Note Covid-19, 15 April.

Gordon, R. (2012). Is US economic growth over? Faltering innovation confronts the six headwinds. NBER W. P. No. 18315.

Gordon, R. (2014a). The turtle's progress: Secular stagnation meets the headwinds. In C. Teulings and R. Baldwin, eds., *Secular Stagnation: Facts, Causes and Cures*. A VoxEU.orgBook, CEPR Press.

Gordon, R. (2014b). US economic growth is over: The short run meets the long run. In Think Tank 20, ed., *Growth, Convergence and Income Distribution: The Road from the Brisbane G-20 Summit*, pp. 185–192. Brookings, November.

Grassia, M., G. Mangioni, S. Schiavo and S. Traverso (2020). (Unintended) Consequences of export restrictions on medical goods during the Covid-19 pandemic. Mimeo.

Gros, D. (2020). EU solidarity in exceptional times: Corona transfers instead of Coronabonds. VOX CEPR Policy Portal, 5 April.

Han, E., and M. Mei Jin Tan (2020). Lessons learnt from easing COVID-19 restrictions: an analysis of countries and regions in Asia Pacific and Europe, September 24, https://doi.org/10.1016/S0140–6736(20)32007-9.

Hansen, A. H. (1939). Economic progress and declining population growth. *American Economic Review*, 29(2): 1–15.

Hein, E. (2015). Secular stagnation or stagnation policy? Steindl after Summers. Levy Economics Institute of Bard College, W. P. No. 846, October.

Held, D., A. McGrew, D. Goldblatt and J. Perraton (1999). *Global Transformations*. Stanford: Stanford University Press.

Hume, M. (2020), Macroeconomic imbalances in the Euro Area: Can they be managed? In N. F. Campos, P. De Grauwe, Y. Ji (eds.), *Economic Growth and Structural Reforms in Europe*. Cambridge: Cambridge University Press.

Humphries, J. E., C. Neilson and G. Ulyssea (2020). The evolving impacts of COVID-19 on small businesses since the CARES Act. Cowles Foundation Discussion Paper No. 2230, April.

Hyun J., D. Kim and S.-R. Shin (2020). The role of global connectedness and market power in crises: Firm-level evidence from the COVID-19 pandemic. Covid Economics: Vetted and Real-Time Papers CEPR Press, Issue 49, 18 September.

Ietto Gillies, G. (2019). *Transnational Corporations and the International Production: Concepts, Theories and Effects*. Cheltenham, UK: Edward Elgar.

Ietto Gillies, G. (2020). Reflections on organizational change and interdependence in a post-Covid-19 society. *Economia e Lavoro*, 54(3): 77–91.

International Labor Organization (2020). A policy framework for tackling the economic and social impact of the COVID-19 crisis. ILO Policy brief 2, Ilo.org, 20 May. https://bit.ly/2WrTnL0.

International Labour Organization (2021). *World Employment and Social Outlook: Trends 2021*. Geneva: International Labour Office.

International Monetary Fund (2018). *World Economic Outlook: Cyclical Upswing, Structural Change.* April. Washington, DC: International Monetary Fund.

International Monetary Fund (2021). World Economic Outlook Update, January. www.imf.org/en/Publications/WEO/Issues/2021/01/26/2021-world-economic-outlook-update.

International Monetary Fund database. www.imf.org/external/datamapper/NGDP_RPCH@WEO/BRA/CIS.

Irwin, D. (2020). The pandemic adds momentum to the deglobalisation trend. VOX CEPR Policy Portal, 5 May.

Irwin, D. A., and K. H. O'Rourke (2011). Coping with shocks and shifts: The Multilateral Trading System in historical perspective. NBER W. P. No. 17598, November.

Jackson, T. (2019). The post-growth challenge: Secular stagnation, inequality and the limits to growth. *Ecological Economics*, 156: 236–246.

Janiri, M. L., and L. Sala (2019). Uno spettro si aggira per il mondo: la de-globalizzazione. Lavoce.info, 22 February. www.lavoce.info/archives/57711/uno-spettro-si-aggira-per-il-mondo-la-de-globalizzazione/.

Jaumotte, F., and C. Osorio Buitron (2015). Inequality and labor market institutions. International Monetary Fund, July.

Johnson, S. (2019). Come ripensare il capitalismo. Project Syndicate, 1 October. In Osservatorio economico e finanziario, Lo specchio internazionale, no. 6, pp. 14–15.

Jones, C. (2018). Aging, secular stagnation and the business cycle. *IMF Working Paper* 18/67, March.

Juselius, M., C. Borio, P. Disyatat and M. Drehmann (2016). Monetary policy, the financial cycle and ultralow interest rates. BIS W. P., July.

Kalecki, M. (1954). *Theory of Economic Dynamics*. London: George Allen and Unwin.

Kalecki, M. (1971). *Selected Essays on the Dynamics of the Capitalist Economy, 1933–1970*. Cambridge: Cambridge University Press.

Kandila, N., O. Battaïab and R. Hammamic (2020). Globalisation vs. Slowbalisation: A literature review of analytical models for sourcing decisions in supply chain management. *Annual Reviews in Control*, 49: 277–287.

Keynes, J. M. (1930). Economic Possibilities for our Grandchildren. in *Essays in Persuasion*, pp. 358–373. New York: Harcourt Brace, 1932.

Kharas, H., and M. Dooley (2021). Long-run impacts of COVID-19. Brookings Institutions, June 2. www.brookings.edu/blog/future-development/2021/06/02/long-run-impacts-of-covid-19-on-extreme-poverty/.

Kharas, H., and B. Seidel (2018). What's happening to the world income distribution? The elephant chart revisited. Global Economy & Development at Brookings, W. P. 114, April.

Kiefer, D., I. Mendieta-Muñoz, C. Rada and R. Von Arnim (2020). Secular stagnation and income distribution dynamics. *Review of Radical Political Economics*, 52(3): 048661341989514.

Kissler, S. M., C. Tedijanto, E. Goldstein, Y. H. Grad and M. Lipsitch (2020). Projecting the transmission dynamics of SARS-CoV-2 through the postpandemic period. *Science*, 22 May, 368(6493): 860–868.

Kobayashi, K., and K. Ueda (2020). Secular stagnation under the fear of a government debt crisis. Australian National University, CAMA W. P. 40/2020, April 17.

Kroll, C. (2020). From trade-offs to synergies: COVID-19, populism. and sustainable development. VOX CEPR Policy Portal, 9 June.

Krugman, P. (2014). Four observations on secular Stagnation. In C. Teulings and R. Baldwin, eds., *Secular Stagnation: Facts, Causes and Cures*. A VoxEU.orgBook, CEPR Press.

Krugman, P. (2020). The case for permanent stimulus. In R. Baldwin and B. Weder di Mauro, eds. *Economics in the Time of COVID-19*. London: CEPR Press.

Laubach, M., and J. Williams (2016). Measuring the natural rate of interest redux. *Business Economics*, 51(2): 57–67.

Le Garrec, G., and V. Touzé (2018). Macroeconomics in the age of secular stagnation. *Revue de l'OFCE*, 157: 69–92.

Le Maire, B. (2020). European industrial sovereignty. Minister Bruno Le Maire's speech, International press conference. Gouvernement.fr, 2 April. https://bit.ly/2CCj6JA.

Lin, H. (2016). Risks of stagnation in the Euro Area. IMF W. P. 16/9, January.

MacEwan, A. (1996). Globalization and stagnation. *Social Justice*, 23(1–2): 49–62.

Mahler, D. G., C. Lakner, R. A. Castaneda Aguilar and H. Wu (2020). The impact of COVID-19 (Coronavirus) on global poverty: Why Sub-Saharan Africa might be the region hardest hit. Blogs.worldbank.org, 20 April. https://bit.ly/2OxCpGw.

Majumdar, R. (2017). Understanding the productivity paradox. Behind the numbers. October. www2.deloitte.com/us/en/insights/economy/behind-the-numbers/decoding-declining-stagnant-productivity-growth.html.

Mann, C. L. (2020). Real and financial lenses to assess the economic consequences of COVID-19. In R. Baldwin, R., and B. Weder di Mauro, eds., *Economics in the Time of COVID-19*. London: CEPR Press.

Mazzucato, M. (2018). *Il valore di tutto: Chi lo produce e chi lo sottrae nell'economia globale*. Roma-Bari: Laterza.

Mazzucato, M., and E. Torreele (2020). How to develop a COVID-19 vaccine for all. Project Syndicate, 27 April.

Meninno, R., and G. Wolff (2020). As the Coronavirus spreads, can the EU afford to close its borders? VOX CEPR Policy Portal, Voxeu.org, 28 February. https://bit .ly/3jc2qtl.

Milanovic, B. (2013). Global income inequality in numbers: In history and now. *Global Policy*, 4(2): 198–208.

Milanovic, B. (2016). *Global Inequality. A New Approach for the Age of Globalization*. Cambridge, MA.: Harvard University Press.

Mill, J. S. (1887). *Principles of Political Economy*. Ist ed. 1848.New York: D. Appleton and Co.

Ministro per il Sud e la Coesione territoriale (2020). Piano Sud 2030. Sviluppo e coesione per l'Italia. Ministroperilsud.gov.it, February. https://bit.ly/32kccUa.

Minsky, H. (1992). The financial instability hypothesis. The Jerome Levy Economics Institute of Bard College, W. P. No. 74, May.

Mokyr, J. (2014). Secular stagnation? Not in your life. In C. Teulings and R. Baldwin, eds., *Secular Stagnation: Facts, Causes and Cures*. A VoxEU. orgBook, CEPR Press.

Neri, S. (2013). The impact of the sovereign debt crisis on bank lending rates in the Euro Area. Bank of Italy, Questioni di Economia e Finanza Occasional Papers 170, June.

Nikiforos, M. (2020). Demand, distribution, productivity, structural change, and (secular?) stagnation. Levy Economics Institute of Bard College, W. P. No. 945, January.

North, D. C., and R. P. Thomas (1973). *The Rise of the Western World: A New Economic History*. Cambridge: Cambridge University Press.

OECD (2012). Looking to 2060: Long-term global growth prospects: A going for growth report. OECD Economic Policy Papers, No. 3, November 7.

OECD (2020a). OECD Economic Outlook. Volume 2020, Issue 1: Preliminary version, No. 107, OECD Publishing, Paris. https://doi.org/10.1787/0d1d1e2e-en.

OECD (2020b). OECD Economic Outlook. Volume 2020, Issue 2: Preliminary version, No. 108. www.politico.eu/wp-content/uploads/2020/12/01/EO108 .PDFO.pdf.

OECD (2020c). *Education at a Glance*. Paris: OECD Publishing. www.oecd.org/ education/education-at-a-glance/

OECD (2021). *Employment Outlook: A Once-in-a-Lifetime Opportunity to Build a Better World of Work*. Paris: OECD Publishing.

Onaran, Ö. (2016). Secular stagnation and progressive economic policy alternatives. PKSG, Post Keynesian Economics Study Group, W. P. 1609, May.

Palomino, J. C., J. G. Rodríguez and R. Sebastian (2020). Inequality and poverty effects of the lockdown in Europe. VOX CEPR Policy Portal, 16 June.

Pariboni, R., W. Paternesi Meloni and P. Tridico (2020). When *Melius Abundare* is no longer true: Excessive financialization and inequality as drivers of stagnation. *Review of Political Economy*, 32(2): 216–242.

Pedone, A. (2016). Ascesa, declino e destino della progressività tributaria. Menabò di Etica ed Economia n. 36, 1 February.

Perotti, R. (2020). Gli aiuti di Bruxelles all'Italia. Quei conti che non tornano. La republica, 29 May.

Perrelli, Branca M. C., and P. Piccioni (2020). *Riprogrammazione degli interventi chirurgici, liste d'attesa e mobilità sanitaria: Il Covid spingerà gli italiani a curarsi vicino casa?* Bologna: Nomisma.

Petach, L., and D. Tavani (2019). Income shares, secular stagnation, and the long-run distribution of wealth. October 10. https://ssrn.com/abstract=3198311 or http://dx.doi.org/10.2139/ssrn.3198311.

Piccioni, P., and M. C. Perrelli (2020). *Il peso del lockdown sugli screening oncologici: Quanto dobbiamo recuperare.* Bologna: Nomisma.

Pichelmann, K. (2015). 'Secular stagnation' meets Piketty's capitalism in the 21st century: Growth and inequality trends in Europe reconsidered. European Economy, Economic Papers 551, June.

Pietrunti, M. (2020). The impact of a coordinated monetary and fiscal policy reaction to a pandemic shock. June 3. Mimeo.

Piketty, T. (2013). *Le capital au XXI siècle*. Paris: Editions du Seuil.

Pisani-Ferry, J. (2020). European Union recovery funds: Strings attached, but not tied up in knots. Policy Contribution 2020/19, Bruegel.

Popović, M. (2018). Technological progress, globalization, and secular stagnation. *Journal of Central Banking Theory and Practice*, 7(1): 59–100.

Portes, J. (2020). The lasting scars of the Covid-19 crisis: Channels and impacts. VoxEU.org, 1 June. https://bit.ly/2ZAhokR.

Posen, A. S. (2020). Containing the economic nationalist virus through global coordination: The case for permanent stimulus. In R. Baldwin and B. Weder di Mauro, eds., *Economics in the Time of COVID-19*. London: CEPR Press.

Putnam, R. D. (1993). The prosperous community: Social capital and public life. *American Prospect*, 4(13): 35–42.

Rachel, Ł., and L. H. Summers (2019). On secular stagnation in the industrialized world. NBER W. P. No. 26198, August.

Rakic, R., et al. (2021). Fostering R&D intensity in the European Union: Policy experiences and lessons learned. Case study contribution to the OECD TIP project on R&D intensity. https://community.oecd.org/community/cstp/tip/rdintensity.

Rajan, R. (2010). *Fault Lines*. Princeton, Princeton University Press.

Ramey, V. A. (2020). Productivity origins of 'Secular Stagnation'. American Economic Association, 3 January.

Rannenberg, A. (2019). Inequality, the risk of secular stagnation and the increase in household debt. National Bank of Belgium, W. P. 375, August.

Razin, A. (2021). Globalization and global crises: Rest of the world vs. Israel. NBER W. P. 28339. www.nber.org/papers/w28339.

Rehman, S. S., P. Della Posta, A. Kulathunga and K. C. Rudd (2020). Post Covid-19 era fused crises and impact on productivity. Mimeo.

Reichlin, P. (2019). Economic stagnation and recession: The difficult Italian transition to the Monetary Union. *Journal of Modern Italian Studies*, 24(3): 402–414. https://doi.org/10.1080/1354571X.2019.1605717.

Reinhart, C., and K. Rogoff (2009). *This Time Is Different: Eight Centuries of Financial Folly*. Princeton: Princeton University Press.

Reinhart, C. M., and R. Subbaraman (2020). Preventing a COVID-19 food crisis. World Economic Forum and Project Syndicate, 15 May.

Reinhart, C., V. Reinhart and K. Rogoff (2015). Dealing with debt. *Journal of International Economics*, 96: S43–S55.

Ricci, M. (2020). Dal coronavirus un nuovo colpo a una globalizzazione già malata. *La repubblica*, 14 March. www.repubblica.it/economia/rubriche/eurobarometro/2020/03/14/news/coronavirus_deglobalizzazione-251263007/.

Rodrigue, J.-P., with C. Comtois and B. Slack (2017). *The Geography of Transport Systems*, 3rd ed.. London, Routledge.

Rodrik, D. (2007). How to Save Globalization from Its Cheerleaders. *Journal of International Trade and Diplomacy*, 1(10). https://ssrn.com/abstract=1019015 or http://dx.doi.org/10.2139/ssrn.1019015.

Rodrik, D. (2011). *The Globalization Paradox: Democracy and the Future of the World Economy*. New York and London: W. W. Norton.

Rodrik, D. (2019). Should we worry about income gaps within or between countries? *Social Europe*, October 2.

Rogoff, K. (2020a). Deglobalization will hurt growth everywhere. Project Syndicate, 3 June.

Rogoff, K. (2020b). Pourquoi il faut aller vers des taux d'intérêt résolument négatifs. Les echos, 13 May.

Romano, B. (2020). Piano Von der Leyen: Recovery Fund da 750 miliardi di cui 500 a fondo perduto. Per l'Italia previsti 82 miliardi di aiuti e 91 di crediti. Il sole 24 ore, 27 May.

Roser, M., and E. Ortiz-Ospina (2019). Income inequality. Our world in data, October. https://ourworldindata.org/income-inequality4.4.2.

Rothstein, B. (2020). Trust is the key to fighting the pandemic. *Scientific American*, 24 March.

Schmelzing, P. (2018). Eight centuries of the risk-free rate: Bond market reversals from the Venetians to the VAR-shock. Bank of England, W. P. 686, October.

Sensoy, A., E. Hacihasanoglu and A. M. Rostom (2015). European Economic and Monetary Union sovereign debt markets. World Bank Policy Research W. P. 7149.

Seric, A., H. Görg, S. Mösle and M. Windisch (2020). Managing COVID-19: How the pandemic disrupts global value chains. Iap.unido.org, 27 April. https://bit.ly/3h3Ih6L.

Steindl, J., (1952). *Maturity and Stagnation in American Capitalism*. Oxford, Blackwell; 2nd ed, New York and London: Monthly Review Press, 1976.

Steindl, J. (1979). Stagnation theory and stagnation policy. *Cambridge Journal of Economics*, 3(1): 1–14.

Stiglitz, J. (2017). Inequality, stagnation, and market power: The need for a new progressive era. Roosevelt Institute W. P., November.

Stiglitz, J. E., A. Jayadev and A. Prabhala (2020). Patents vs. the pandemic. Project Syndicate, 23 April.

Stockhammer, E. (2015). Rising inequality as a cause of the present crisis. *Cambridge Journal of Economics*, 39(3): 935–958.

Summers, L. H. (2014). Reflections on the 'New Secular Stagnation Hypothesis'. In C. Teulings and R. Baldwin, eds., *Secular Stagnation: Facts, Causes and Cures*. A VoxEU.orgBook, CEPR Press.

Summers, L. H. (2020). Accepting the reality of secular stagnation. *Finance & Development*, 57(1): 17–19.

Sumner, A., C. Hoy and E. Ortiz-Juarez (2020). Estimates of the impact of COVID-19 on global poverty. United Nations University World Institute for development economics research, WIDER W. P. 2020/43, April.

Tancioni, M. (2020). Le conseguenze macroeconomiche del SARS-CoV-2: Incertezza e scenari di policy. Sinistrainrete.info, 2 April. https://bit.ly/32qNUbg.

Tax Justice Network (2020). The State of Tax Justice 2020. 20 November. www.taxjustice.net/reports/the-state-of-tax-justice-2020/.

Terzi, A., and P. M. Marrazzo (2020). Structural reforms and growth: The elusive quest for the silver bullet. In N. F. Campos, P. De Grauwe and Y Ji (eds.), *Economic Growth and Structural Reforms in Europe*. Cambridge, Cambridge University Press.

Teulings, C., and R. Baldwin (2014a). eds. *Secular Stagnation: Facts, Causes and Cures*. A VoxEU.orgBook, CEPR Press.

Teulings, C., and R. Baldwin (2014b). Introduction. In C. Teulings and, R. Baldwin, eds., *Secular Stagnation: Facts, Causes and Cures*. A VoxEU.orgBook, CEPR Press.

Timmer, M., B. Los, R. Stehrer and G. De Vries (2013). Fragmentation, incomes and jobs: An analysis of European competitiveness. *Economic Policy*, 28(76): 613–661.

Terzi, A., and P. M. Marrazzo (2020). Structural reforms and growth: The elusive quest for the silver bullet. In N. F. Campos, P. De Grauwe and Y. Ji (eds.), *Economic Growth and Structural Reforms in Europe*. Cambridge: Cambridge University Press.

Tørsløv, T., L. Wier and G. Zucman (2020). The missing profits of nations. Gabriel-zucman.eu, 22 April. http://gabriel-zucman.eu/missingprofits/.

Unctad (2012). *Trade and Development Report*. New York and Geneva: World Trade Organization. https://unctad.org/system/files/official-document/tdr2012_en.pdf.

Unctad (2013). *World Investment Report 2013: Global Value Chains: Investment and Trade for Development*. Geneva: World Trade Organization.

Unctad (2020). *World Investment Report 2020: International Production beyond the Pandemic*. Geneva: World Trade Organization.

UNIDO (2020). Coronavirus: The economic impact. Unido.org, 26 May. https://bit.ly/2OubTOe.

van Treeck, T. (2015). Inequality, the crisis, and stagnation. *European Journal of Economics and Economic Policies: Intervention*, 12(2): 158–169.

Visser, J. (2016). What happened to collective bargaining during the great recession? *IZA Journal of Labor Policy*, 5:9.

WHO (2021). Health Emergency Dashboard. 5 June hour 10.41 a.m.

World Bank (2021a). Covid-19: Debt Service Suspension Initiative. 8 April. www.worldbank.org/en/topic/debt/brief/covid-19-debt-service-suspension-initiative.

World Bank (2021b). Global Economic Prospects. January.

World Bank (2021c). Global Economic Prospects. June.

World Inequality Database. https://wid.world/world/#sptinc_p90p100_z/US;FR;DE;CN;ZA;GB;WO/last/eu/k/p/yearly/s/false/24.339999999999996/80/curve/false/country.

World Trade Organization (2008). *World Trade Report: Trade in a Globalizing World*. Geneva: World Trade Organization.

World Trade Organization (2019). *Technological Innovation, Supply Chain Trade, and Workers in a Globalized World*. Geneva: World Trade Organization.

World Trade Organization (2021). World trade primed for strong but uneven recovery after COVID-19 pandemic shock. www.wto.org/english/news_e/pres21_e/pr876_e.htm.

Wren-Lewis, S. (2015). We already have a simple and conventional story to explain the weak recovery. VoxEU, 30th January. http://voxeu.org/article/fiscal--policy--explains--weak--recovery.

Wu, X., R. C. Nethery, B. M. Sabath, D. Braun and F. Dominici (2020). Exposure to air pollution and COVID-19 mortality in the United States. Medrxiv.org. https://bit.ly/3fCCAw7.

Wyplosz, C. (2006). European Monetary Union: The dark sides of a major success. *Economic Policy*, 21(46): 208–261.

Wyplosz, C. (2020). The good thing about Coronavirus. In R. Baldwin and B. Weder di Mauro, eds., *Economics in the Time of COVID-19*. London: CEPR Press.

Yonzan, N., C. Lakner, D. Gerszon Mahler, R. Andres Castaneda Aguilar and H. Wu (2021). Available data and estimates of the impact of the COVID-19 pandemic on global poverty. www.un.org › 2021/05 ›.

Index

Author Index

Printed in the United States
by Baker & Taylor Publisher Services